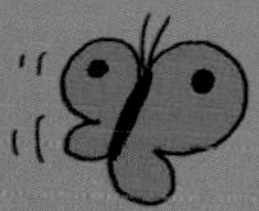

the Awkward Yeti™ Presents

Heart and Brain

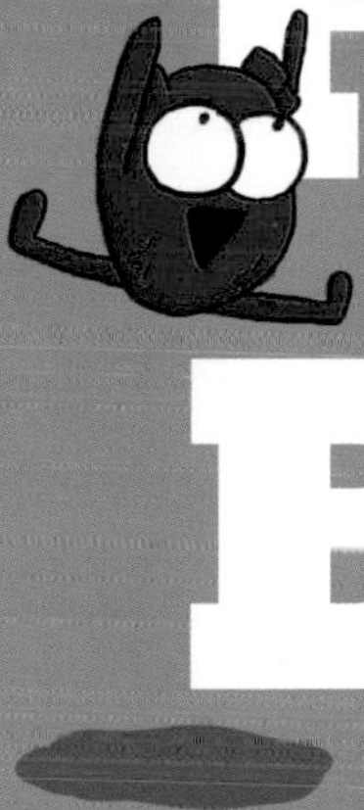

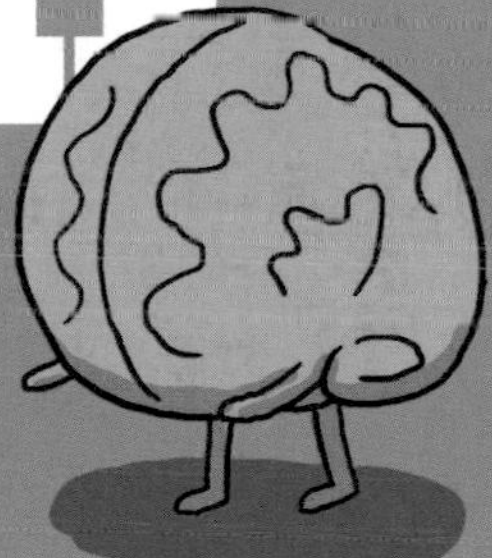

NICK SELUK

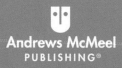

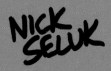

Andrews McMeel
PUBLISHING®

Cast of Characters

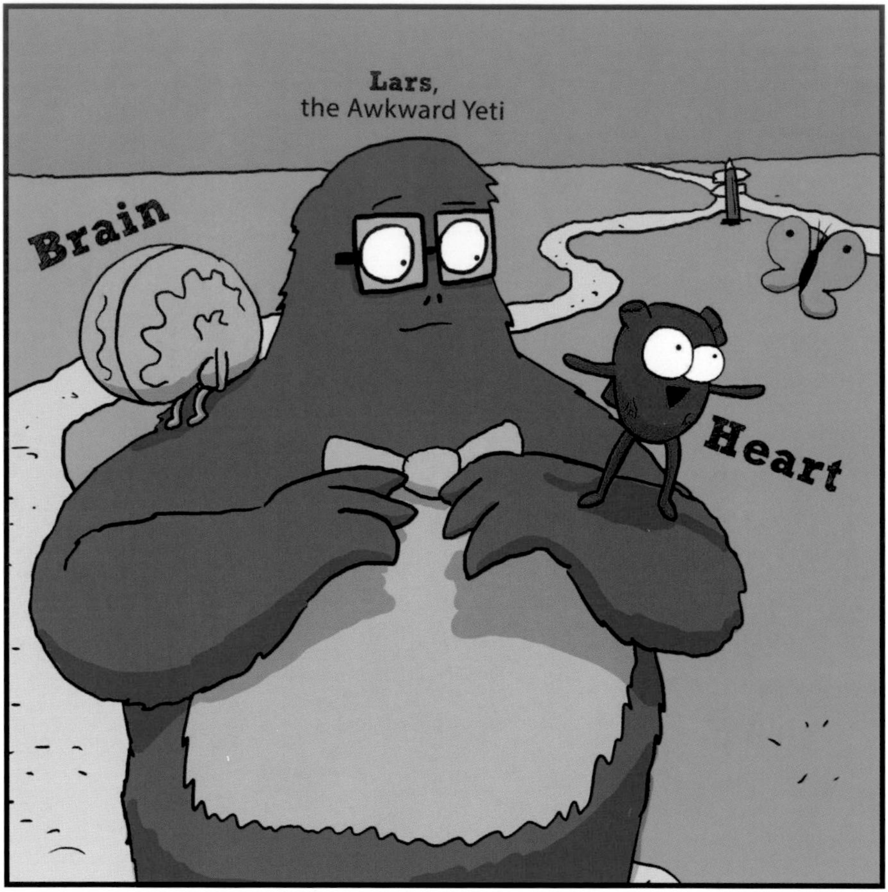
Lars,
the Awkward Yeti
Brain
Heart

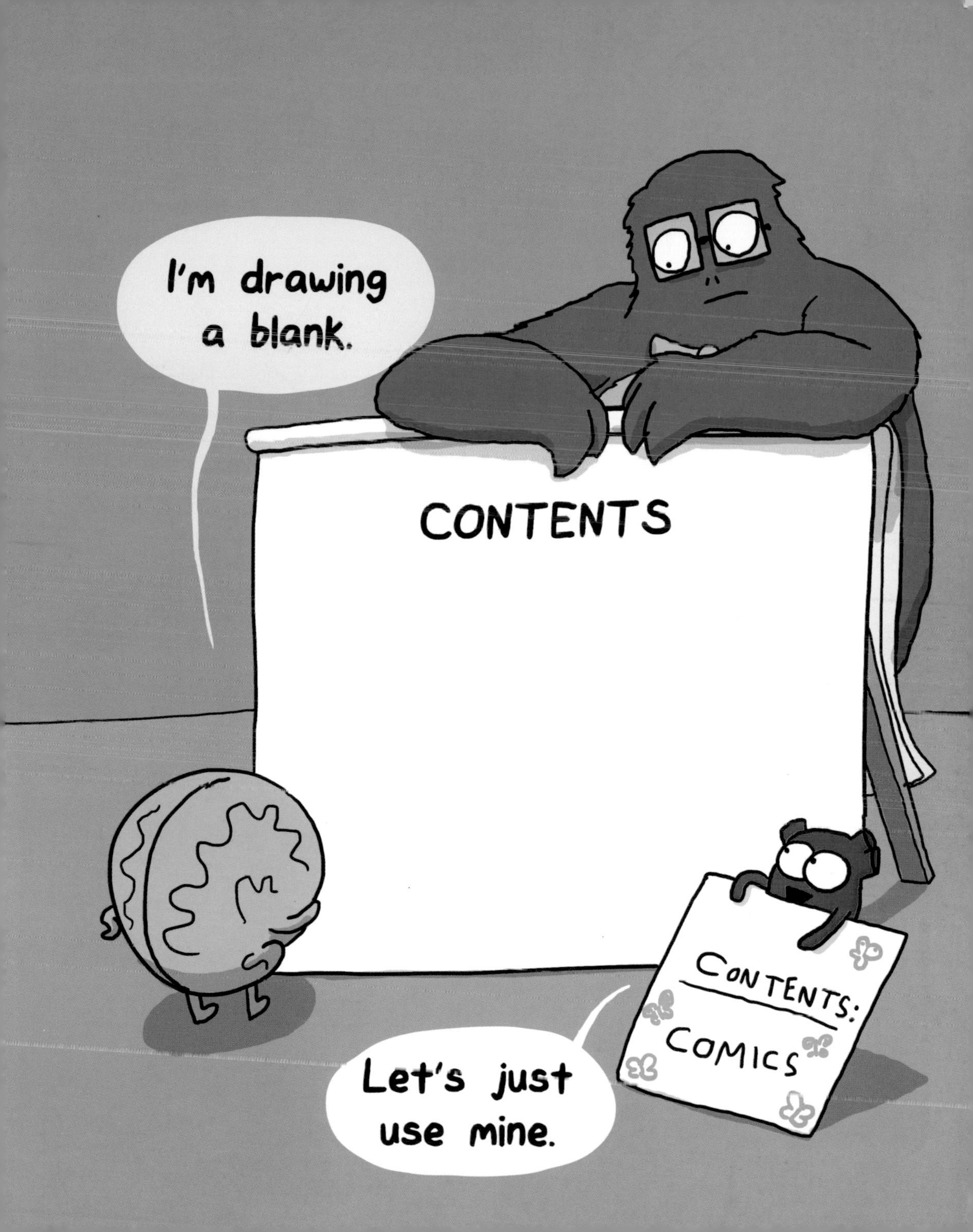
I'm drawing a blank.
CONTENTS
CONTENTS:
COMICS
Let's just use mine.

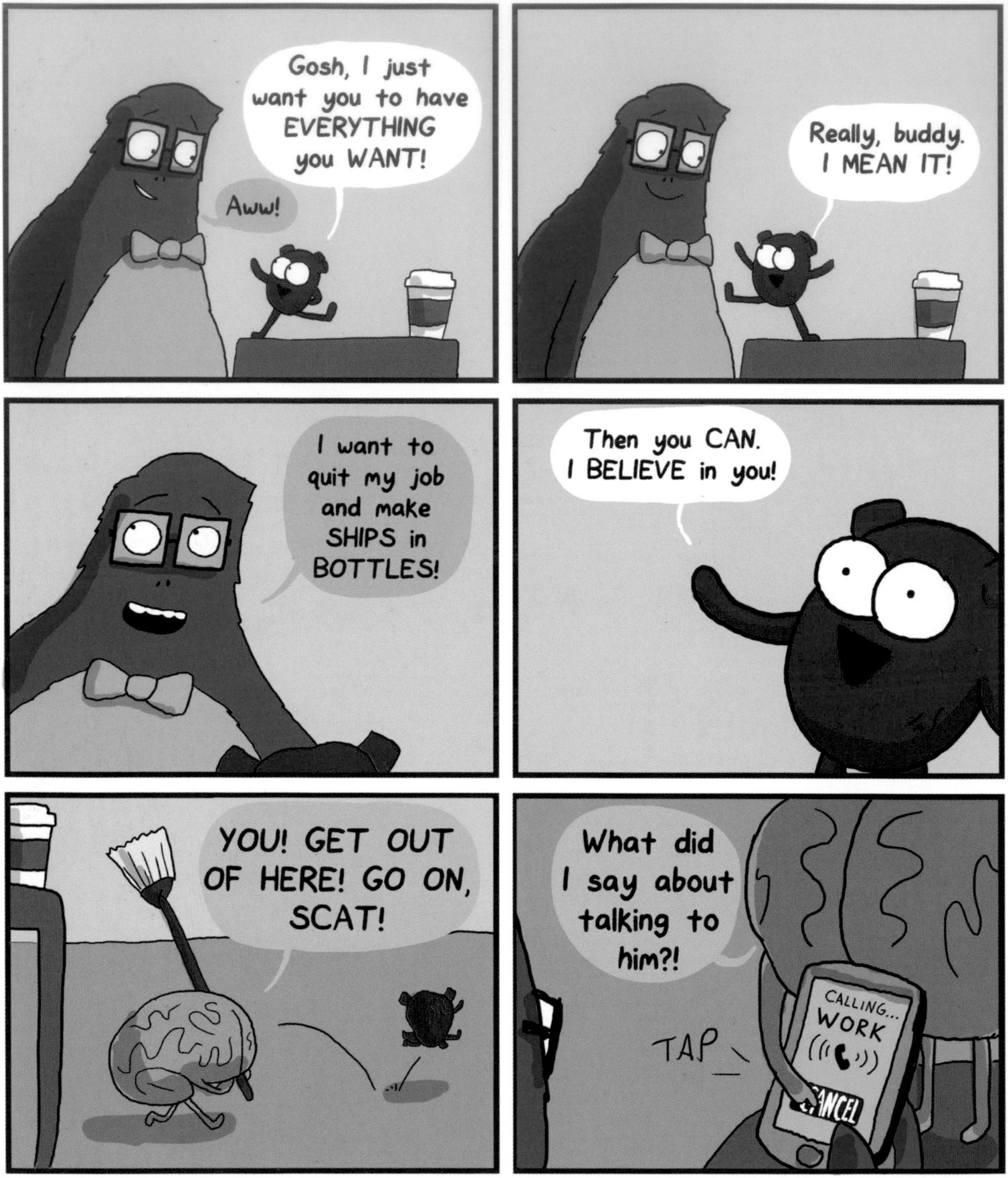
Gosh, I just want you to have EVERYTHING you WANT!
Aww!
Really, buddy. I MEAN IT!
I want to quit my job and make SHIPS in BOTTLES!
Then you CAN. I BELIEVE in you!
YOU! GET OUT OF HERE! GO ON, SCAT!
What did I say about talking to him?!
CALLING... WORK
TAP
CANCEL

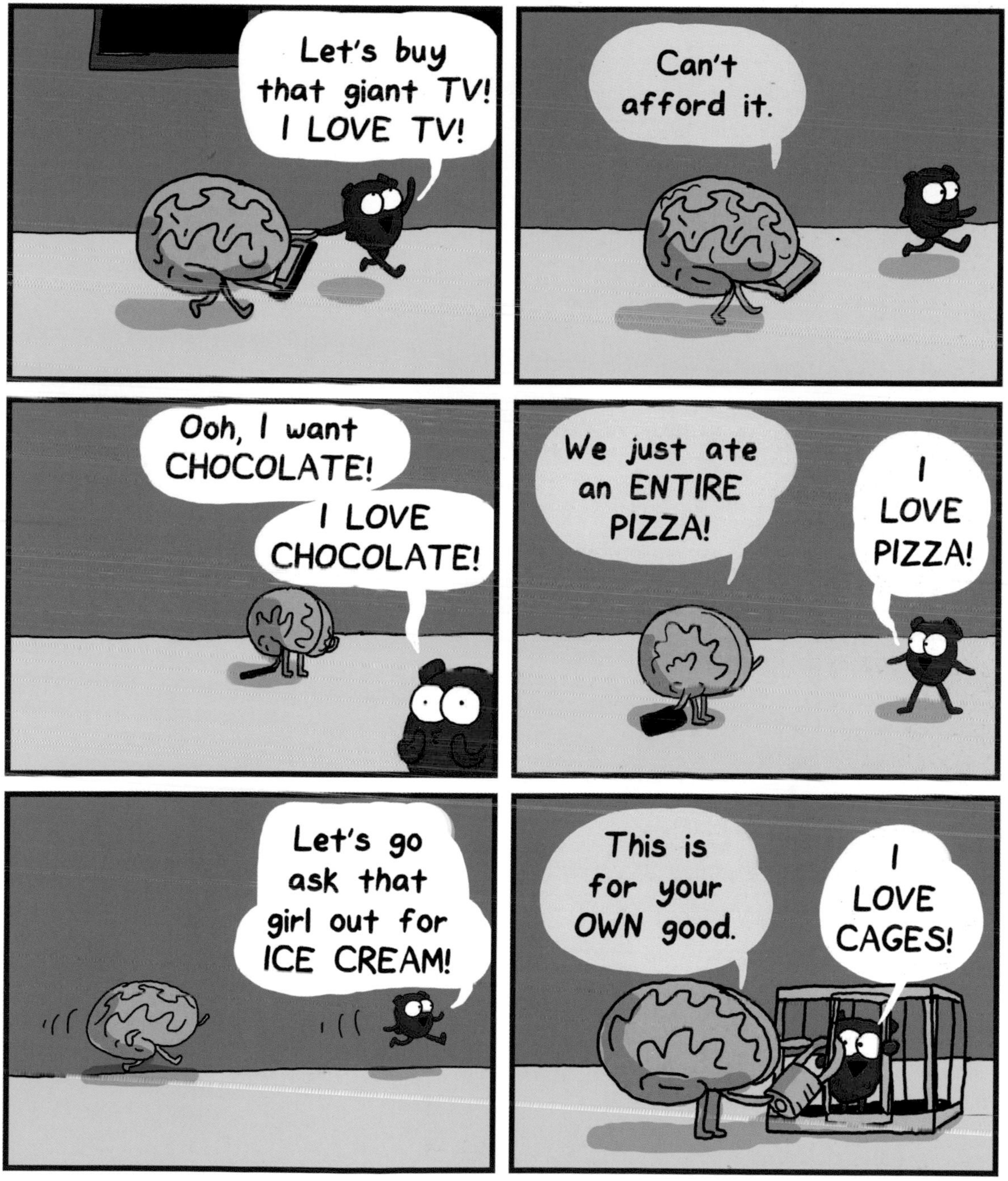
Let's buy that giant TV! I LOVE TV!
Can't afford it.
Ooh, I want CHOCOLATE!
I LOVE CHOCOLATE!
We just ate an ENTIRE PIZZA!
I LOVE PIZZA!
Let's go ask that girl out for ICE CREAM!
This is for your OWN good.
I LOVE CAGES!

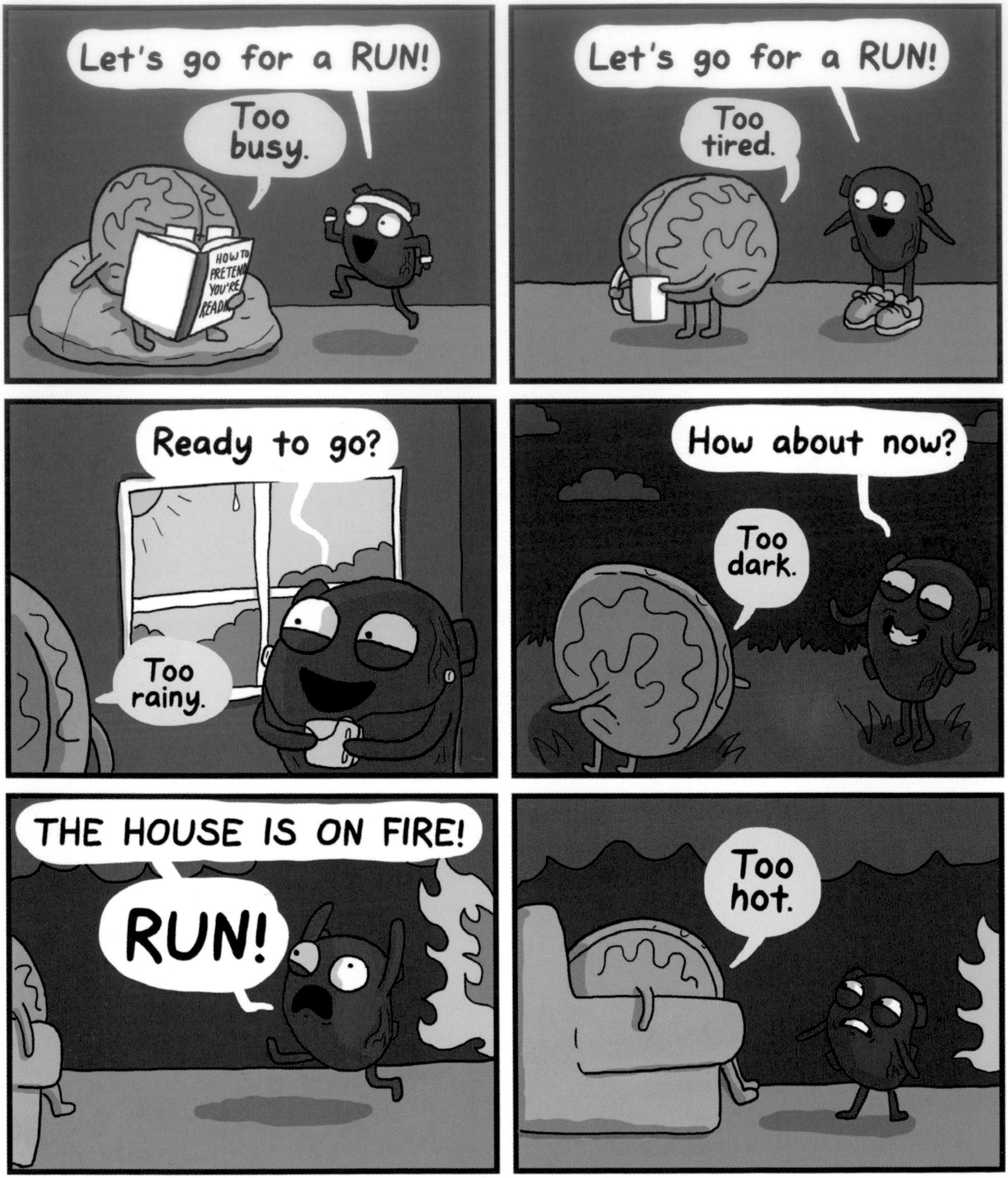
Let's go for a RUN!
Too busy.
HOW TO PRETEND YOU'RE READIN
Let's go for a RUN!
Too tired.
Ready to go?
Too rainy.
How about now?
Too dark.
THE HOUSE IS ON FIRE!
RUN!
Too hot.

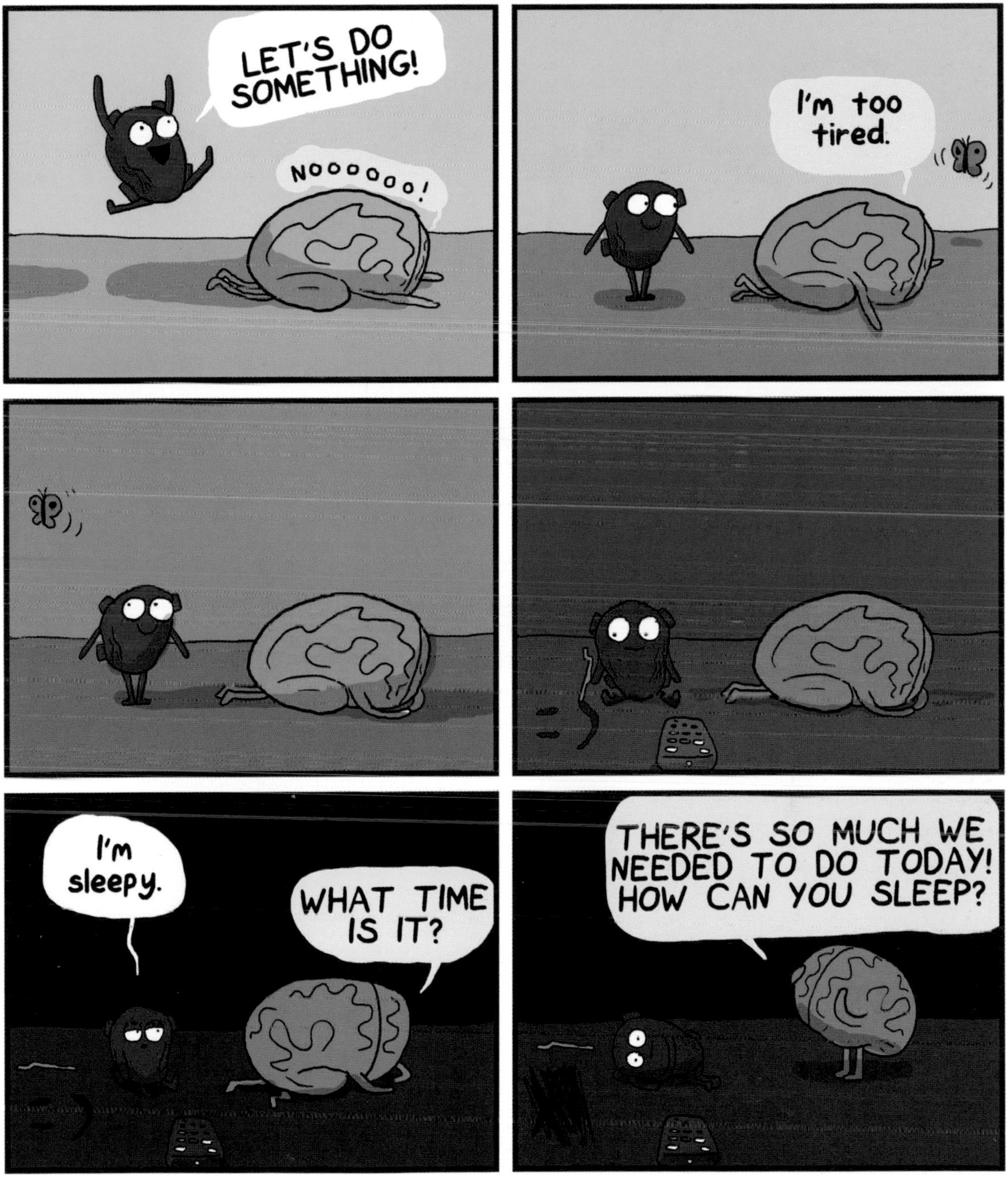
LET'S DO SOMETHING!
NOOOOOOO!
I'm too tired.
I'm sleepy.
WHAT TIME IS IT?
THERE'S SO MUCH WE NEEDED TO DO TODAY! HOW CAN YOU SLEEP?

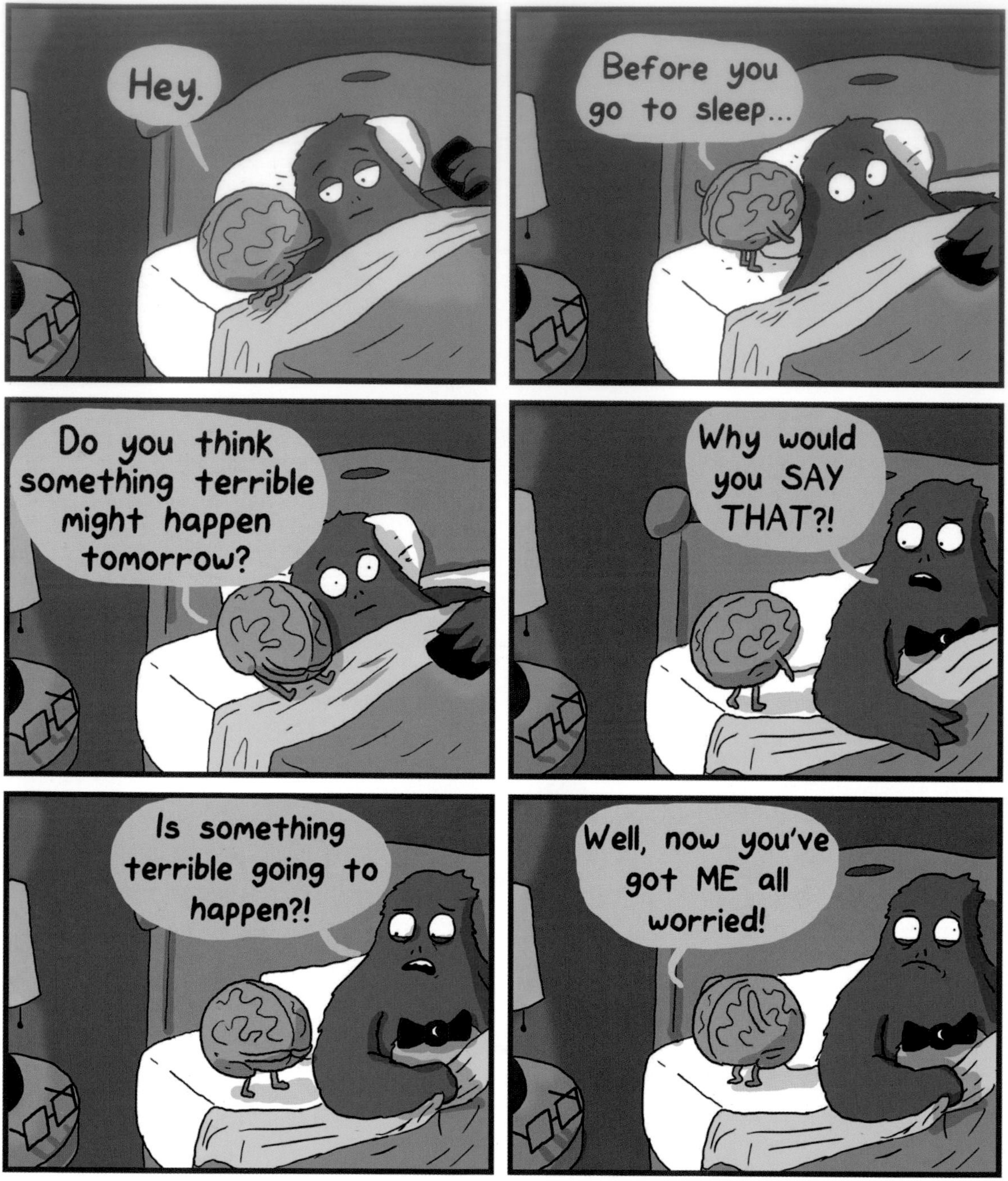
Hey.
Before you go to sleep...
Do you think something terrible might happen tomorrow?
Why would you SAY THAT?!
Is something terrible going to happen?!
Well, now you've got ME all worried!

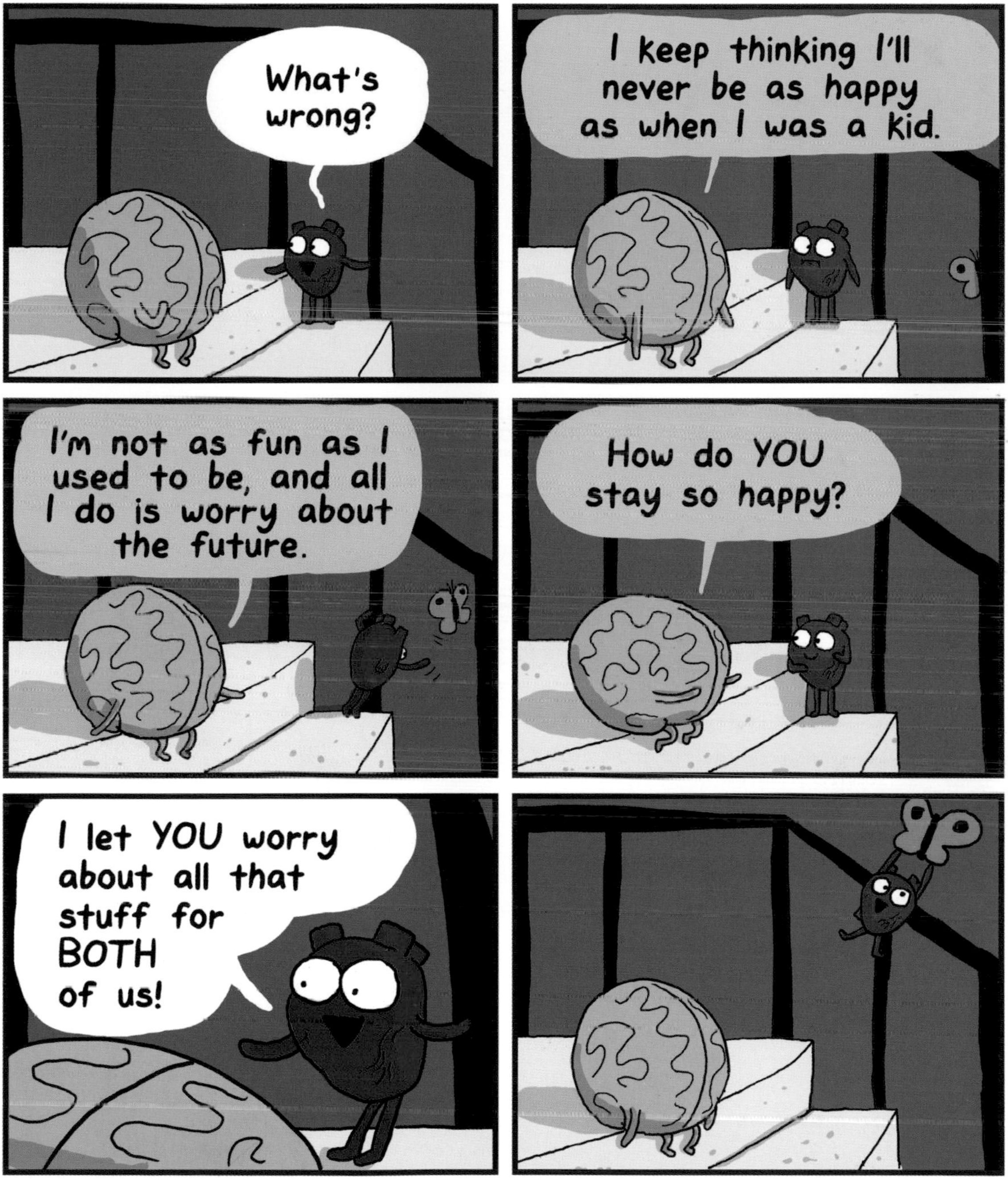
What's wrong?
I keep thinking I'll never be as happy as when I was a kid.
I'm not as fun as I used to be, and all I do is worry about the future.
How do YOU stay so happy?
I let YOU worry about all that stuff for BOTH of us!

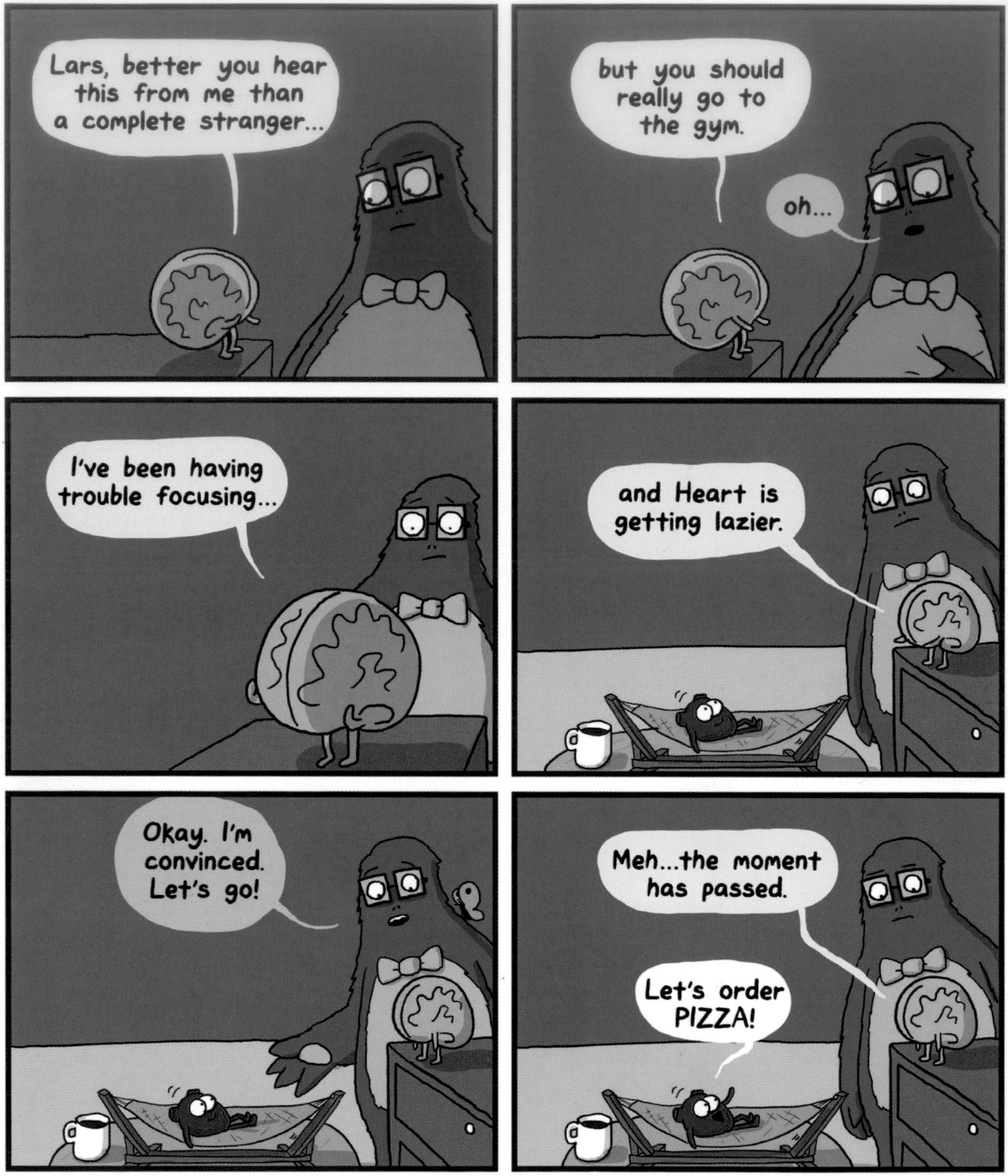
Lars, better you hear this from me than a complete stranger...
but you should really go to the gym.
oh...
I've been having trouble focusing...
and Heart is getting lazier.
Okay. I'm convinced. Let's go!
Meh...the moment has passed.
Let's order PIZZA!

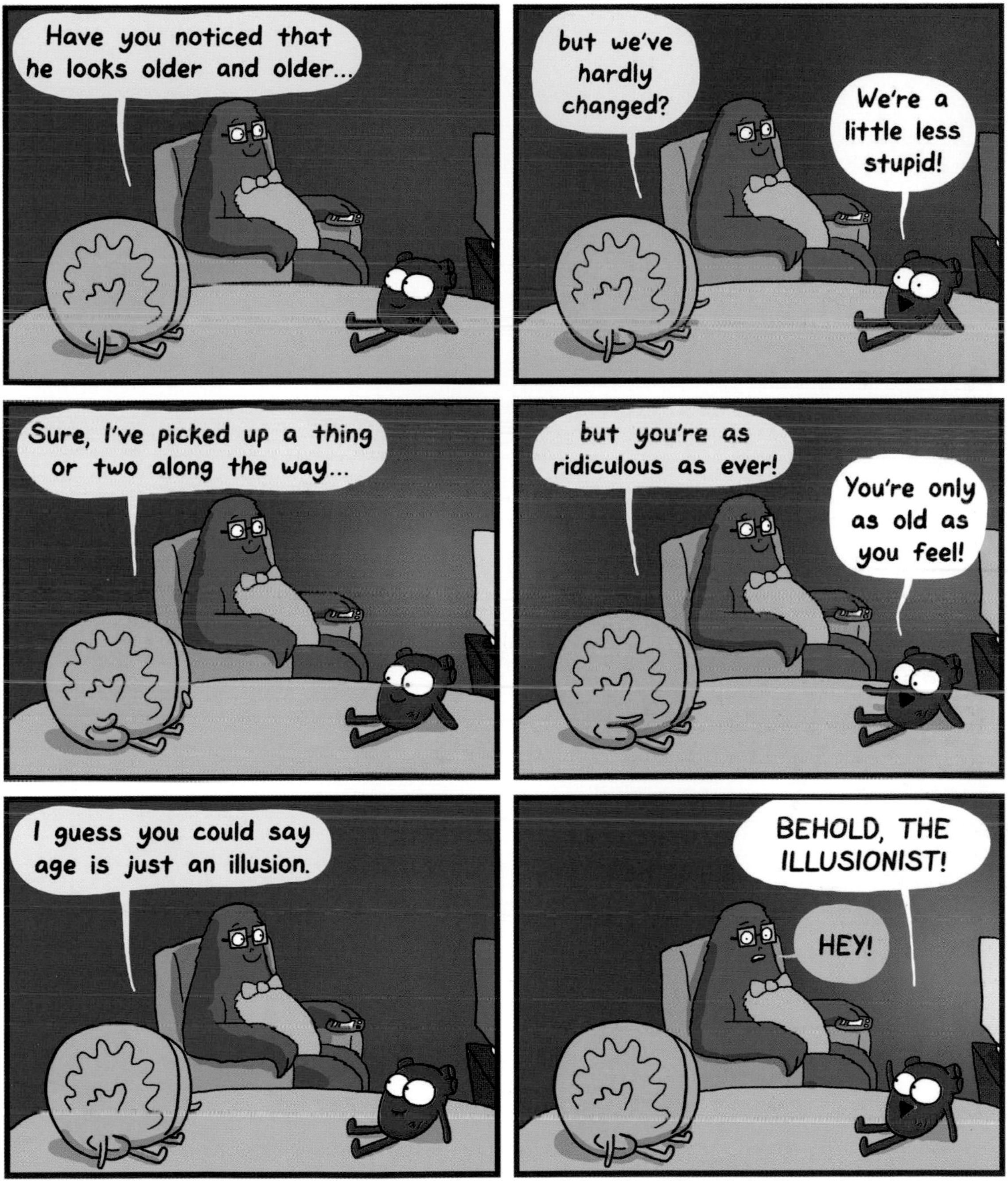
Have you noticed that he looks older and older...
but we've hardly changed?
We're a little less stupid!
Sure, I've picked up a thing or two along the way...
but you're as ridiculous as ever!
You're only as old as you feel!
I guess you could say age is just an illusion.
BEHOLD, THE ILLUSIONIST!
HEY!

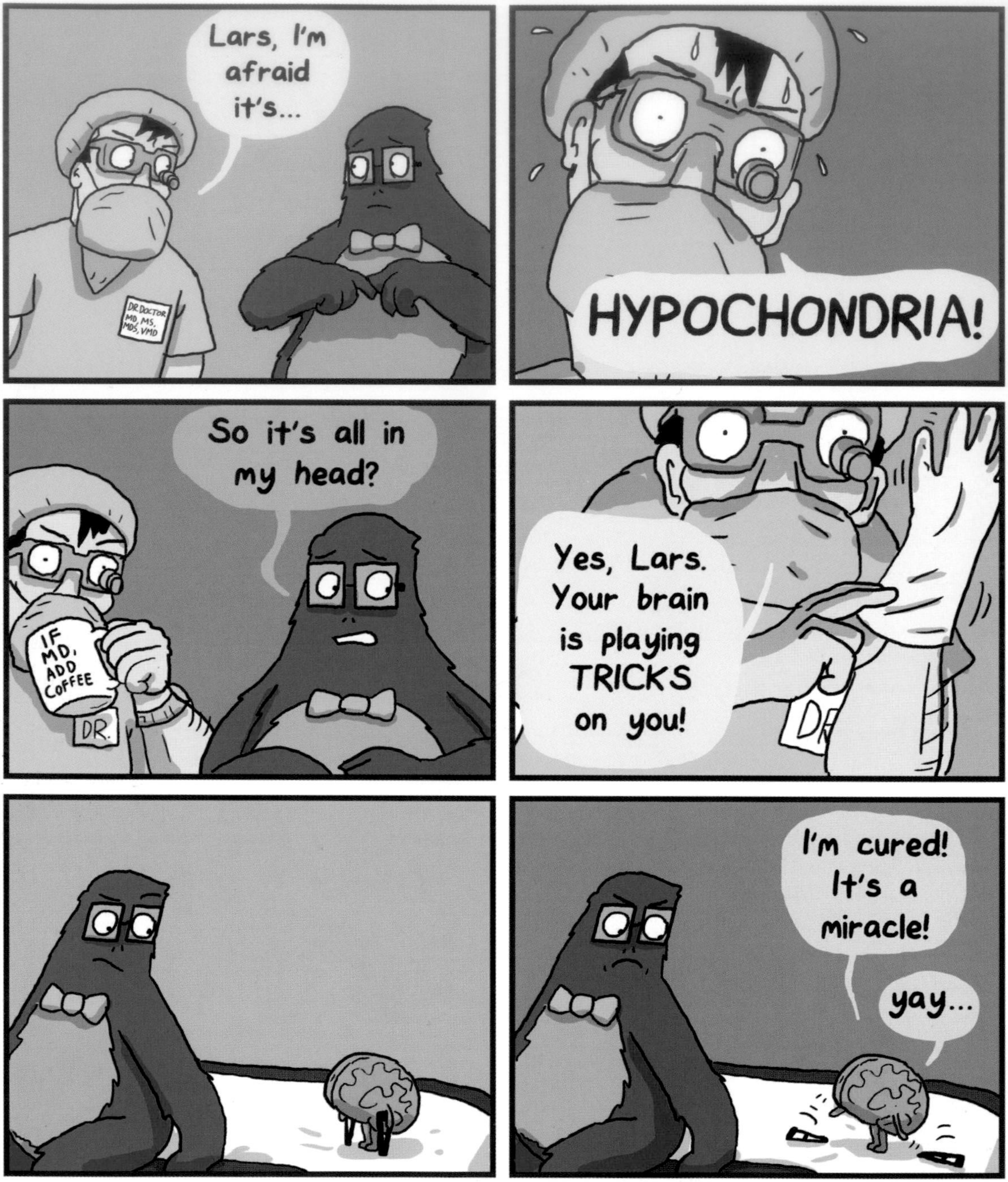
Lars, I'm afraid it's...
DR. DOCTOR MD, MS, MDS, VMD
HYPOCHONDRIA!
So it's all in my head?
IF MD, ADD COFFEE
DR.
Yes, Lars. Your brain is playing TRICKS on you!
I'm cured! It's a miracle!
yay...

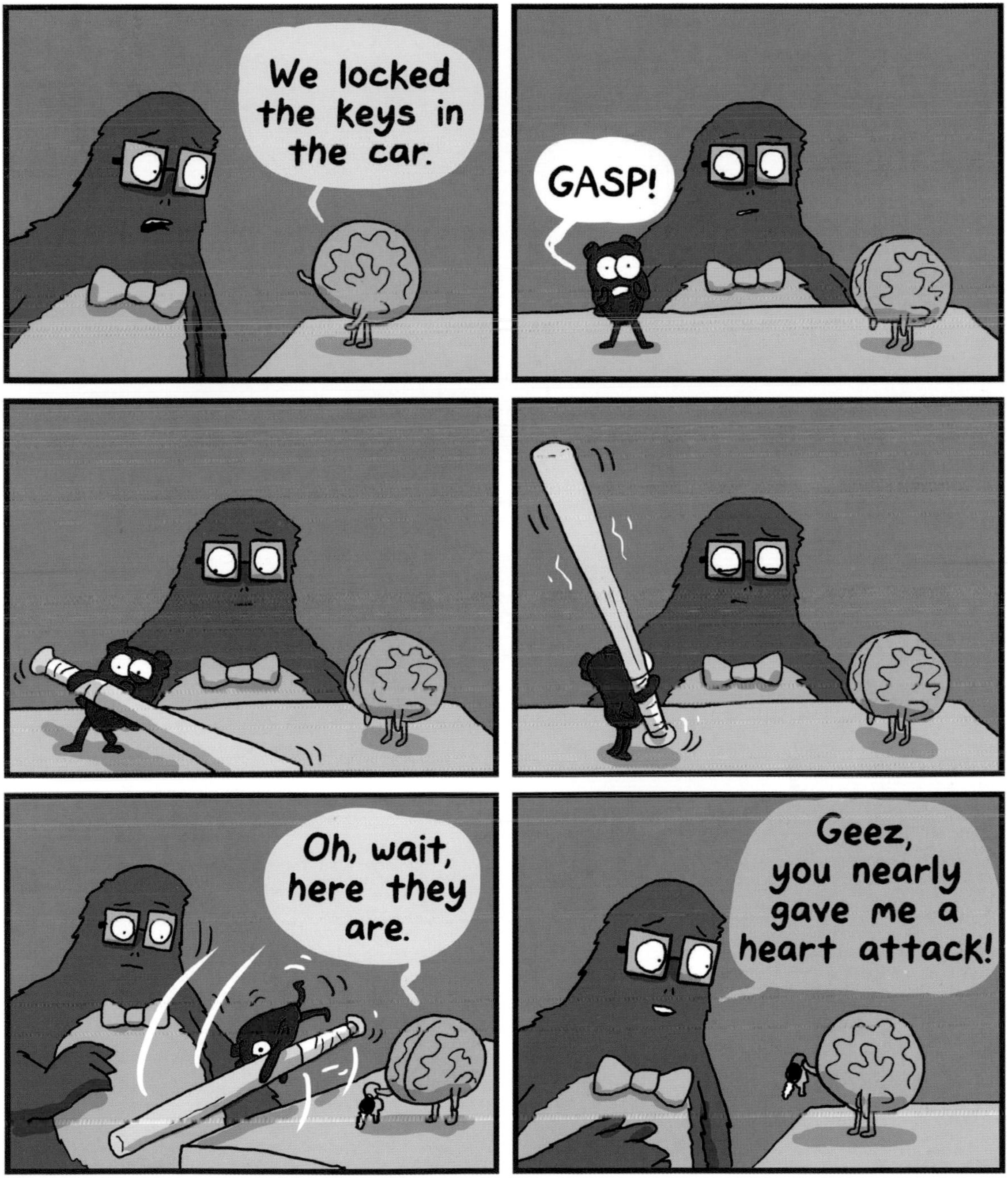
We locked the keys in the car.
GASP!
Oh, wait, here they are.
Geez, you nearly gave me a heart attack!

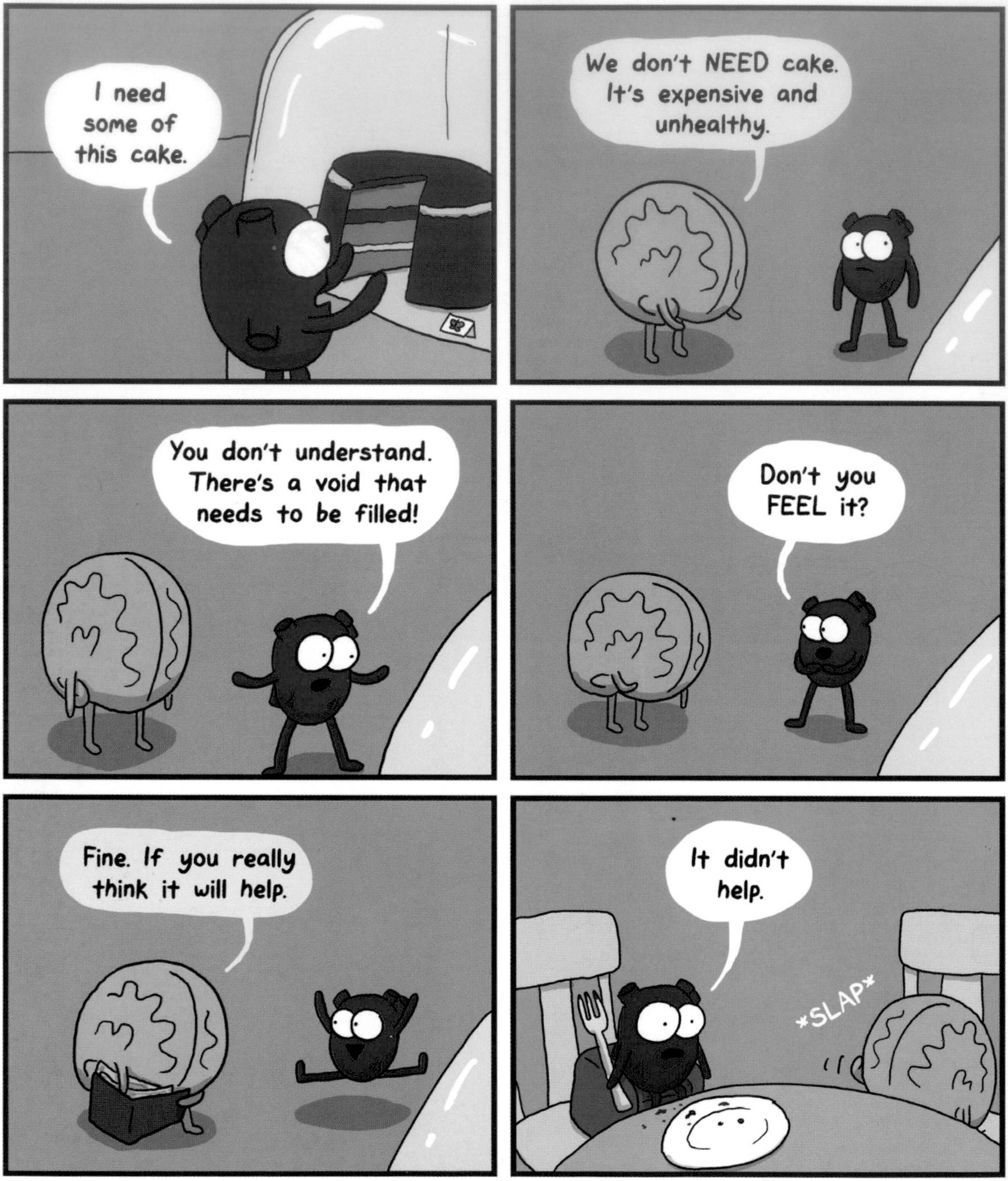
I need some of this cake.
We don't NEED cake. It's expensive and unhealthy.
You don't understand. There's a void that needs to be filled!
Don't you FEEL it?
Fine. If you really think it will help.
It didn't help.
SLAP

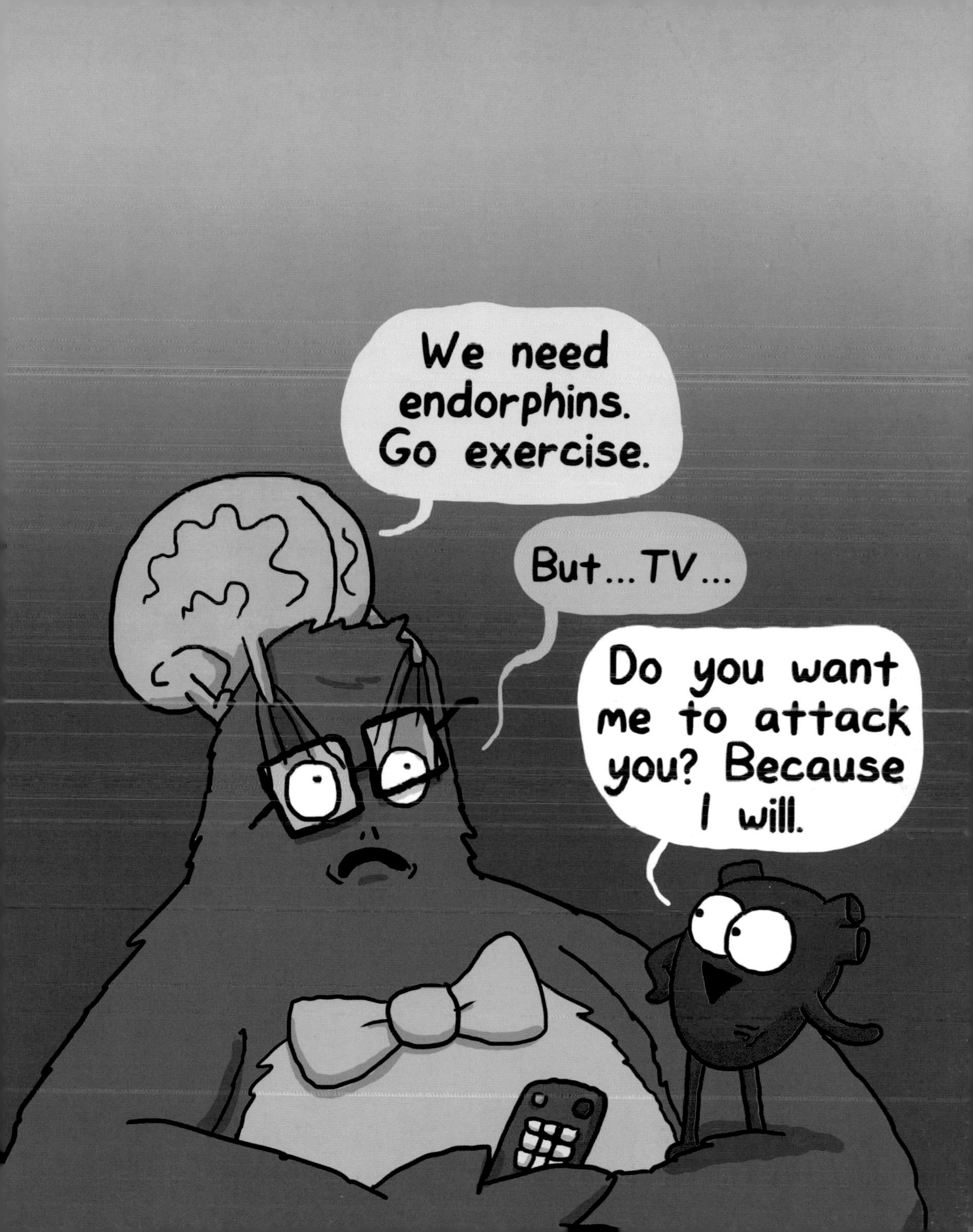
We need endorphins. Go exercise.
But... TV...
Do you want me to attack you? Because I will.

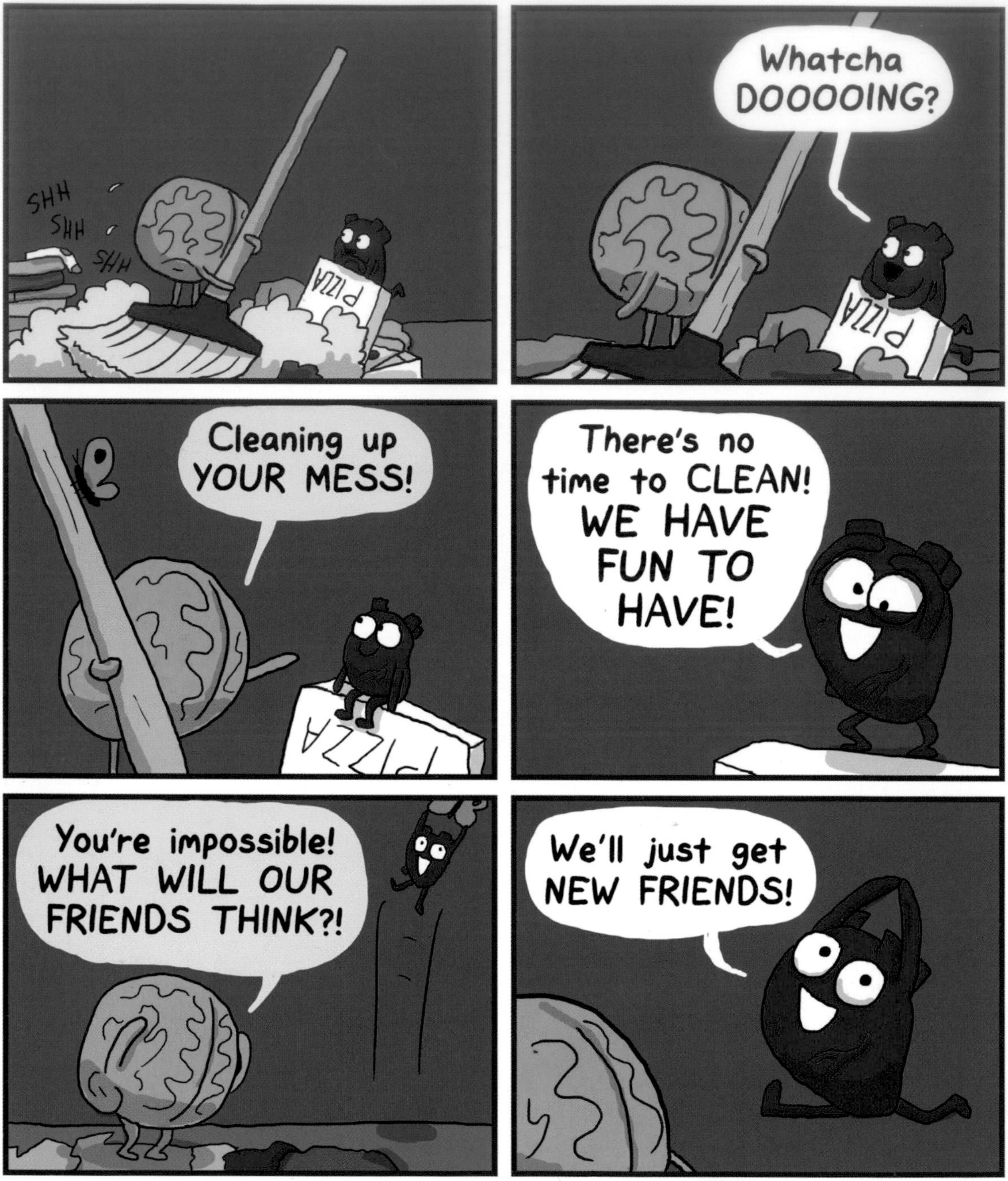
SHH
SHH
SHH
PIZZA
Whatcha DOOOOING?
PIZZA
Cleaning up YOUR MESS!
PIZZA
There's no time to CLEAN! WE HAVE FUN TO HAVE!
You're impossible! WHAT WILL OUR FRIENDS THINK?!
We'll just get NEW FRIENDS!

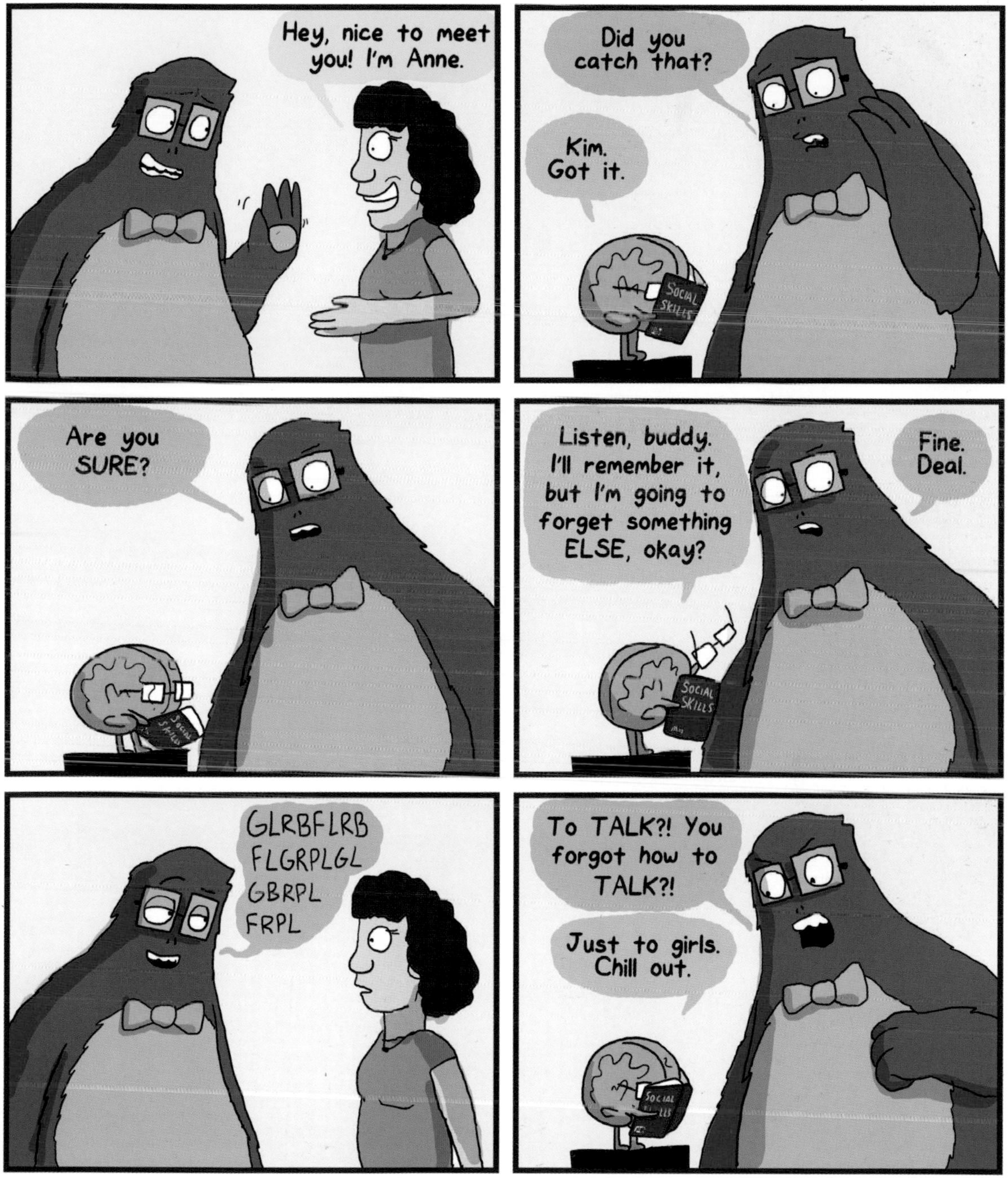
Hey, nice to meet you! I'm Anne.
Did you catch that?
Kim. Got it.
SOCIAL SKILLS
Are you SURE?
Listen, buddy. I'll remember it, but I'm going to forget something ELSE, okay?
Fine. Deal.
GLRBFLRB FLGRPLGL GBRPL FRPL
To TALK?! You forgot how to TALK?!
Just to girls. Chill out.

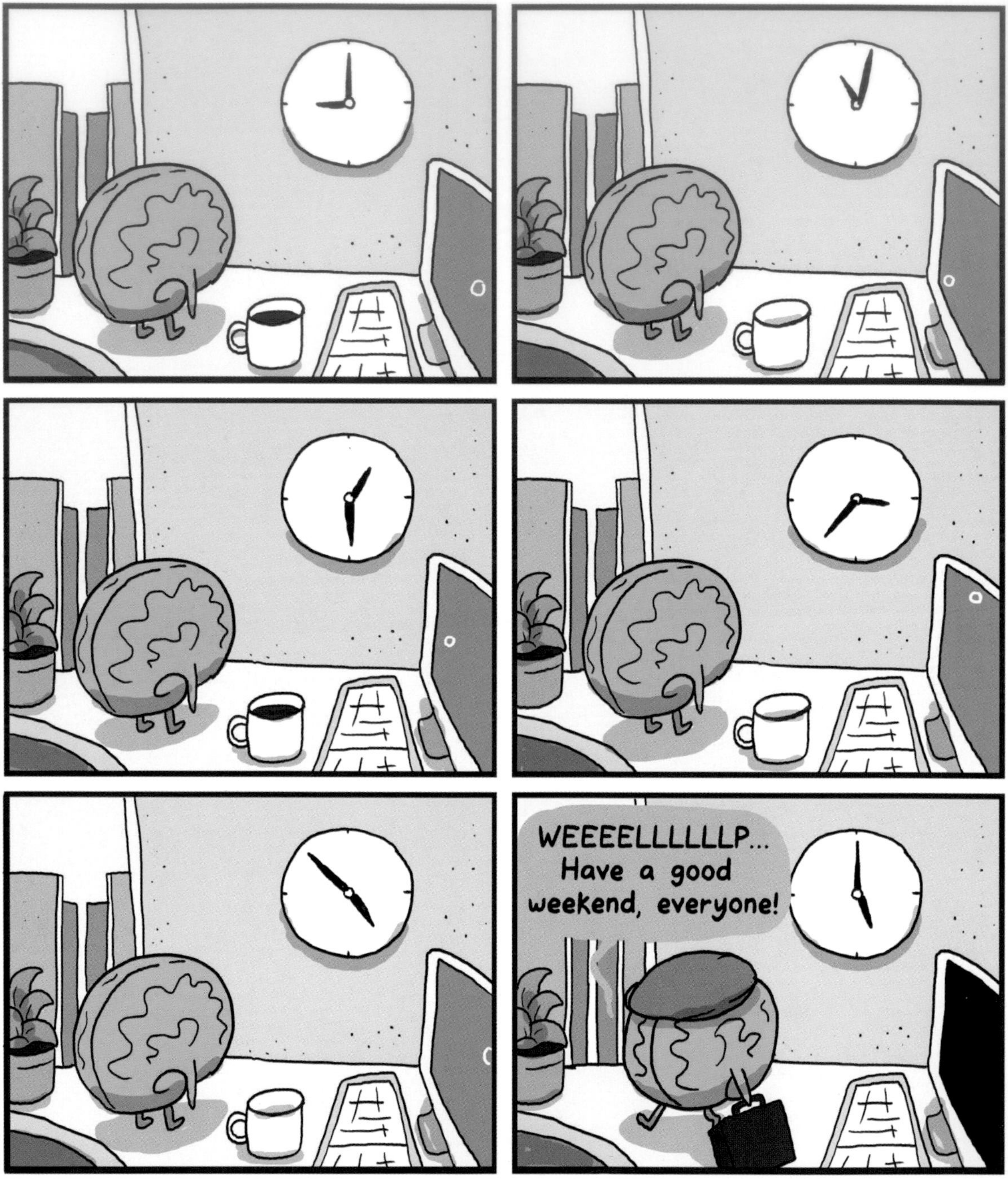
WEEEELLLLLLP... Have a good weekend, everyone!

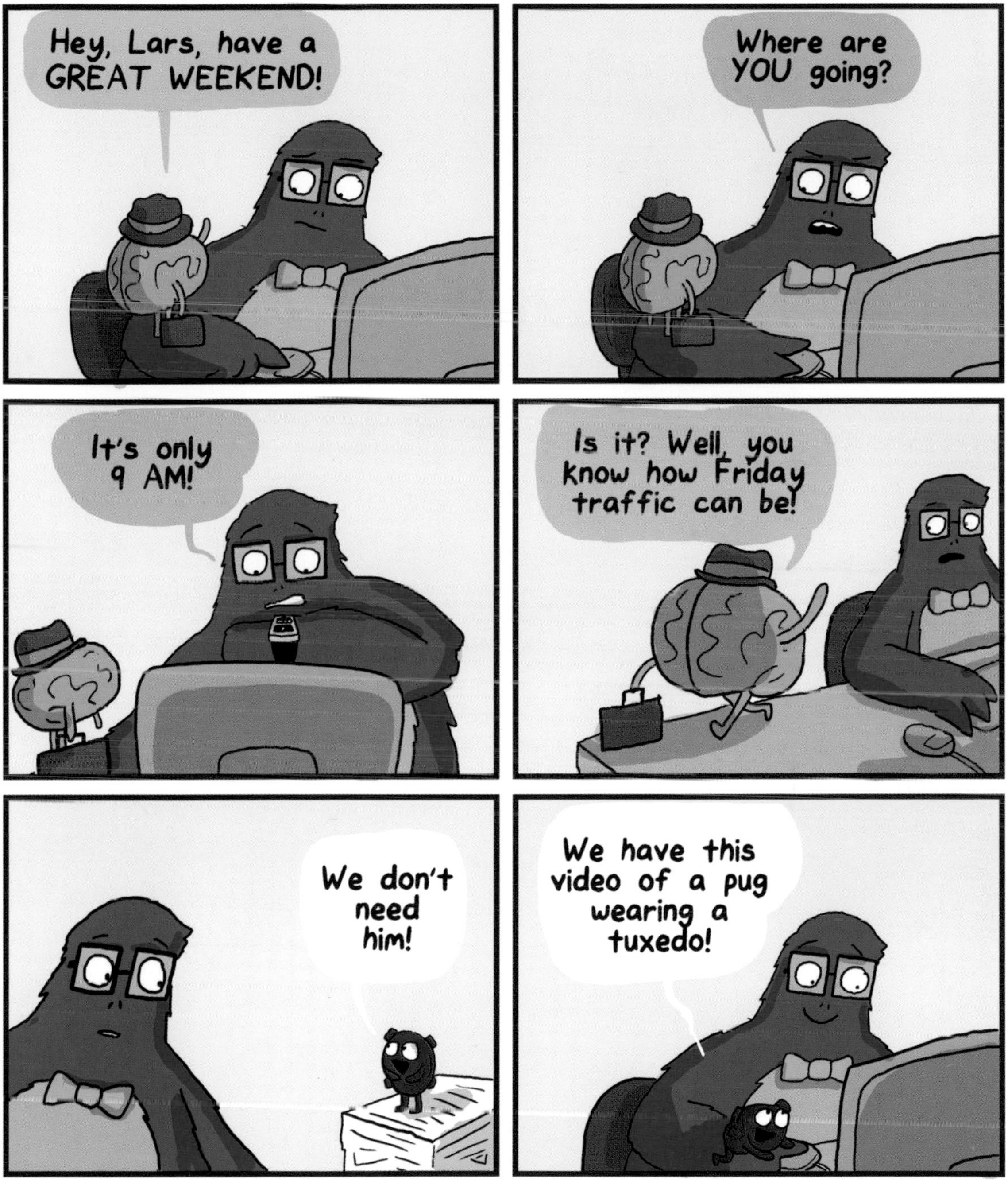
Hey, Lars, have a GREAT WEEKEND!
Where are YOU going?
It's only 9 AM!
Is it? Well, you know how Friday traffic can be!
We don't need him!
We have this video of a pug wearing a tuxedo!

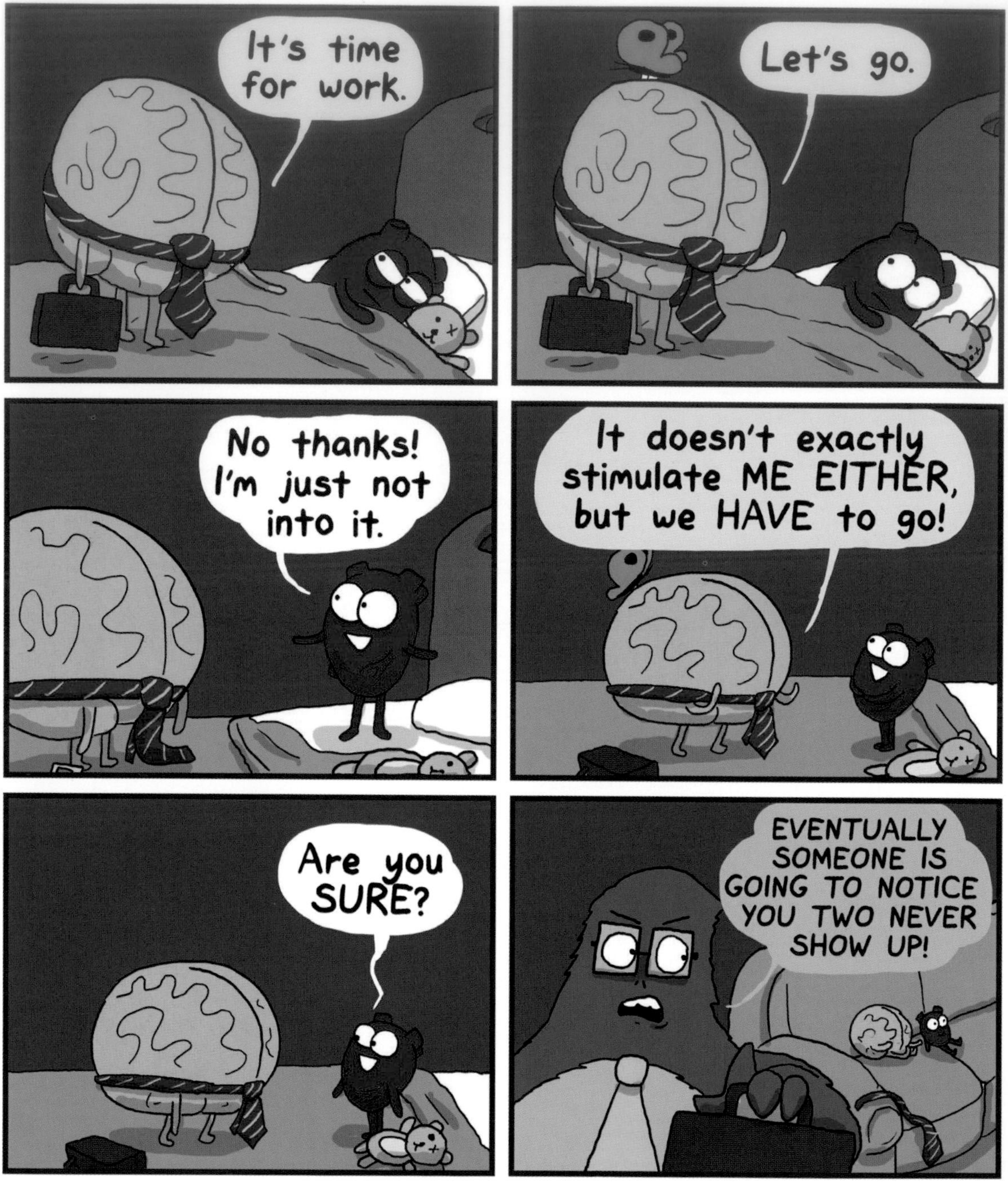
It's time for work.
Let's go.
No thanks! I'm just not into it.
It doesn't exactly stimulate ME EITHER, but we HAVE to go!
Are you SURE?
EVENTUALLY SOMEONE IS GOING TO NOTICE YOU TWO NEVER SHOW UP!

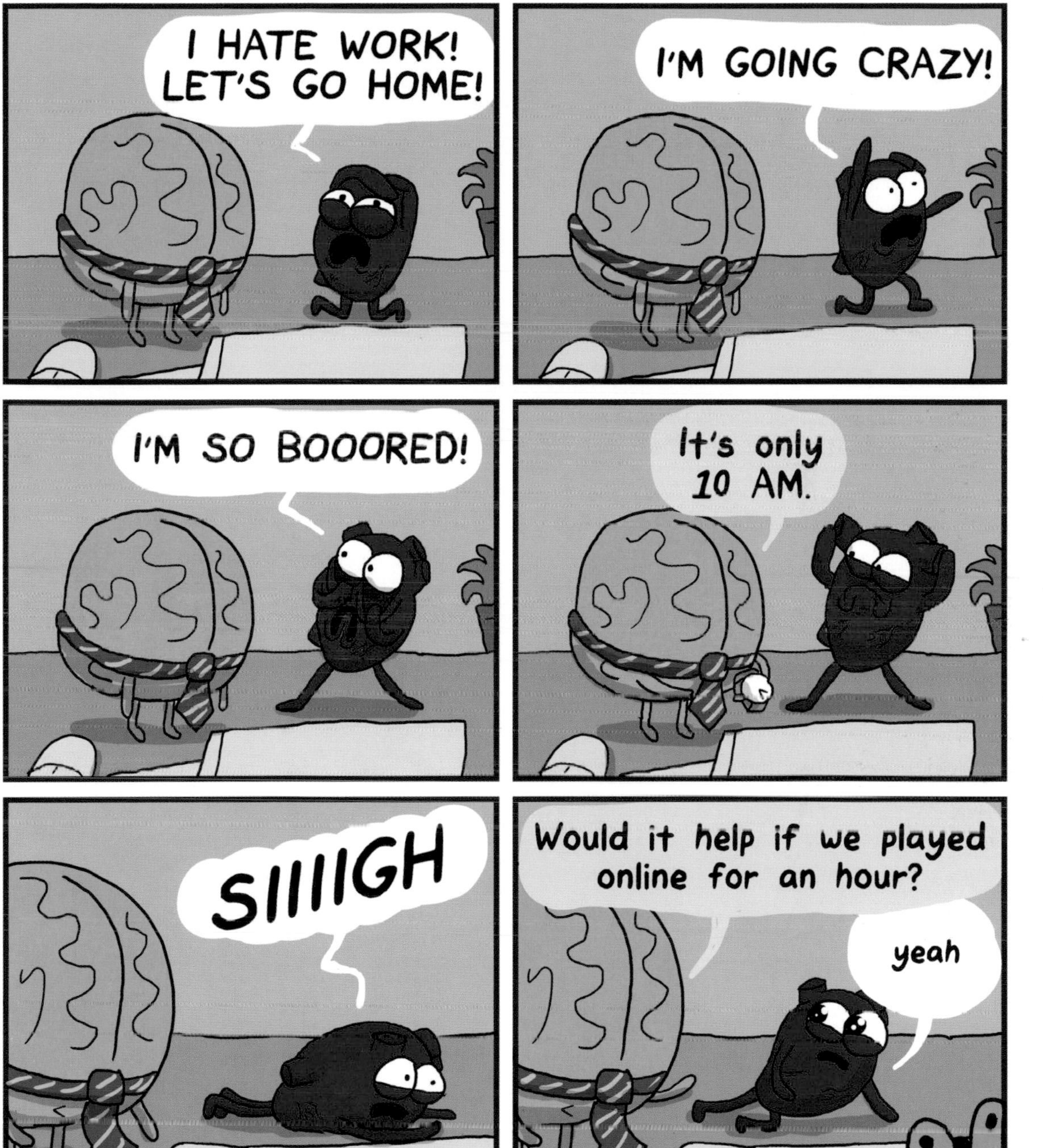

I HATE WORK! LET'S GO HOME!
I'M GOING CRAZY!
I'M SO BOOORED!
It's only 10 AM.
SIIIIGH
Would it help if we played online for an hour?
yeah

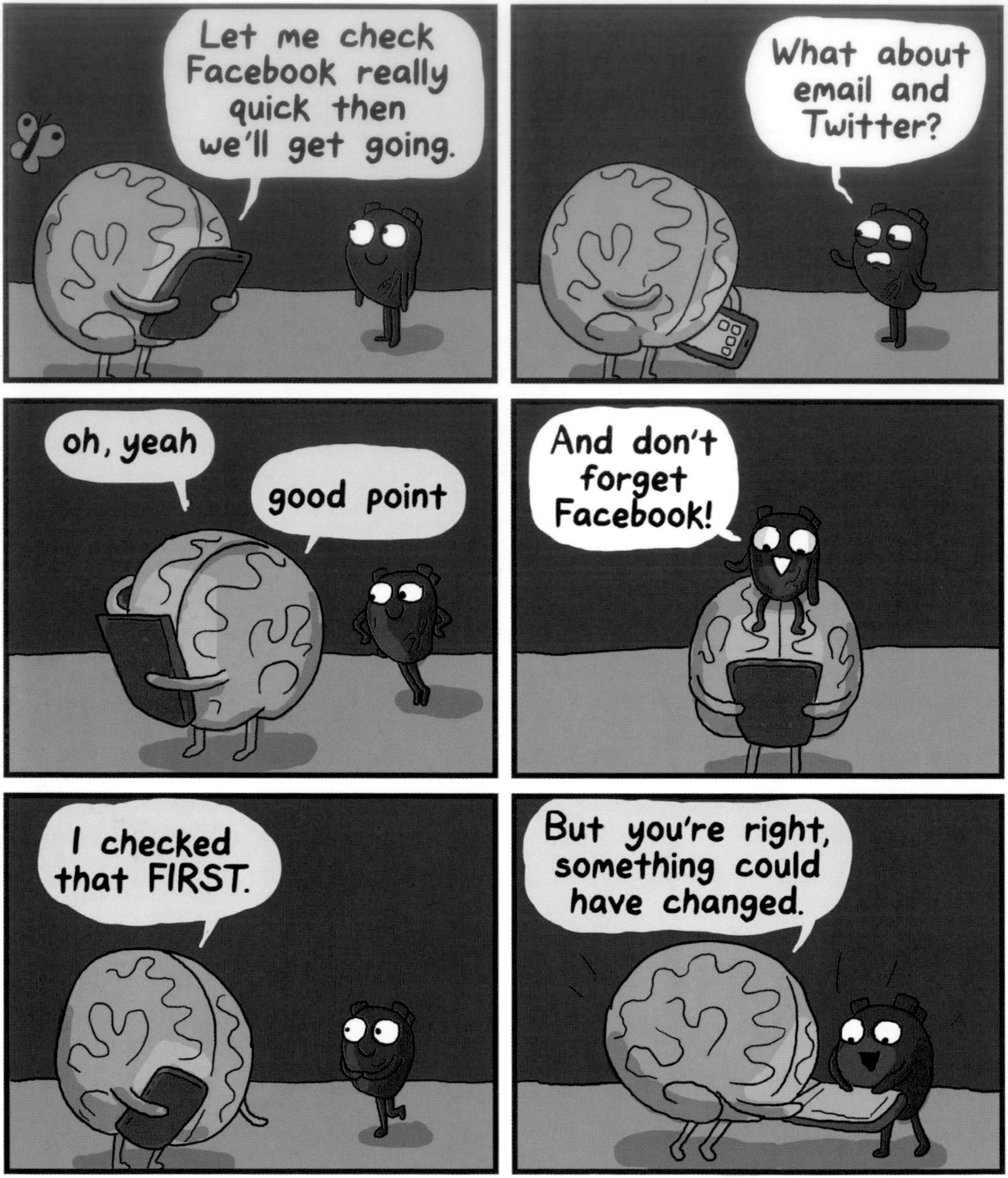
Let me check Facebook really quick then we'll get going.
What about email and Twitter?
oh, yeah
good point
And don't forget Facebook!
I checked that FIRST.
But you're right, something could have changed.

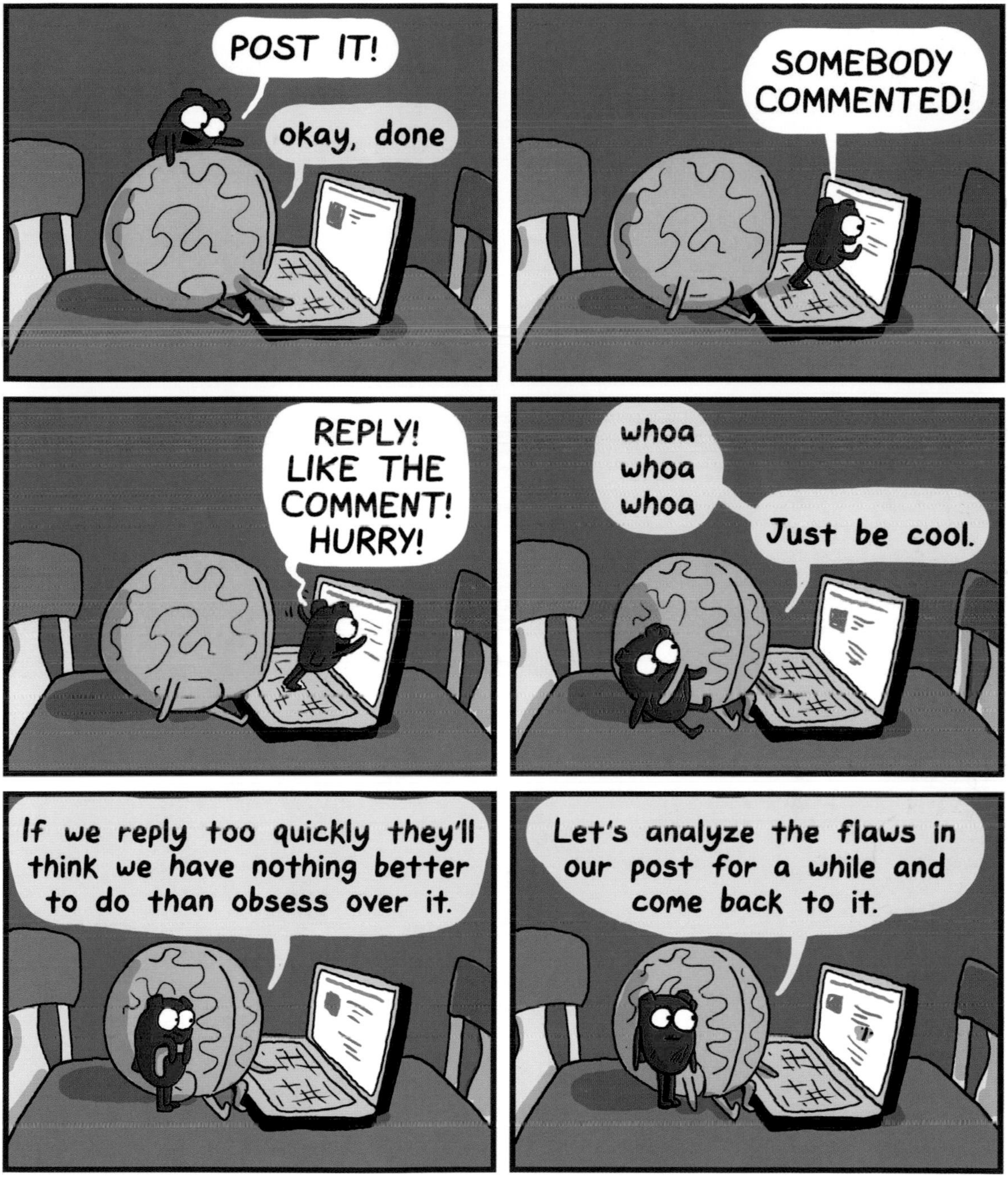
POST IT!
okay, done
SOMEBODY COMMENTED!
REPLY! LIKE THE COMMENT! HURRY!
whoa whoa whoa
Just be cool.
If we reply too quickly they'll think we have nothing better to do than obsess over it.
Let's analyze the flaws in our post for a while and come back to it.

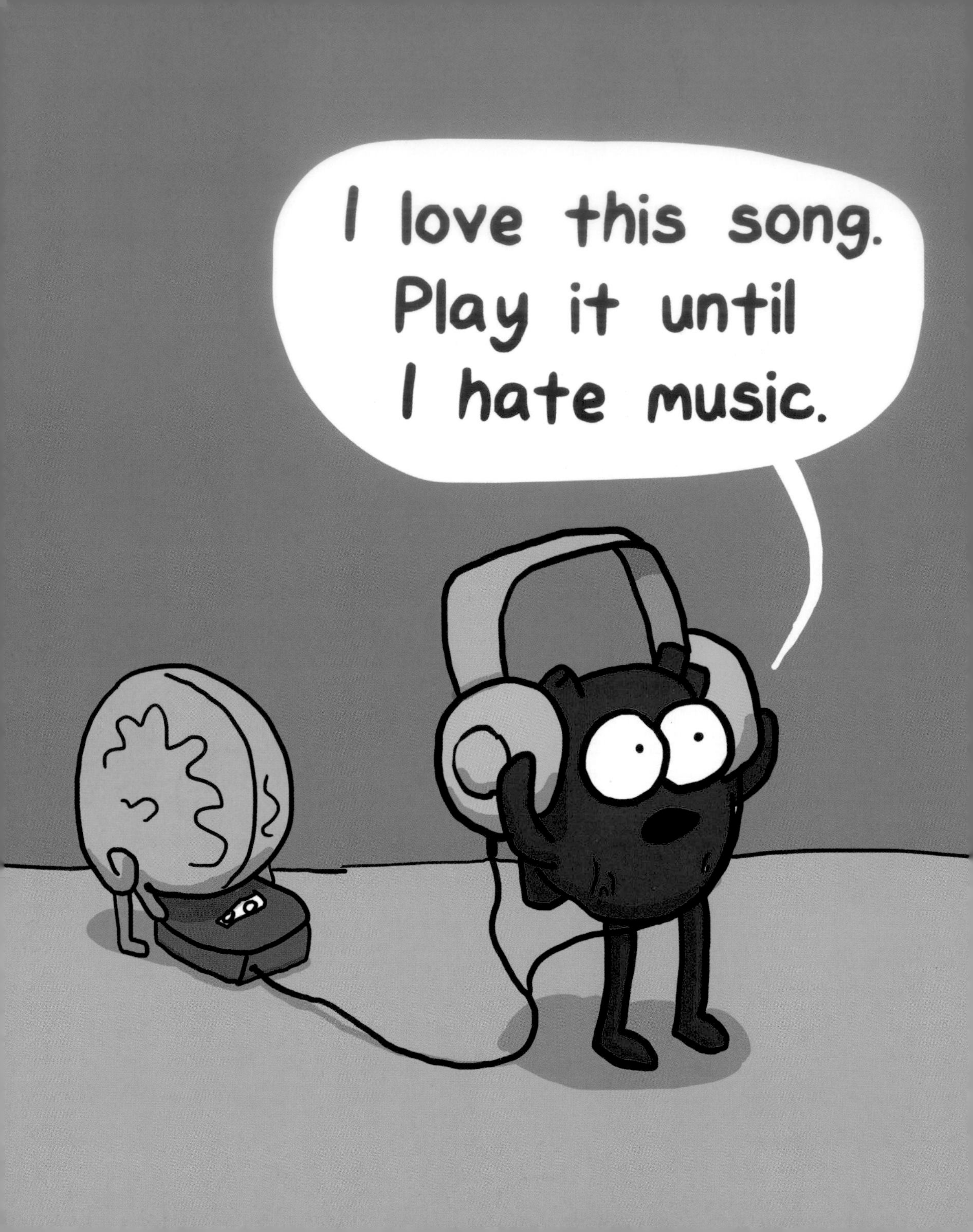
I love this song. Play it until I hate music.

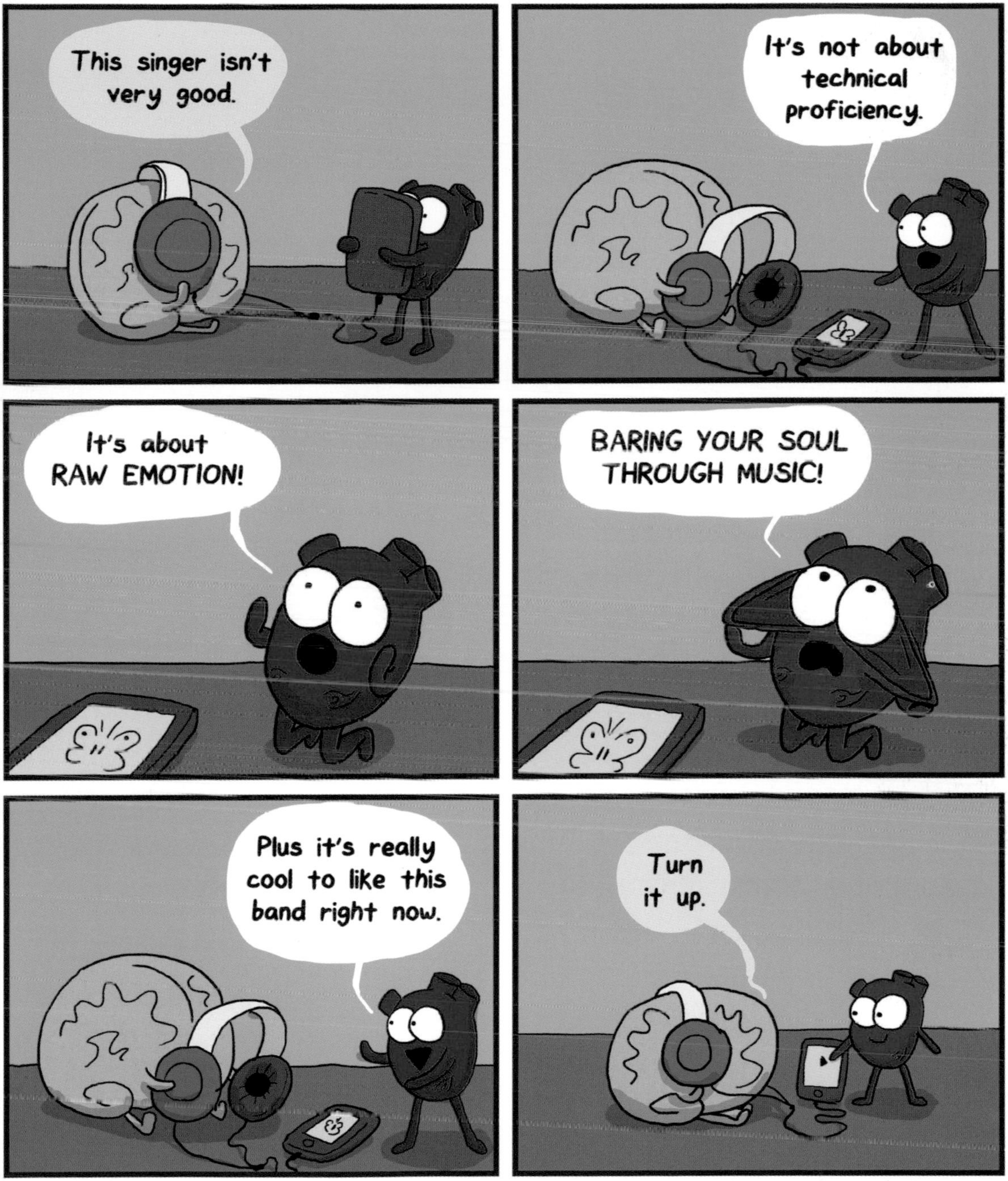
This singer isn't very good.
It's not about technical proficiency.
It's about RAW EMOTION!
BARING YOUR SOUL THROUGH MUSIC!
Plus it's really cool to like this band right now.
Turn it up.

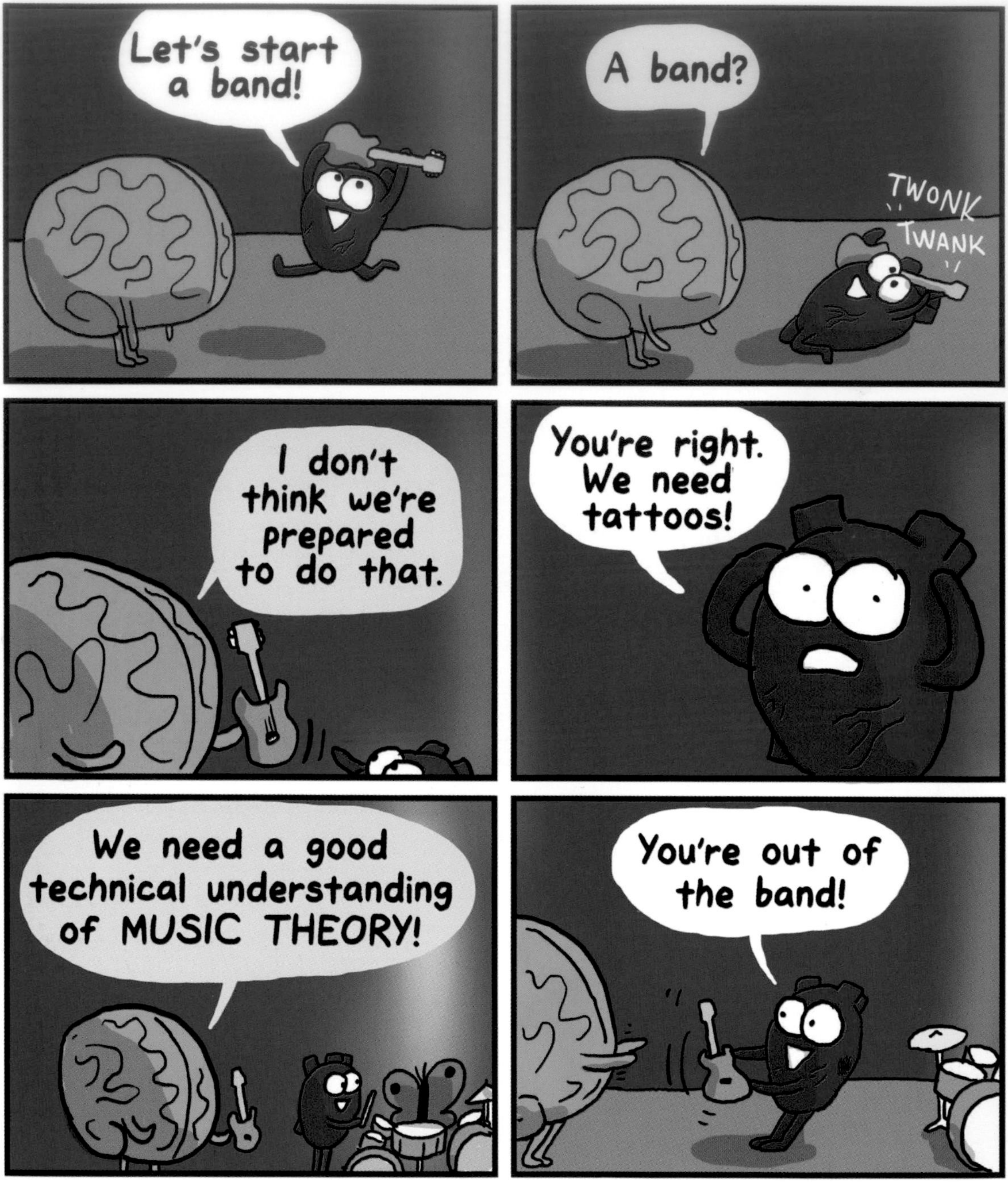
Let's start a band!
A band?
TWONK
TWANK
I don't think we're prepared to do that.
You're right. We need tattoos!
We need a good technical understanding of MUSIC THEORY!
You're out of the band!

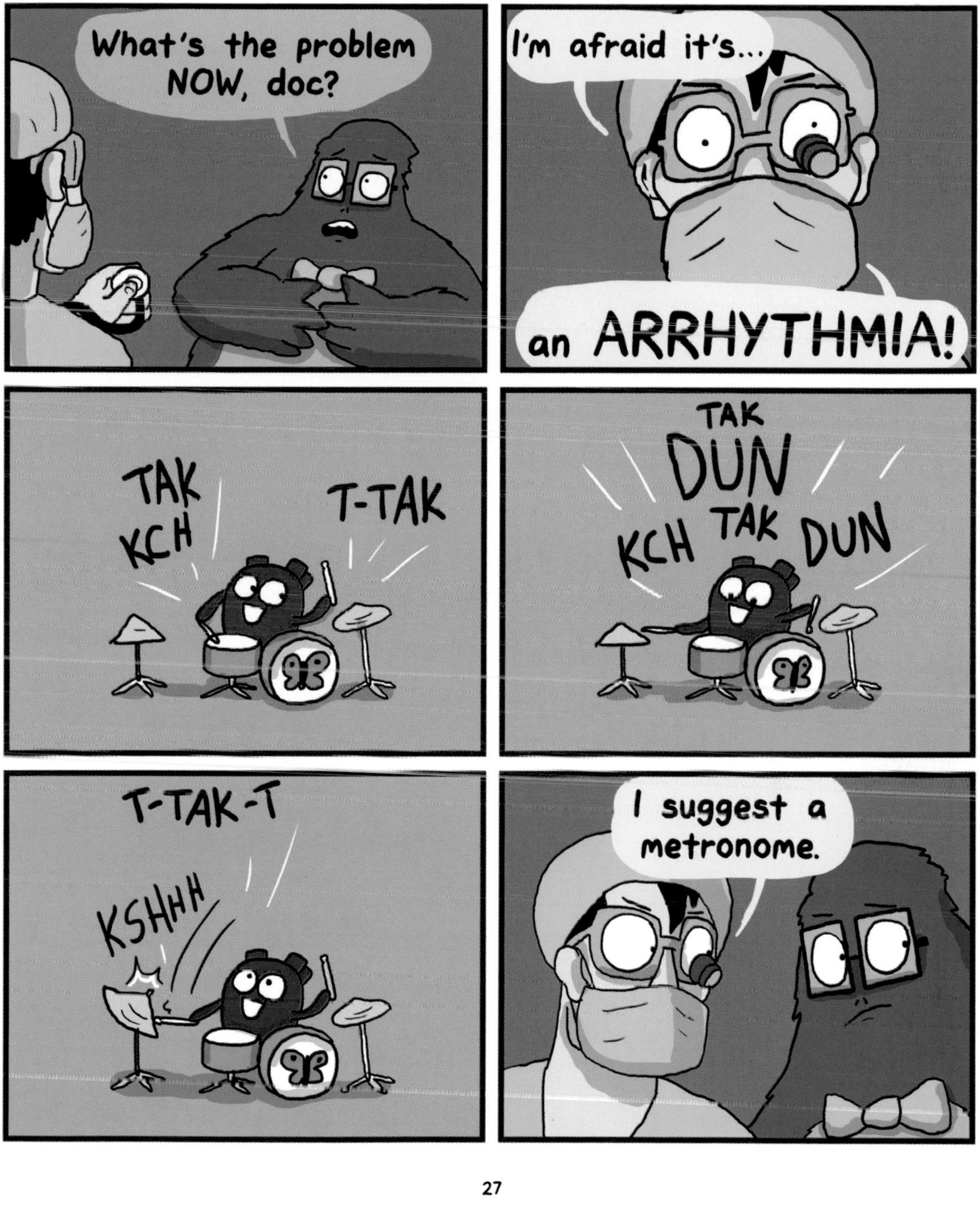
What's the problem NOW, doc?
I'm afraid it's...
an ARRHYTHMIA!
TAK KCH
T-TAK
TAK
DUN
KCH TAK DUN
T-TAK-T
KSHHH
I suggest a metronome.

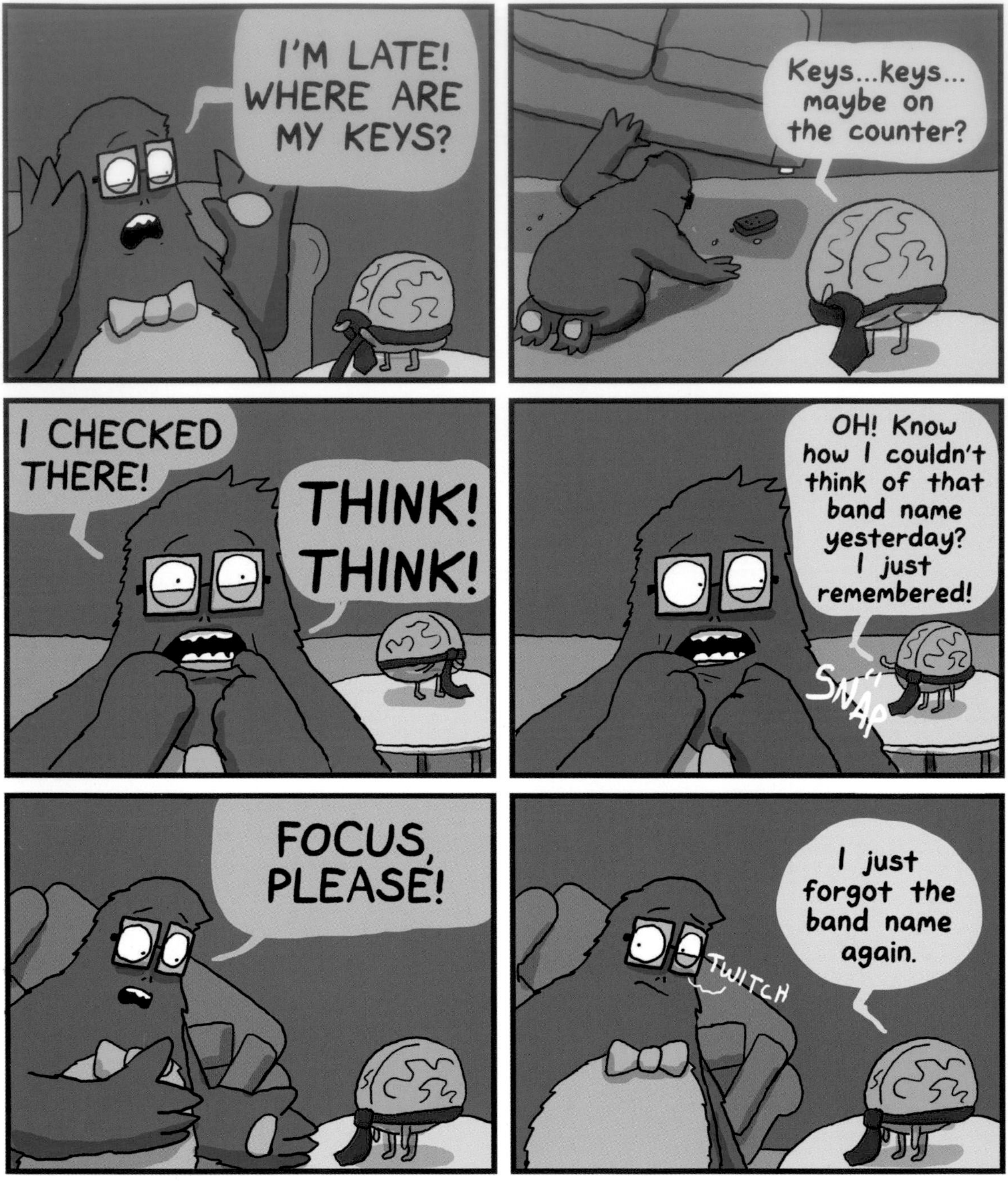
I'M LATE! WHERE ARE MY KEYS?
Keys...keys... maybe on the counter?
I CHECKED THERE!
THINK! THINK!
OH! Know how I couldn't think of that band name yesterday? I just remembered!
SNAP
FOCUS, PLEASE!
TWITCH
I just forgot the band name again.

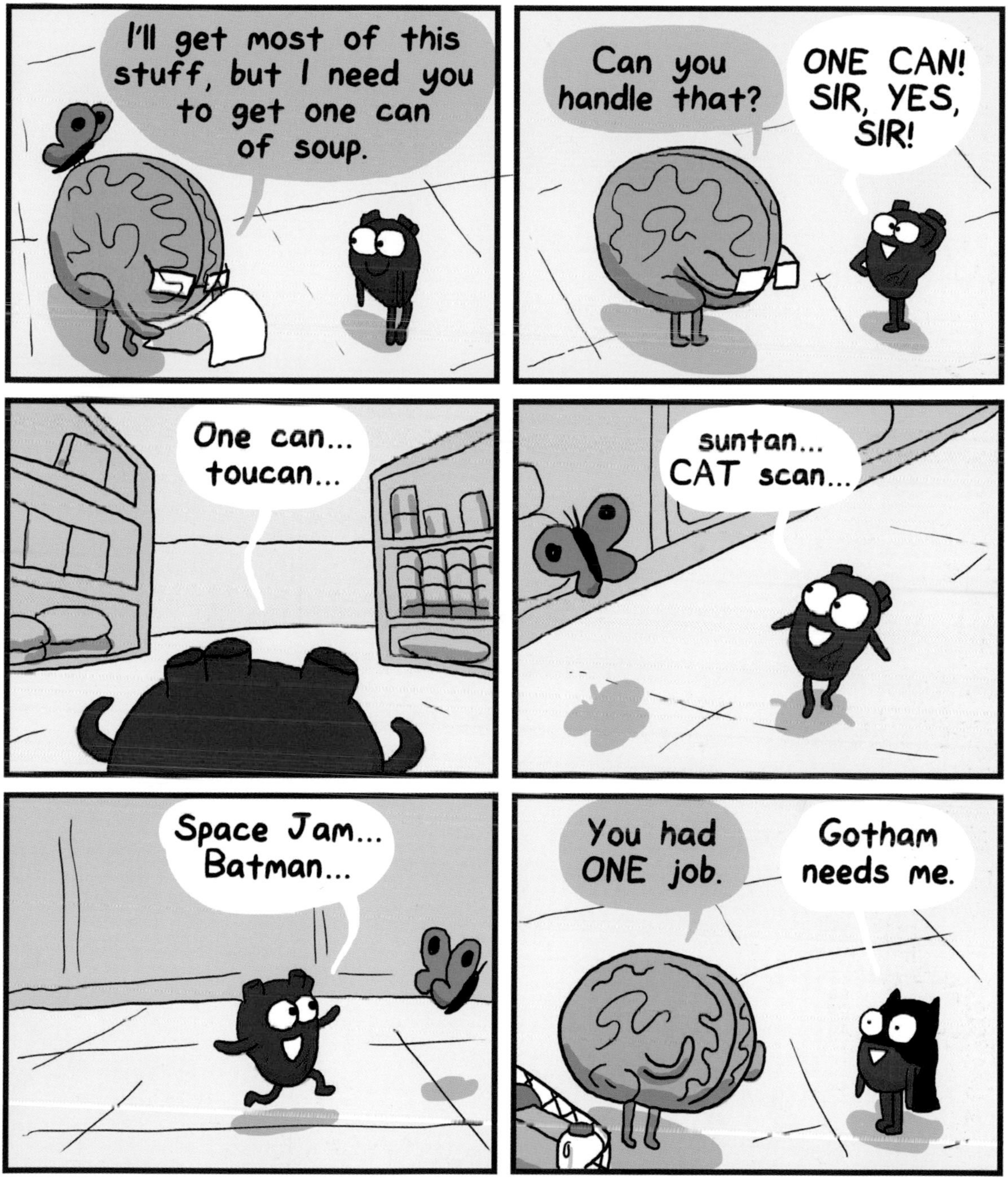
I'll get most of this stuff, but I need you to get one can of soup.
Can you handle that?
ONE CAN! SIR, YES, SIR!
One can... toucan...
suntan... CAT scan...
Space Jam... Batman...
You had ONE job.
Gotham needs me.

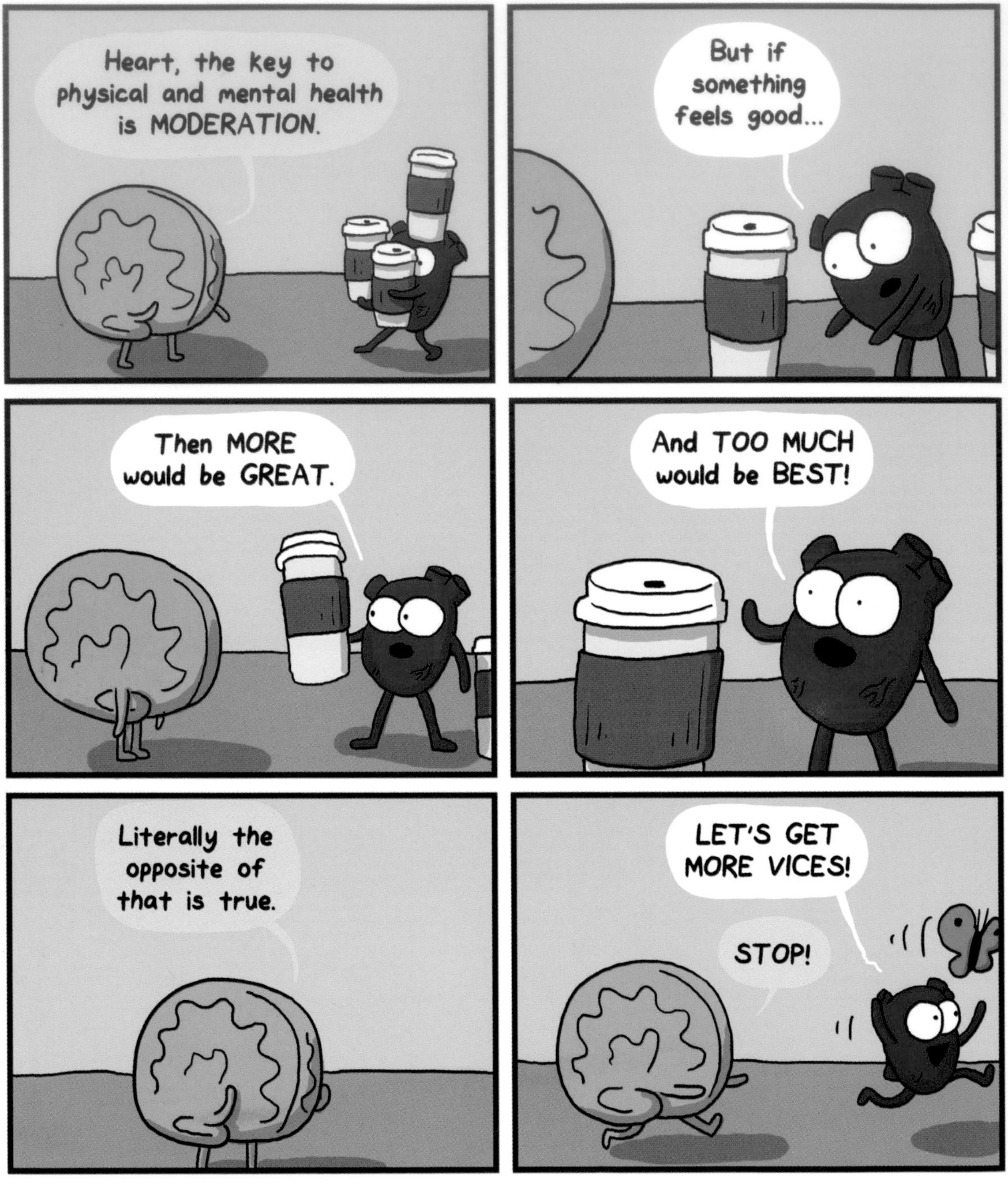
Heart, the key to physical and mental health is MODERATION.
But if something feels good...
Then MORE would be GREAT.
And TOO MUCH would be BEST!
Literally the opposite of that is true.
LET'S GET MORE VICES!
STOP!

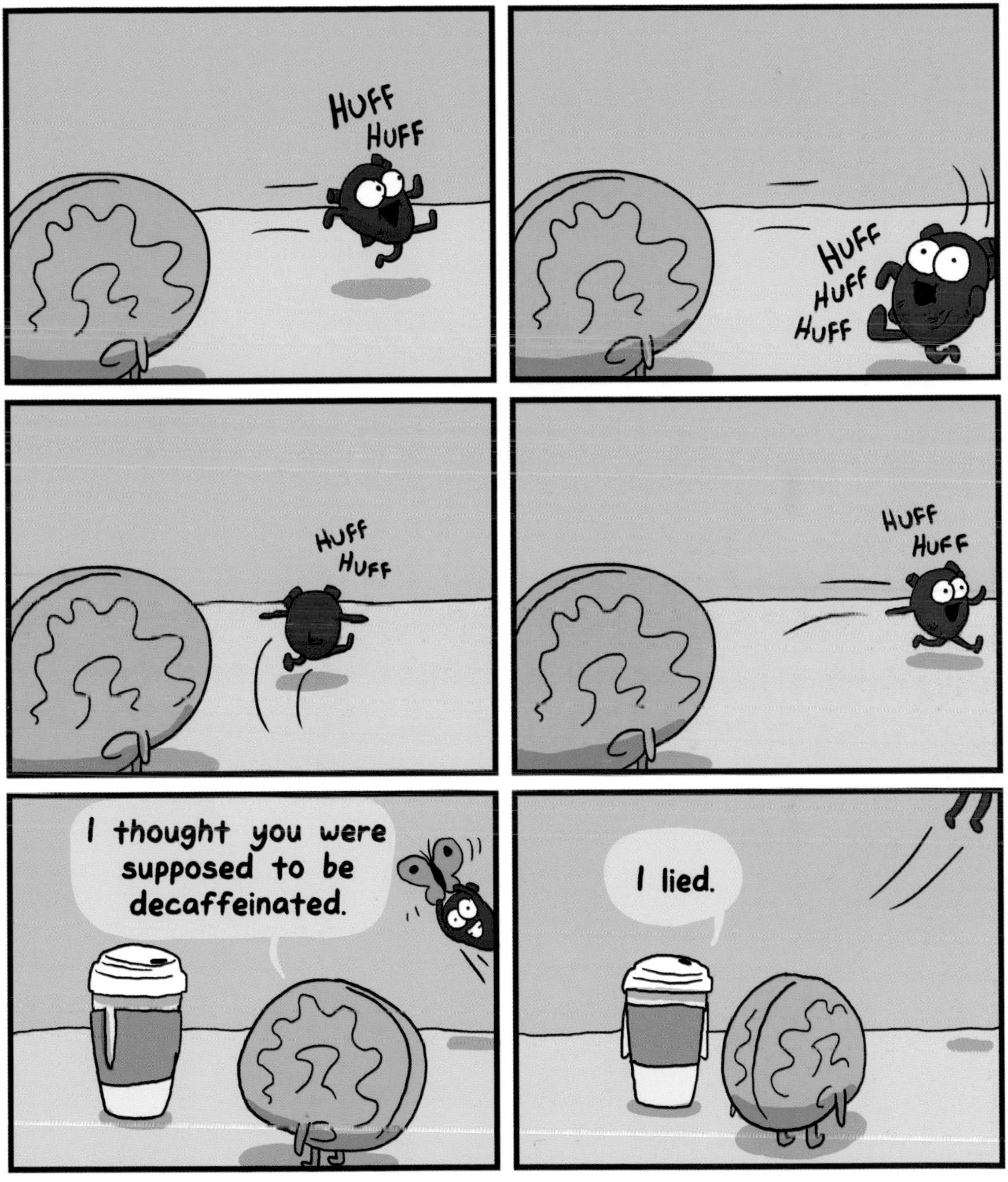
HUFF HUFF
HUFF HUFF HUFF
HUFF HUFF
HUFF HUFF
I thought you were supposed to be decaffeinated.
I lied.

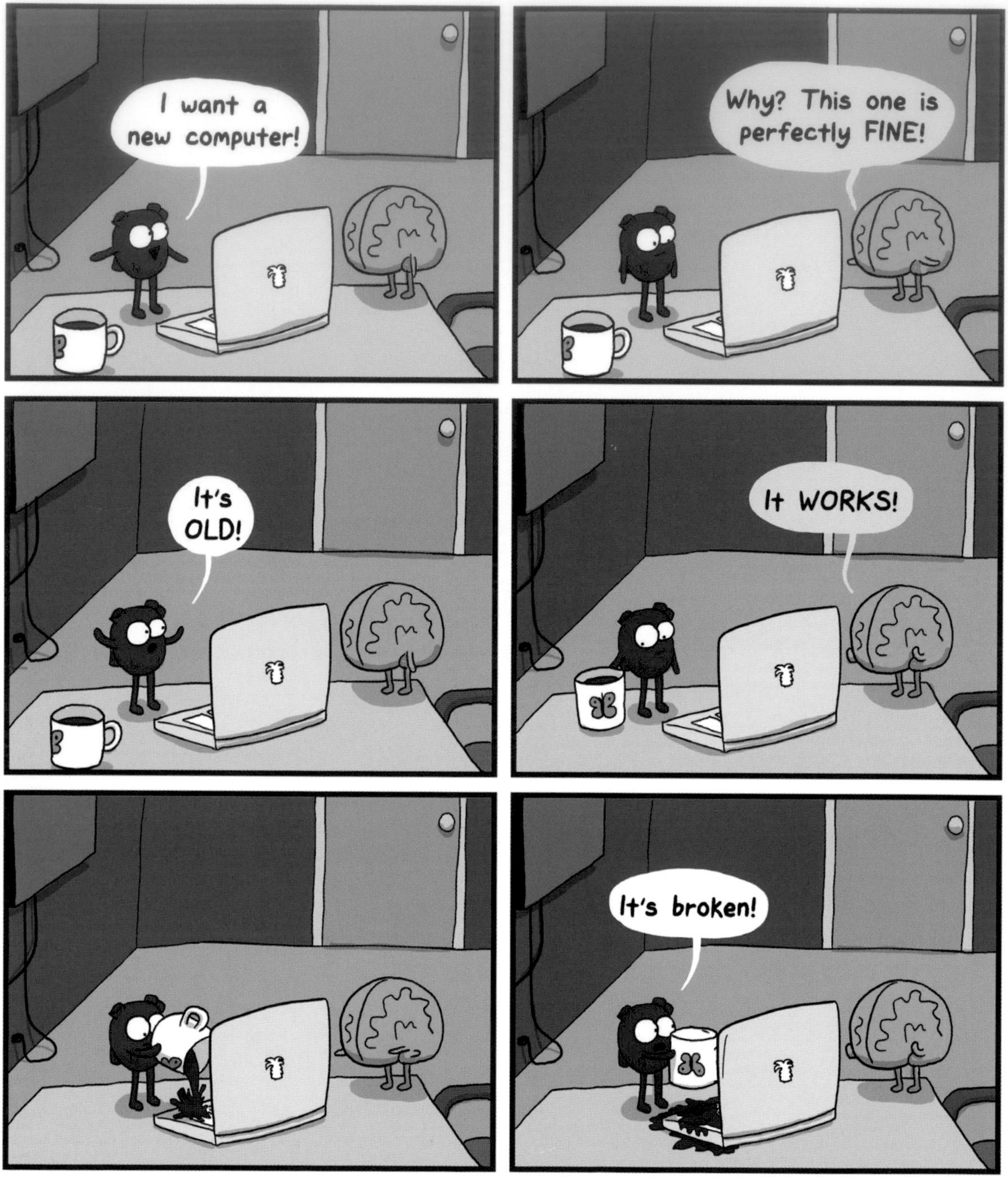
I want a new computer!
Why? This one is perfectly FINE!
It's OLD!
It WORKS!
It's broken!

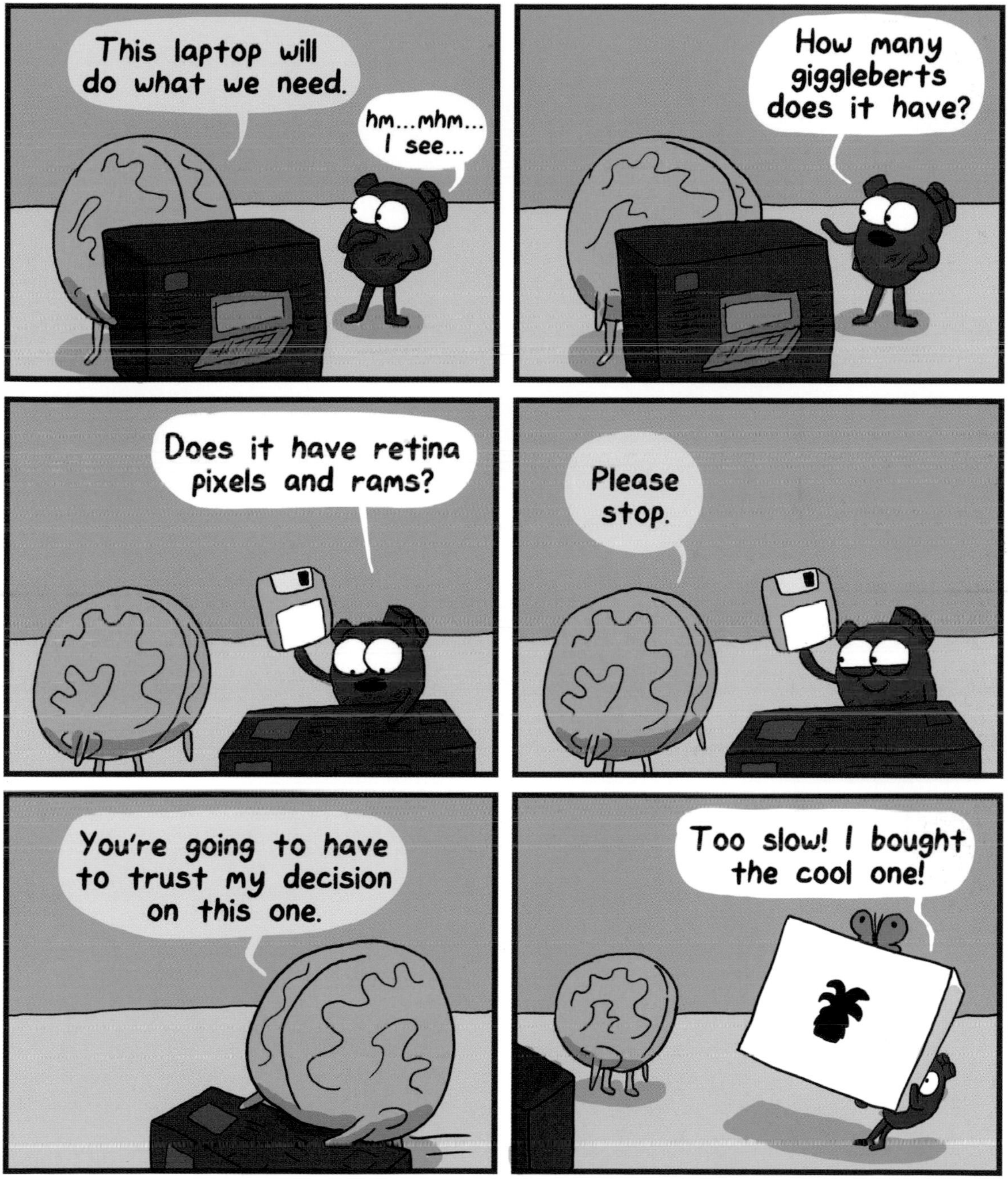
This laptop will do what we need.
hm...mhm... I see...
How many giggleberts does it have?
Does it have retina pixels and rams?
Please stop.
You're going to have to trust my decision on this one.
Too slow! I bought the cool one!

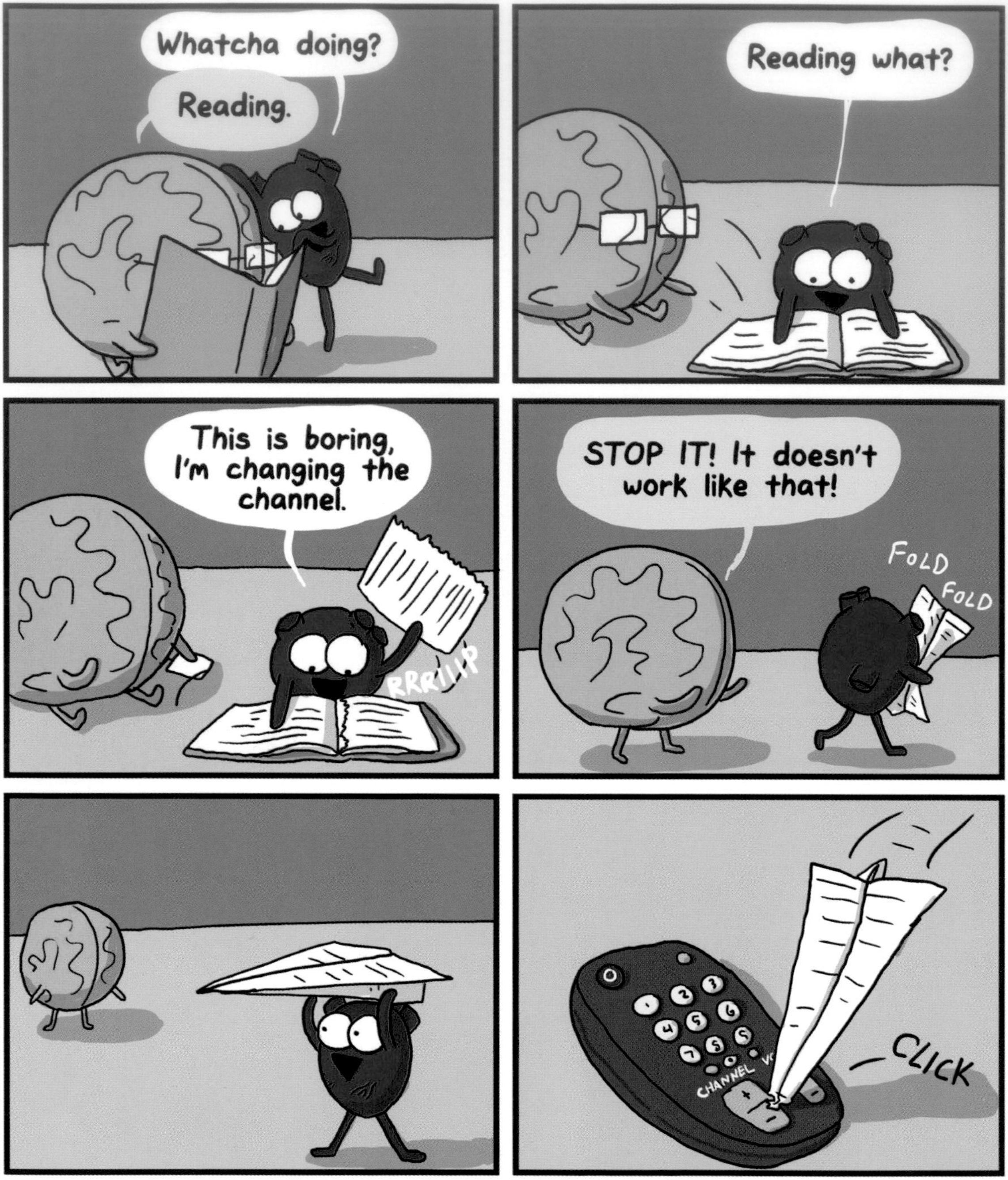
Whatcha doing?
Reading.
Reading what?
This is boring, I'm changing the channel.
RRRIIIP
STOP IT! It doesn't work like that!
FOLD
FOLD
CLICK

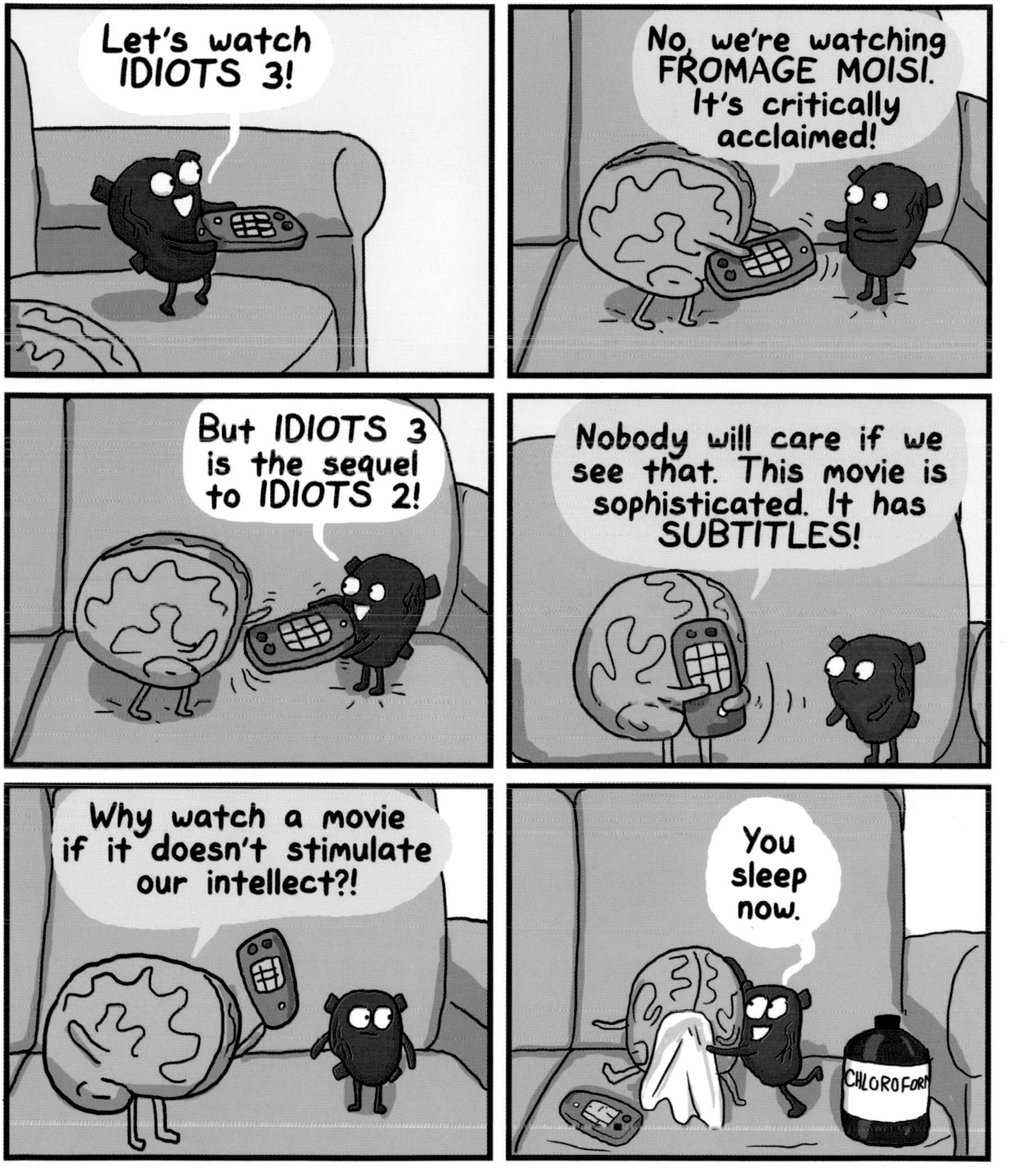
Let's watch IDIOTS 3!
No, we're watching FROMAGE MOISI. It's critically acclaimed!
But IDIOTS 3 is the sequel to IDIOTS 2!
Nobody will care if we see that. This movie is sophisticated. It has SUBTITLES!
Why watch a movie if it doesn't stimulate our intellect?!
You sleep now.
CHLOROFORM

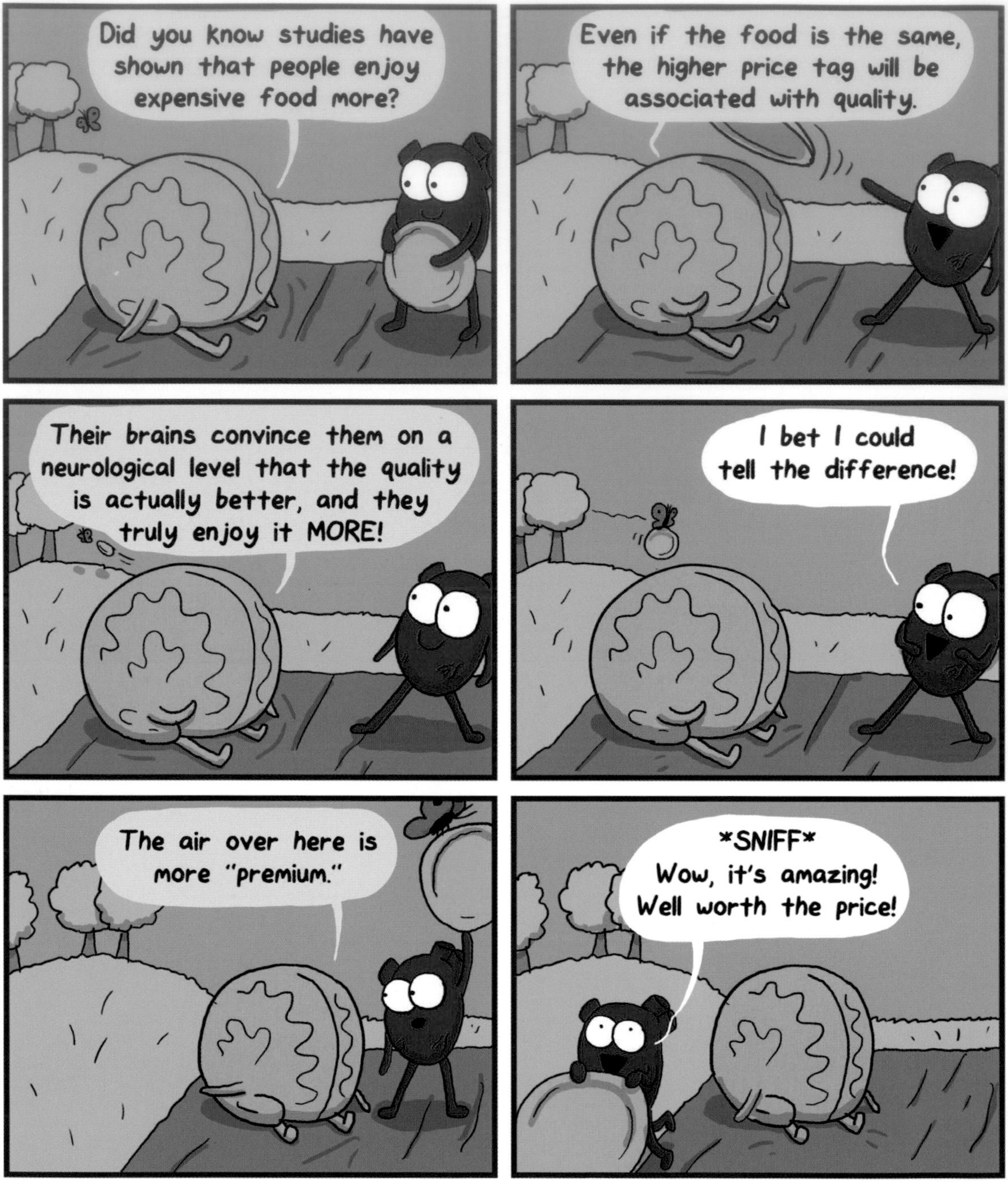
Did you know studies have shown that people enjoy expensive food more?
Even if the food is the same, the higher price tag will be associated with quality.
Their brains convince them on a neurological level that the quality is actually better, and they truly enjoy it MORE!
I bet I could tell the difference!
The air over here is more "premium."
SNIFF
Wow, it's amazing! Well worth the price!

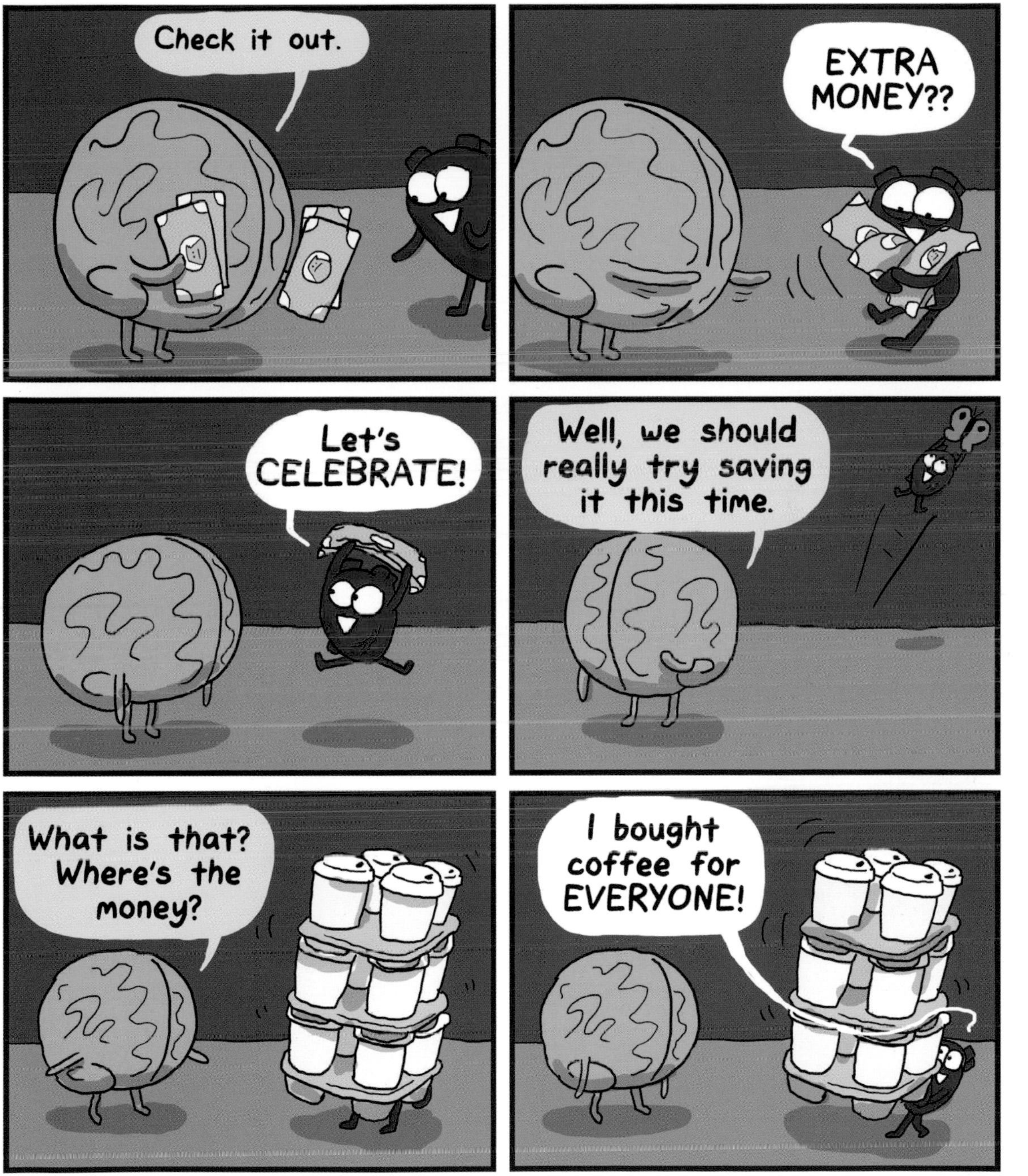
Check it out.
EXTRA MONEY??
Let's CELEBRATE!
Well, we should really try saving it this time.
What is that? Where's the money?
I bought coffee for EVERYONE!

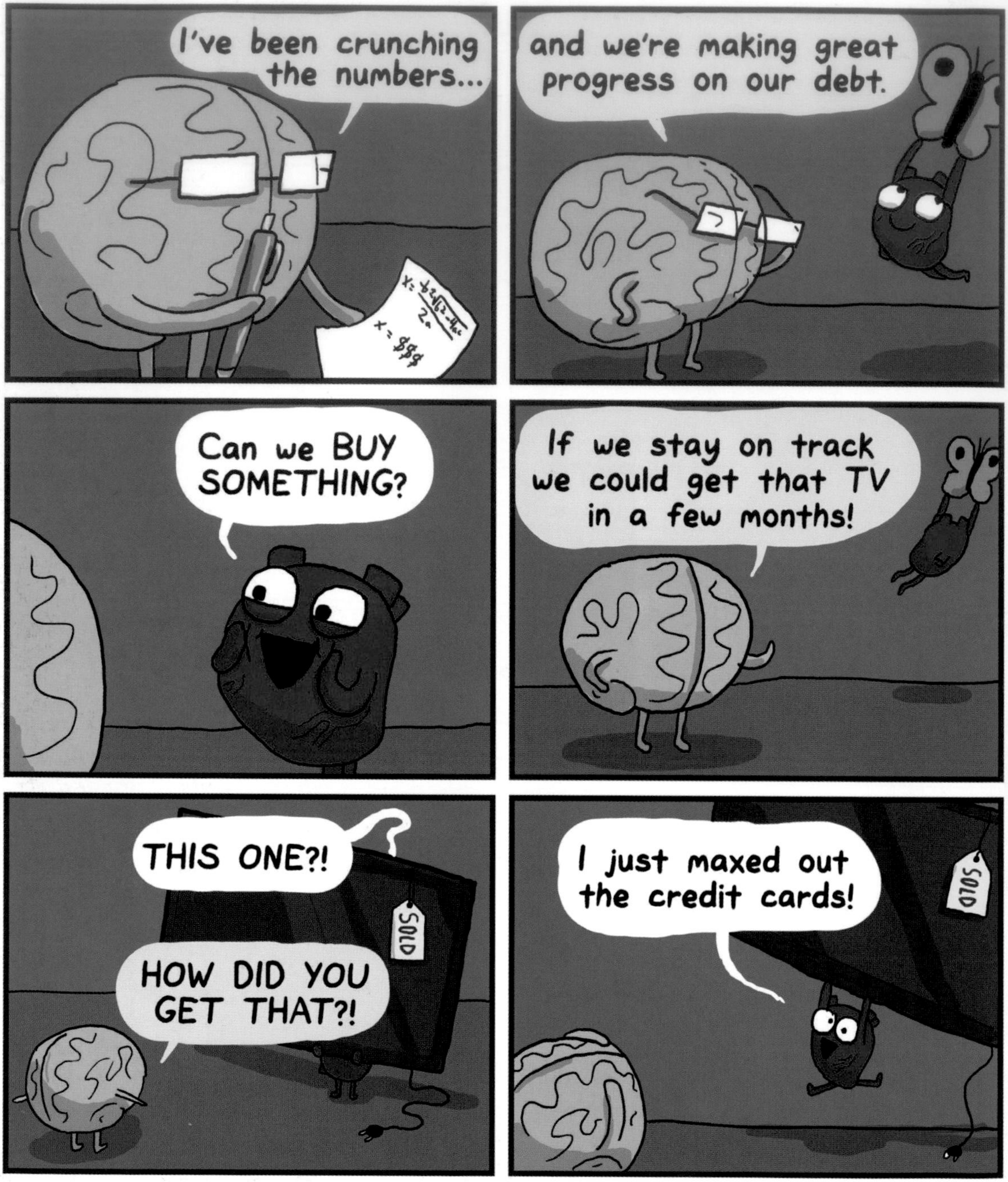
I've been crunching the numbers...
and we're making great progress on our debt.
Can we BUY SOMETHING?
If we stay on track we could get that TV in a few months!
THIS ONE?!
SOLD
HOW DID YOU GET THAT?!
I just maxed out the credit cards!
SOLD

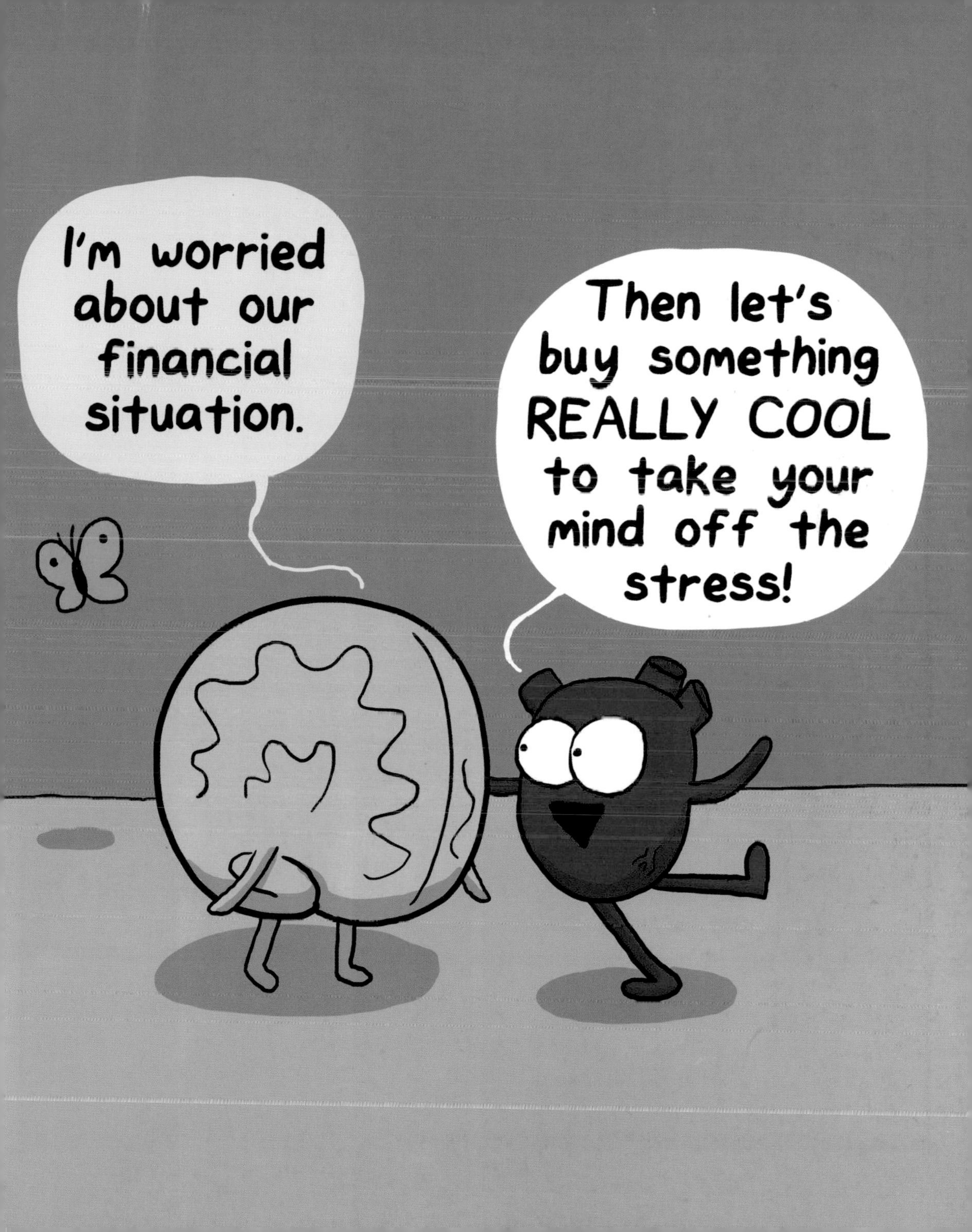
I'm worried about our financial situation.
Then let's buy something REALLY COOL to take your mind off the stress!

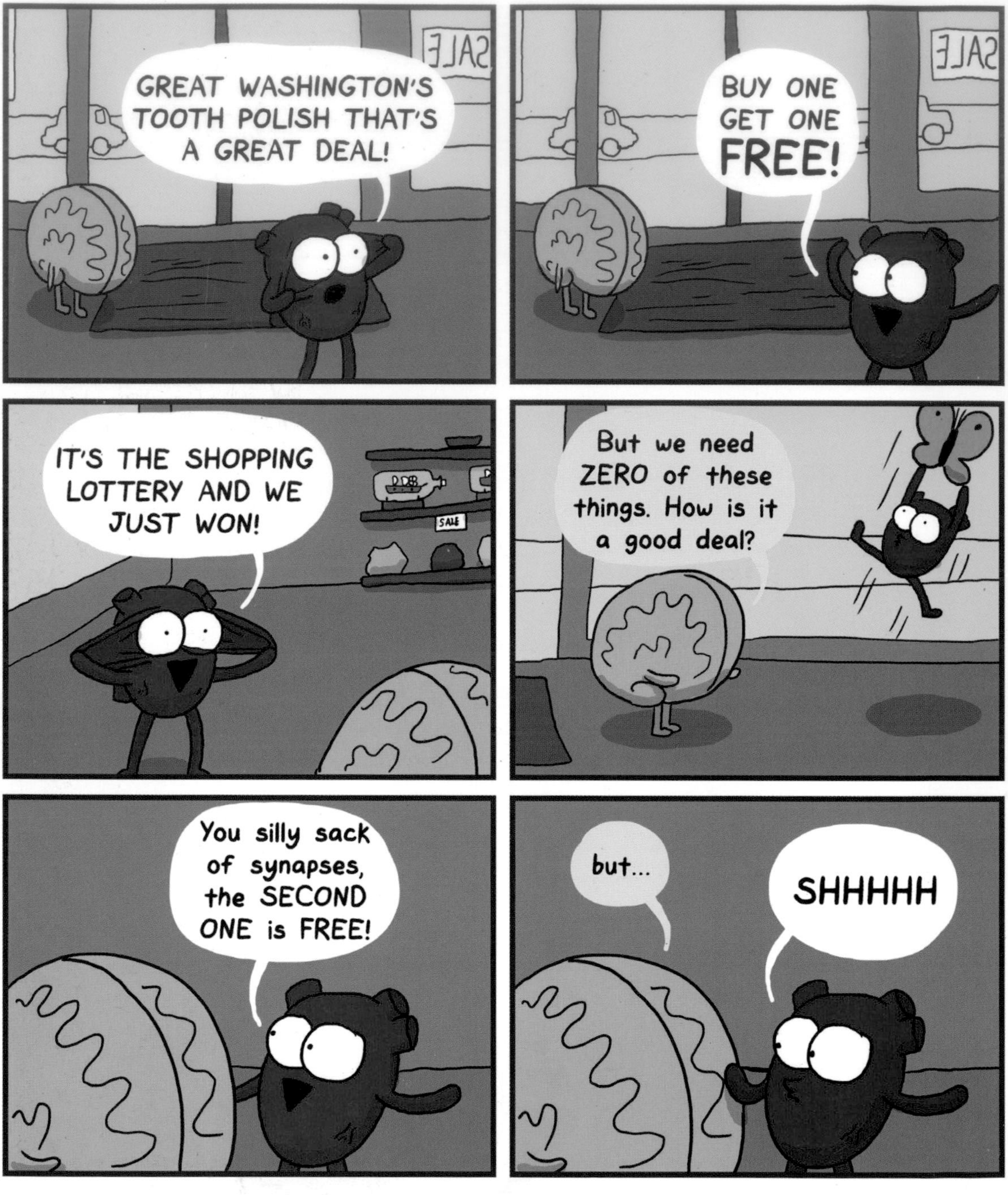
SALE
GREAT WASHINGTON'S TOOTH POLISH THAT'S A GREAT DEAL!
SALE
BUY ONE GET ONE FREE!
IT'S THE SHOPPING LOTTERY AND WE JUST WON!
SALE
But we need ZERO of these things. How is it a good deal?
You silly sack of synapses, the SECOND ONE is FREE!
but...
SHHHHH

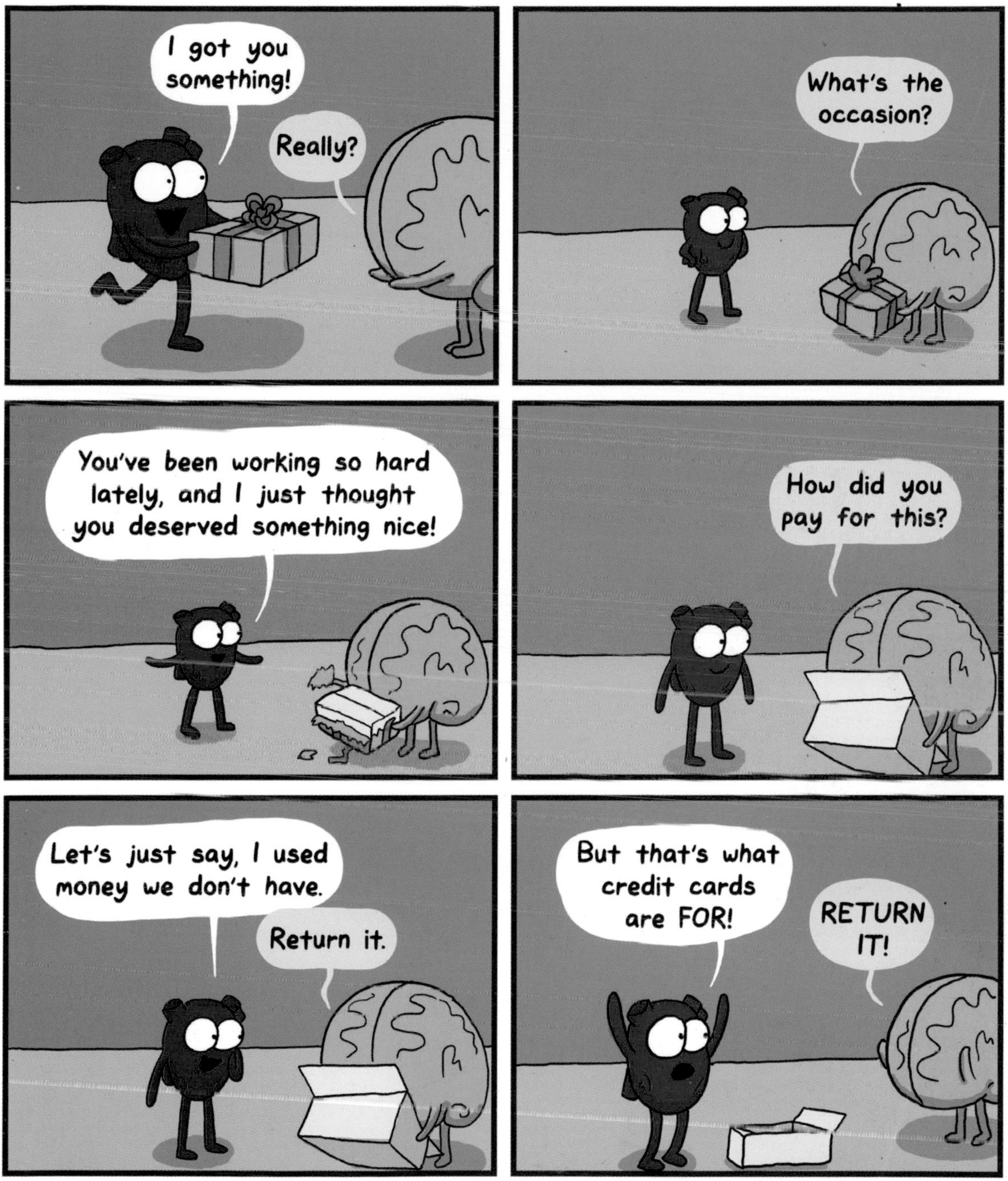
I got you something!
Really?
What's the occasion?
You've been working so hard lately, and I just thought you deserved something nice!
How did you pay for this?
Let's just say, I used money we don't have.
Return it.
But that's what credit cards are FOR!
RETURN IT!

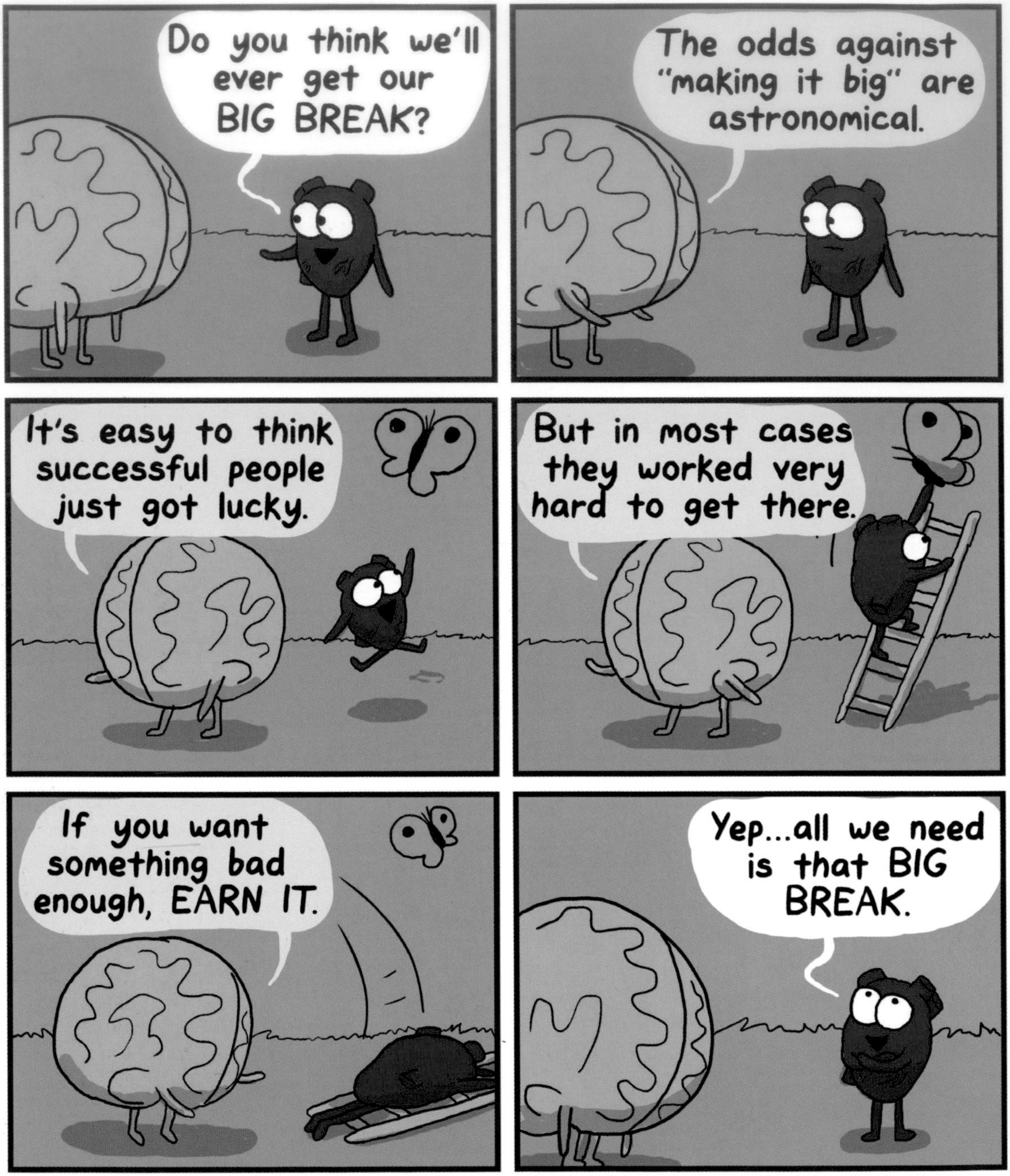
Do you think we'll ever get our BIG BREAK?
The odds against "making it big" are astronomical.
It's easy to think successful people just got lucky.
But in most cases they worked very hard to get there.
If you want something bad enough, EARN IT.
Yep...all we need is that BIG BREAK.

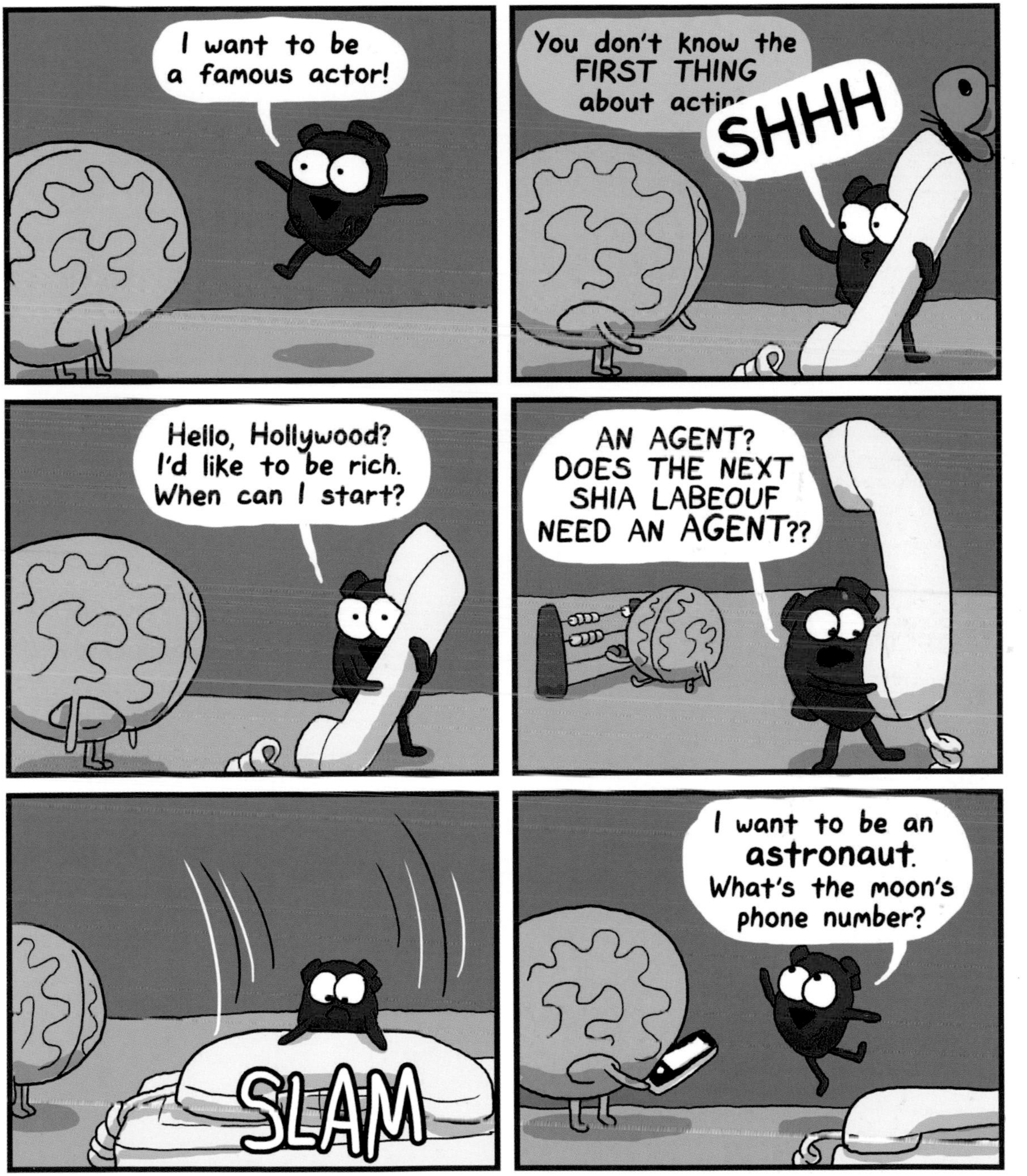
I want to be a famous actor!
You don't know the FIRST THING about actin
SHHH
Hello, Hollywood? I'd like to be rich. When can I start?
AN AGENT? DOES THE NEXT SHIA LABEOUF NEED AN AGENT??
SLAM
I want to be an astronaut. What's the moon's phone number?

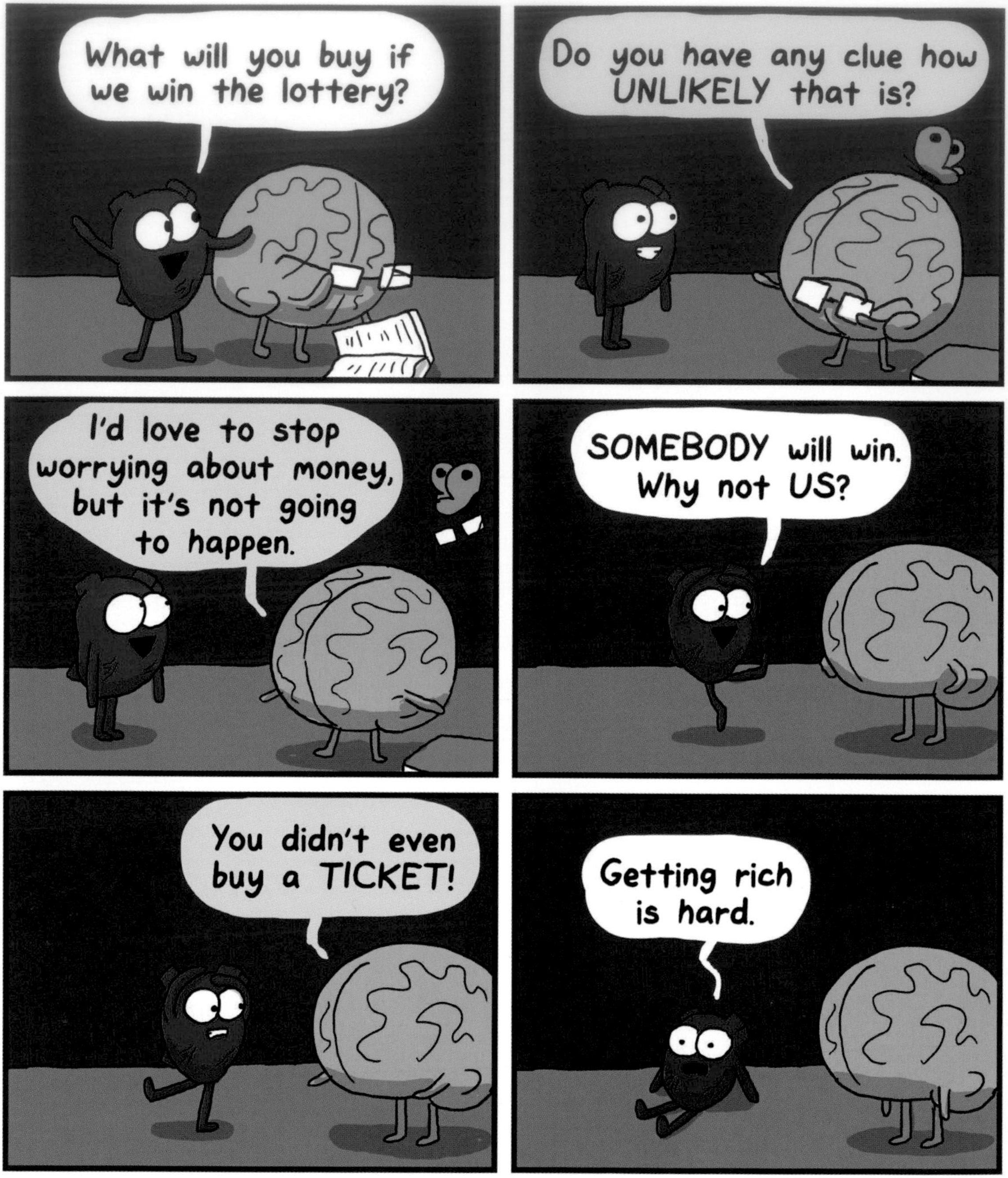

What will you buy if we win the lottery?
Do you have any clue how UNLIKELY that is?
I'd love to stop worrying about money, but it's not going to happen.
SOMEBODY will win. Why not US?
You didn't even buy a TICKET!
Getting rich is hard.

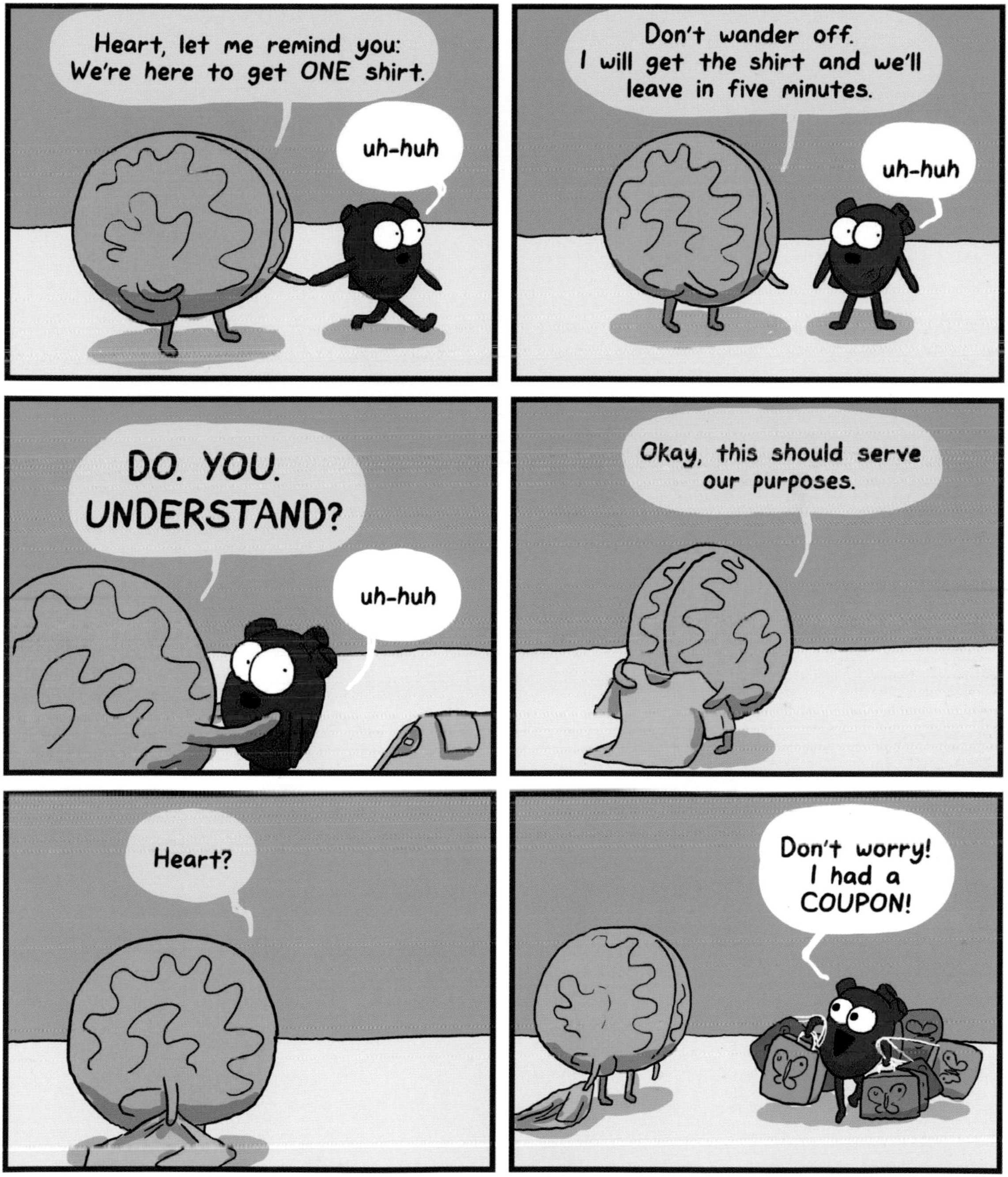
Heart, let me remind you: We're here to get ONE shirt.
uh-huh
Don't wander off. I will get the shirt and we'll leave in five minutes.
uh-huh
DO. YOU. UNDERSTAND?
uh-huh
Okay, this should serve our purposes.
Heart?
Don't worry! I had a COUPON!

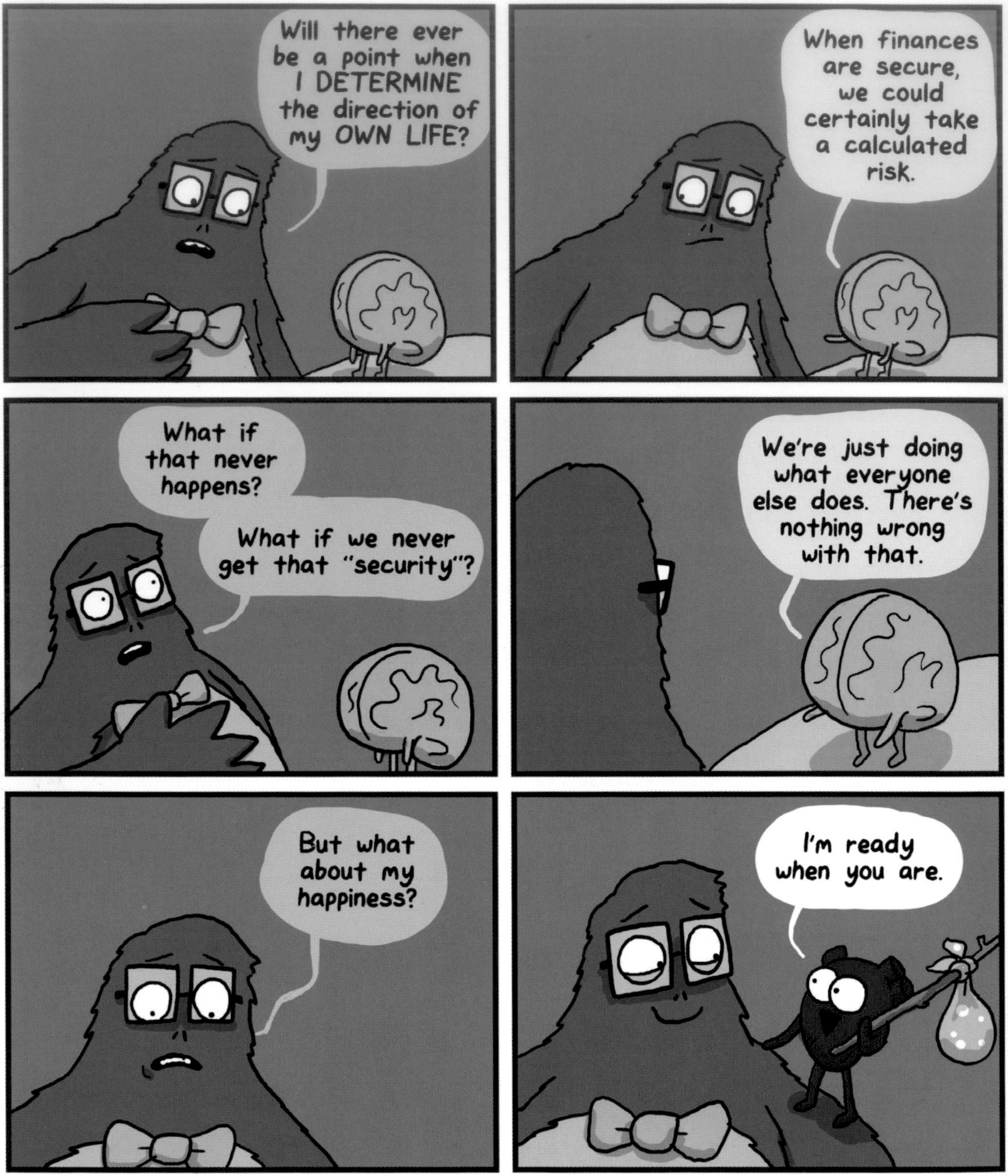
Will there ever be a point when I DETERMINE the direction of my OWN LIFE?
When finances are secure, we could certainly take a calculated risk.
What if that never happens?
What if we never get that "security"?
We're just doing what everyone else does. There's nothing wrong with that.
But what about my happiness?
I'm ready when you are.

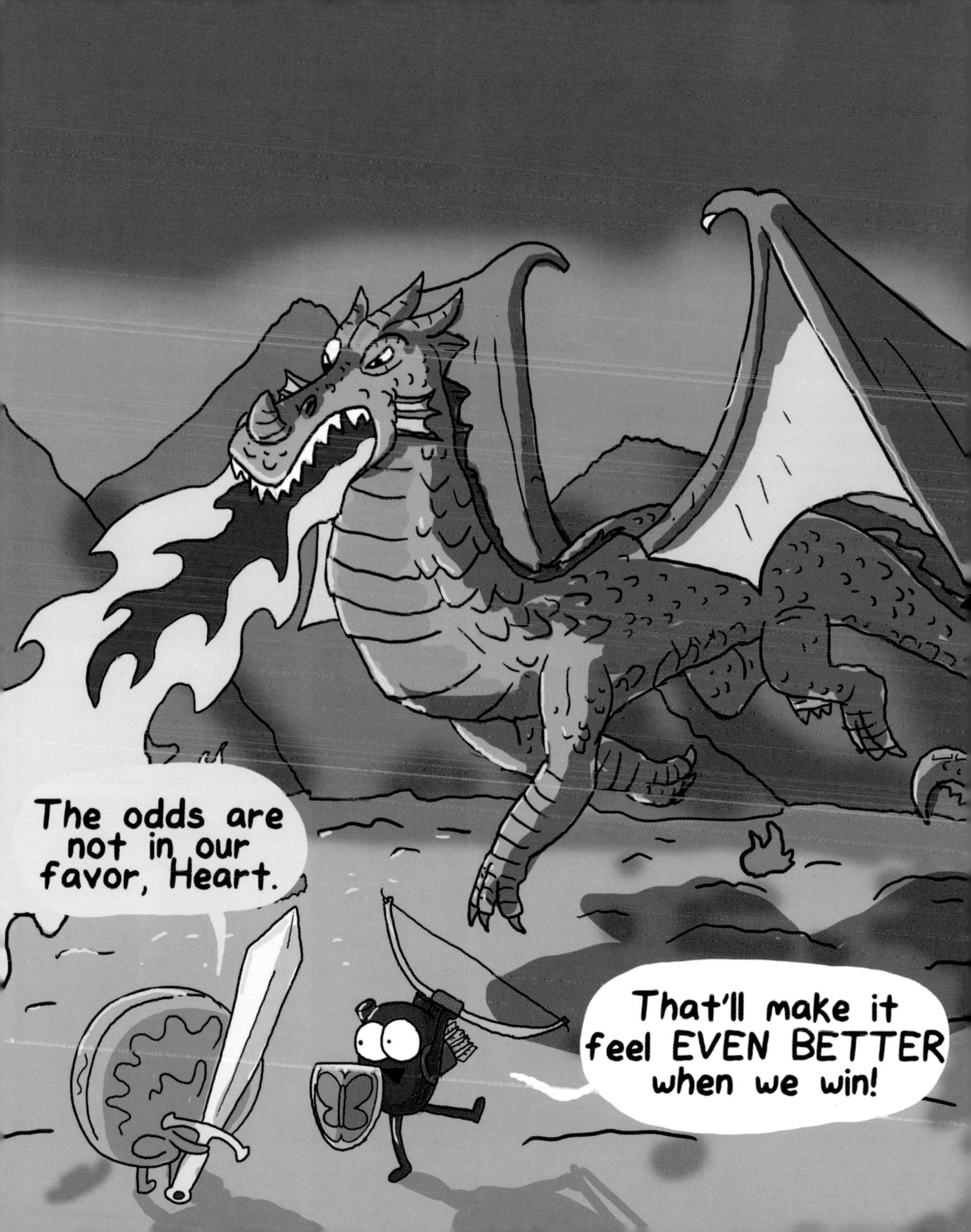
The odds are not in our favor, Heart.
That'll make it feel EVEN BETTER when we win!

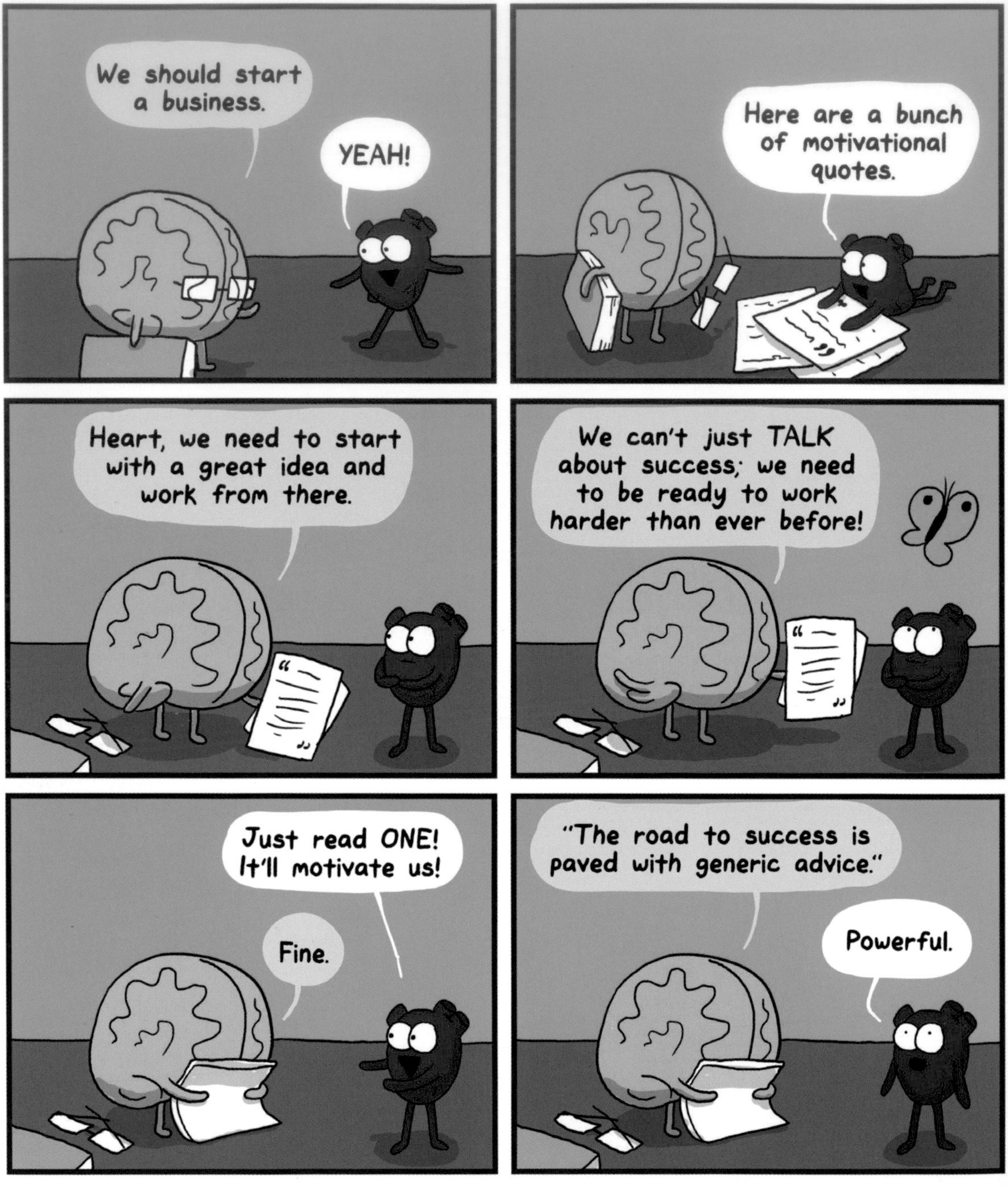
We should start a business.
YEAH!
Here are a bunch of motivational quotes.
Heart, we need to start with a great idea and work from there.
We can't just TALK about success; we need to be ready to work harder than ever before!
Just read ONE! It'll motivate us!
Fine.
"The road to success is paved with generic advice."
Powerful.

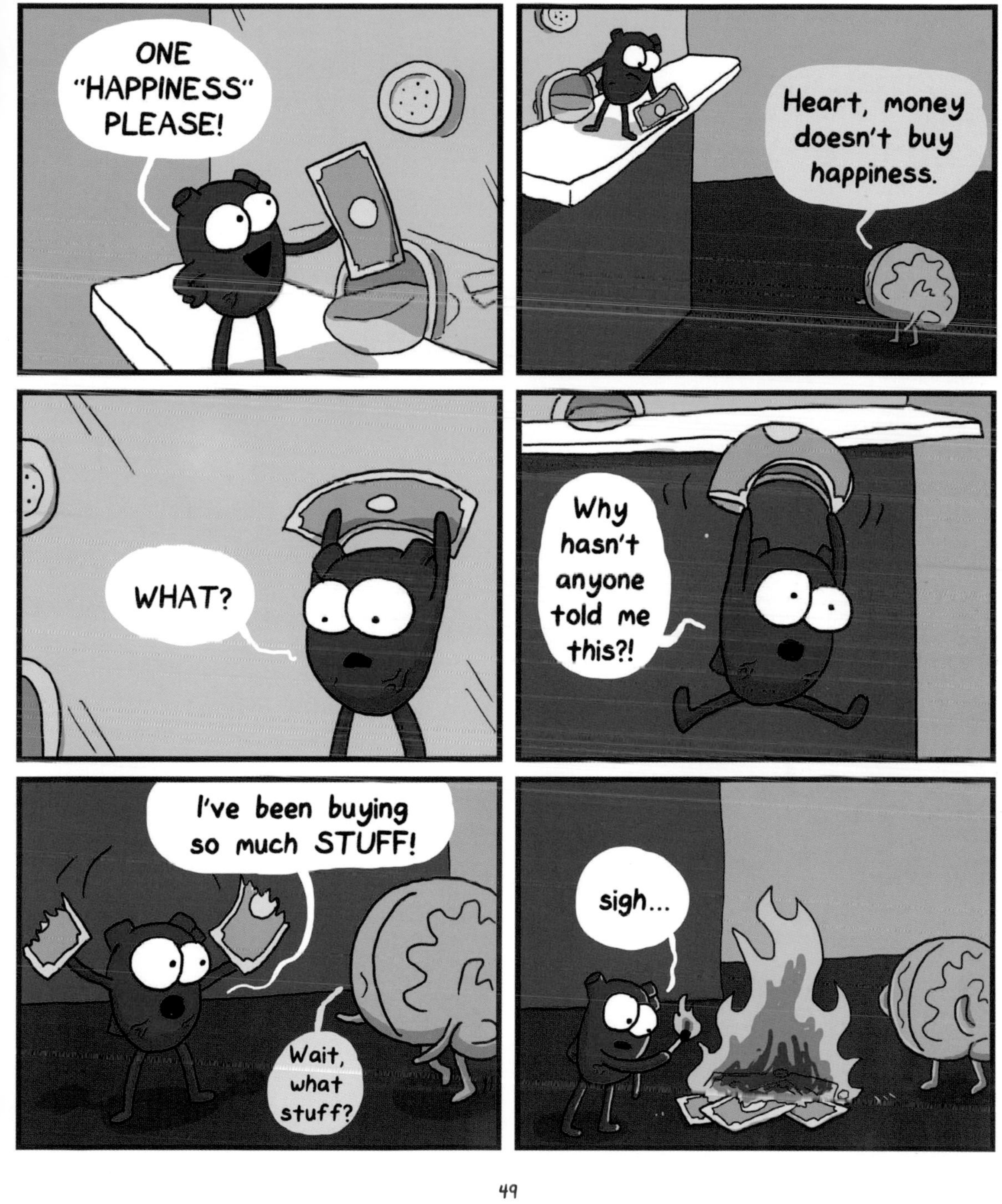
ONE "HAPPINESS" PLEASE!
Heart, money doesn't buy happiness.
WHAT?
Why hasn't anyone told me this?!
I've been buying so much STUFF!
Wait, what stuff?
sigh...

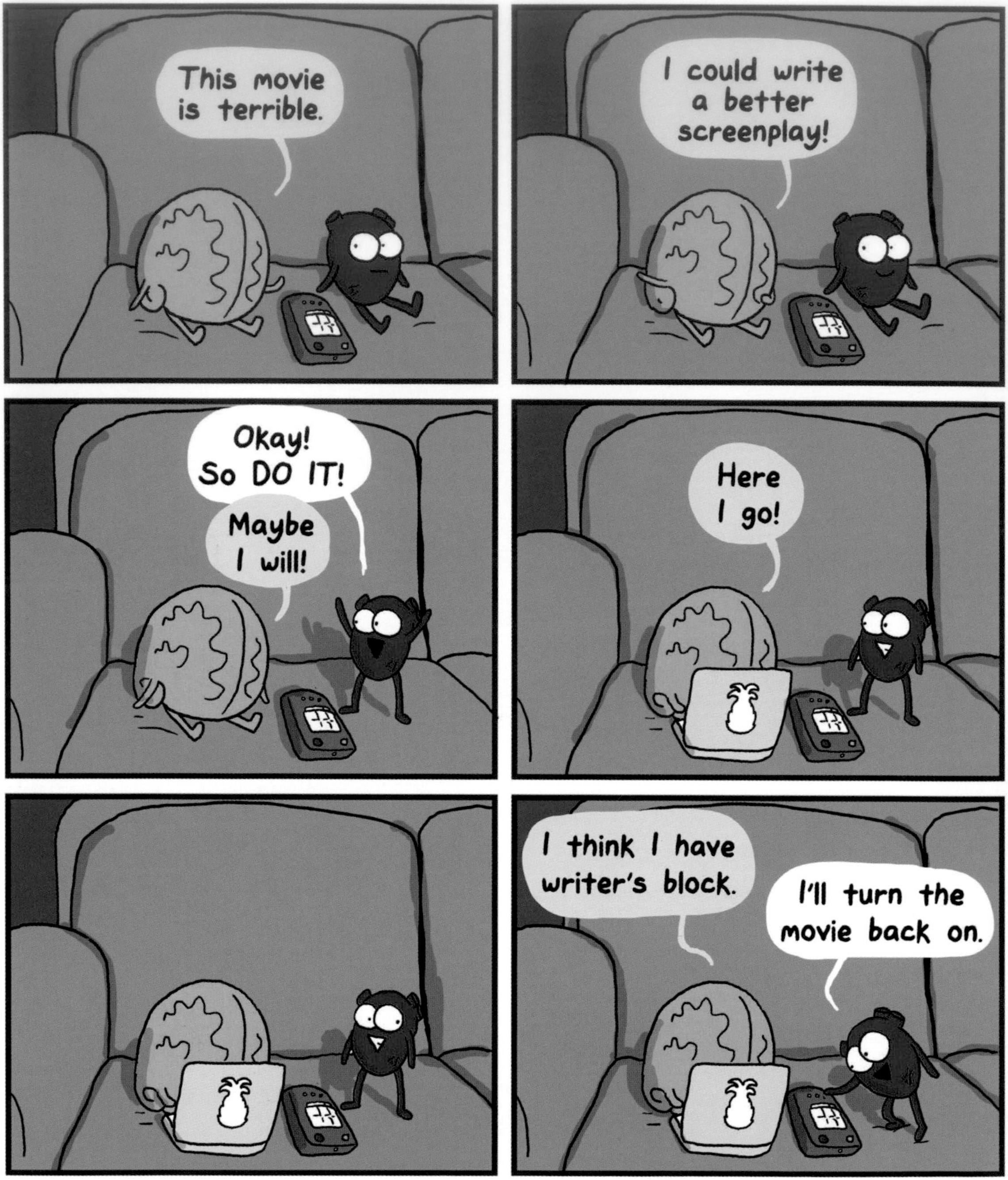
This movie is terrible.
I could write a better screenplay!
Okay! So DO IT!
Maybe I will!
Here I go!
I think I have writer's block.
I'll turn the movie back on.

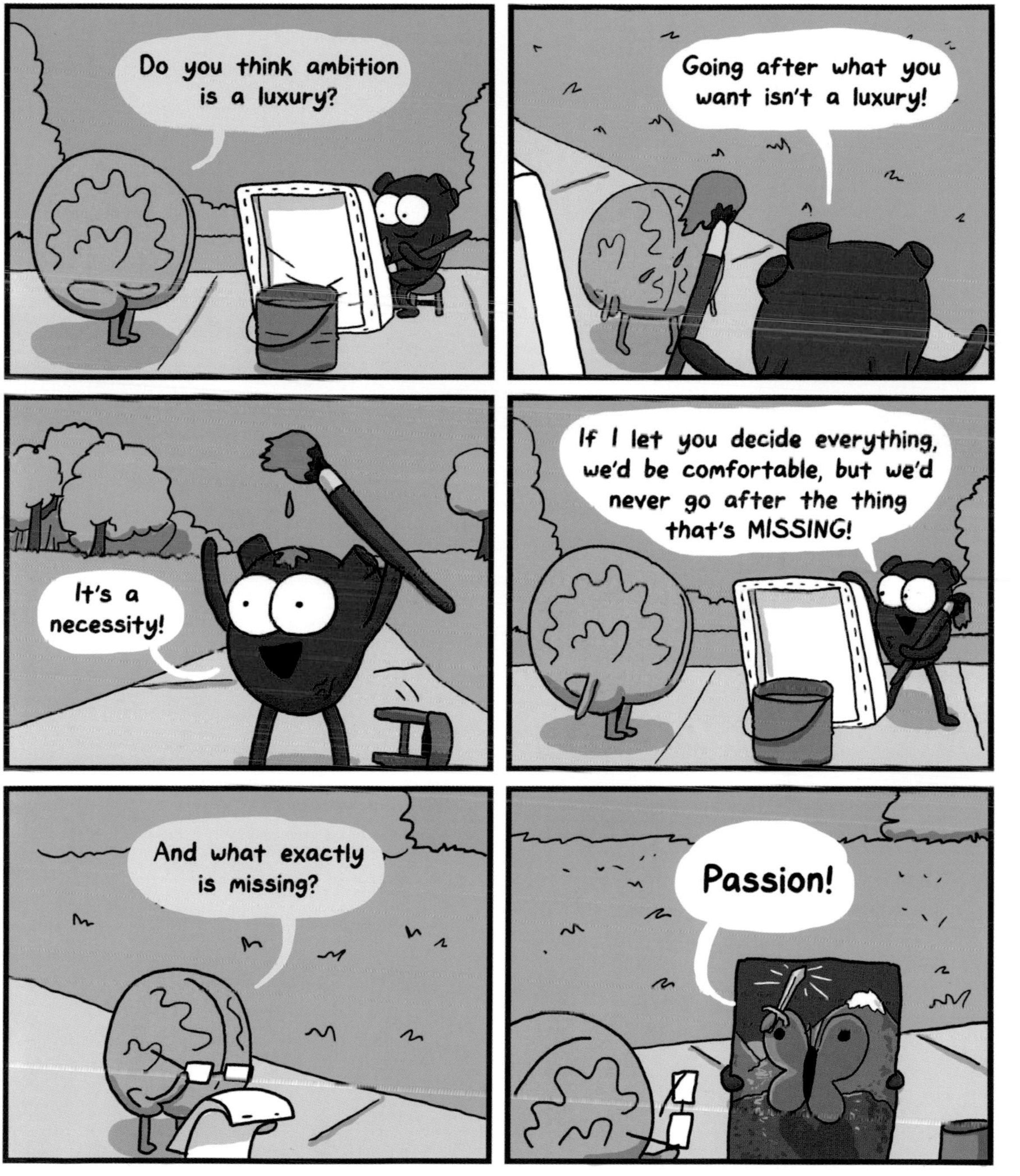
Do you think ambition is a luxury?
Going after what you want isn't a luxury!
It's a necessity!
If I let you decide everything, we'd be comfortable, but we'd never go after the thing that's MISSING!
And what exactly is missing?
Passion!

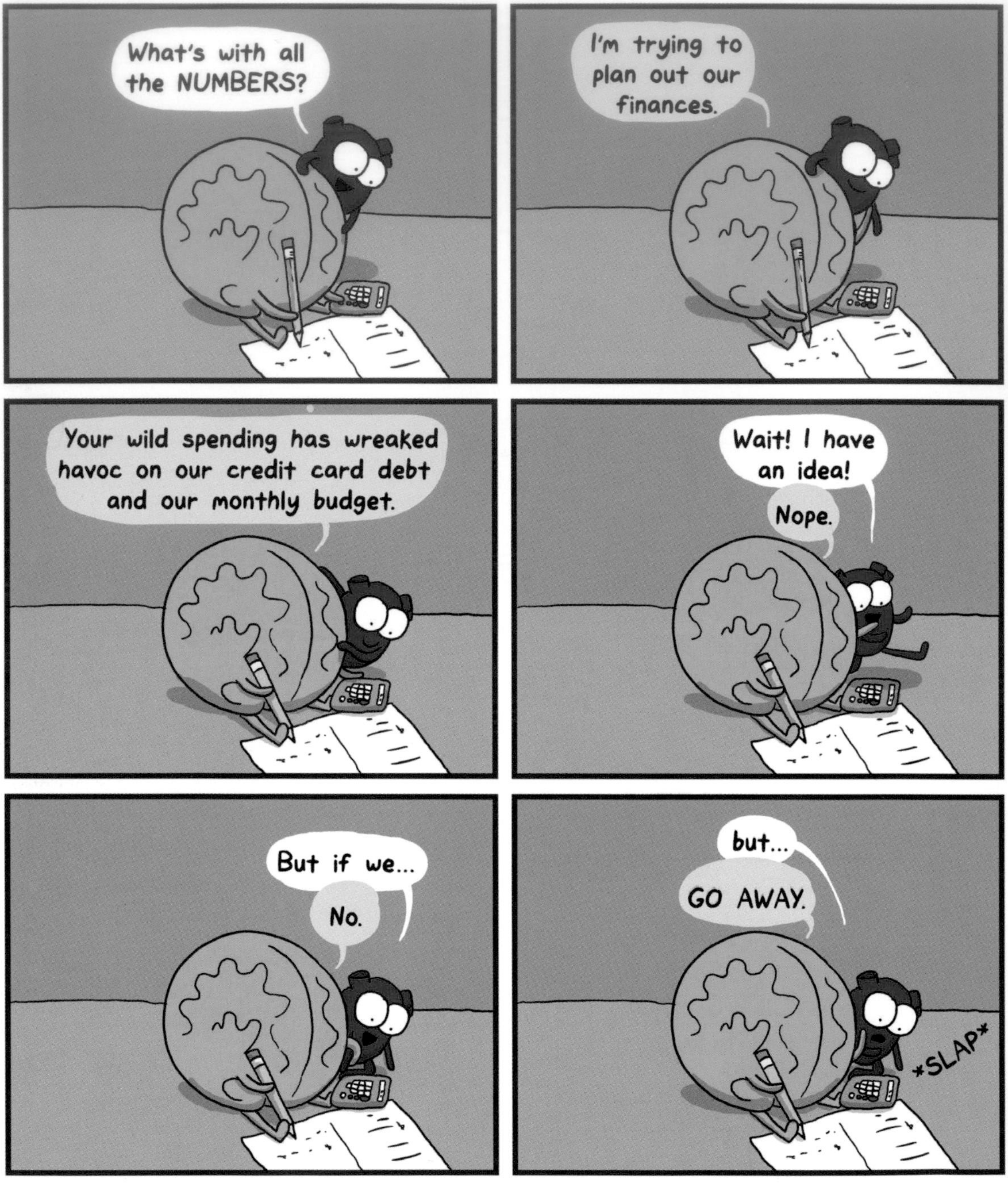
What's with all the NUMBERS?
I'm trying to plan out our finances.
Your wild spending has wreaked havoc on our credit card debt and our monthly budget.
Wait! I have an idea!
Nope.
But if we...
No.
but...
GO AWAY.
SLAP

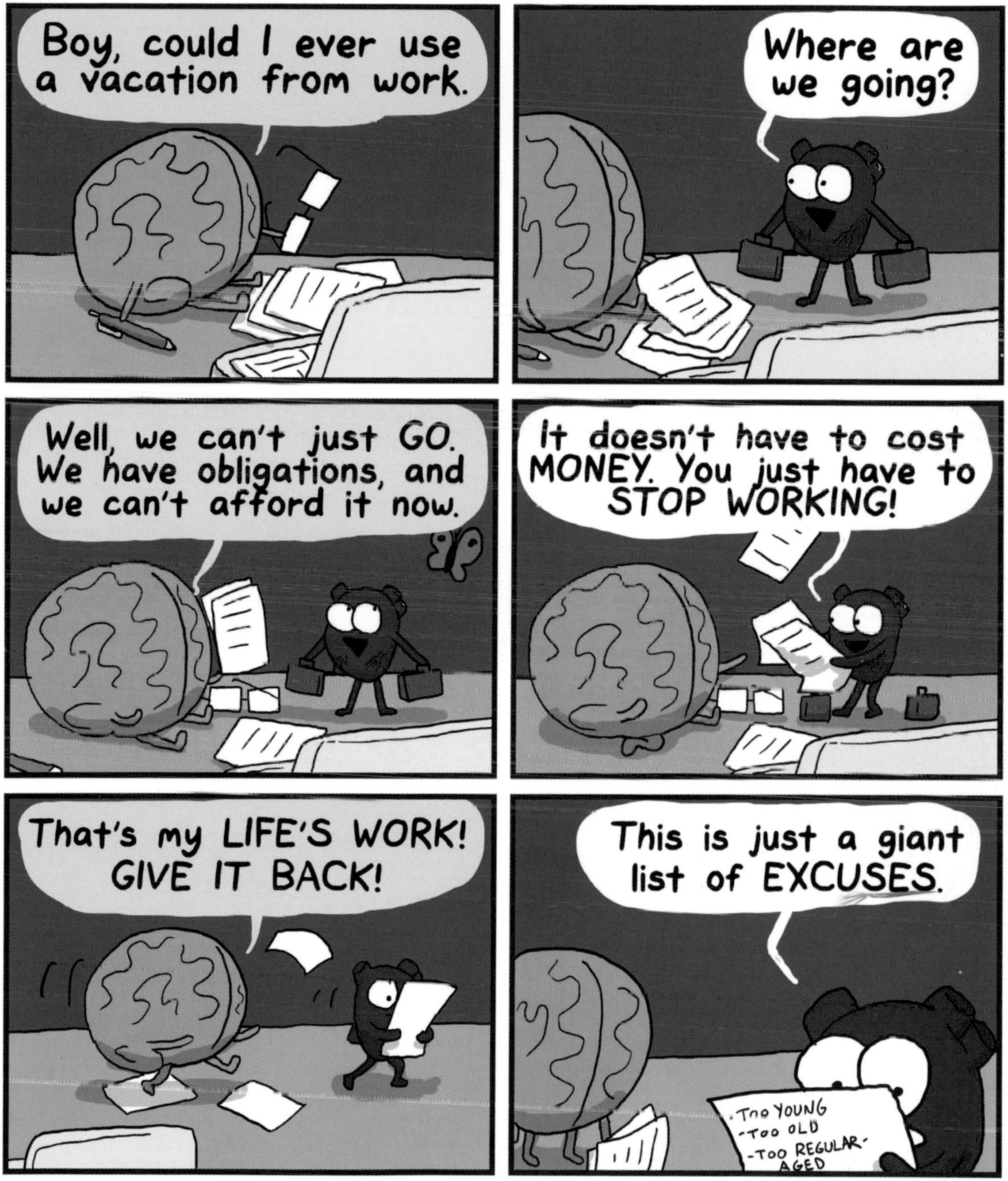
Boy, could I ever use a vacation from work.
Where are we going?
Well, we can't just GO. We have obligations, and we can't afford it now.
It doesn't have to cost MONEY. You just have to STOP WORKING!
That's my LIFE'S WORK! GIVE IT BACK!
This is just a giant list of EXCUSES.
-TOO YOUNG
-TOO OLD
-TOO REGULAR-AGED

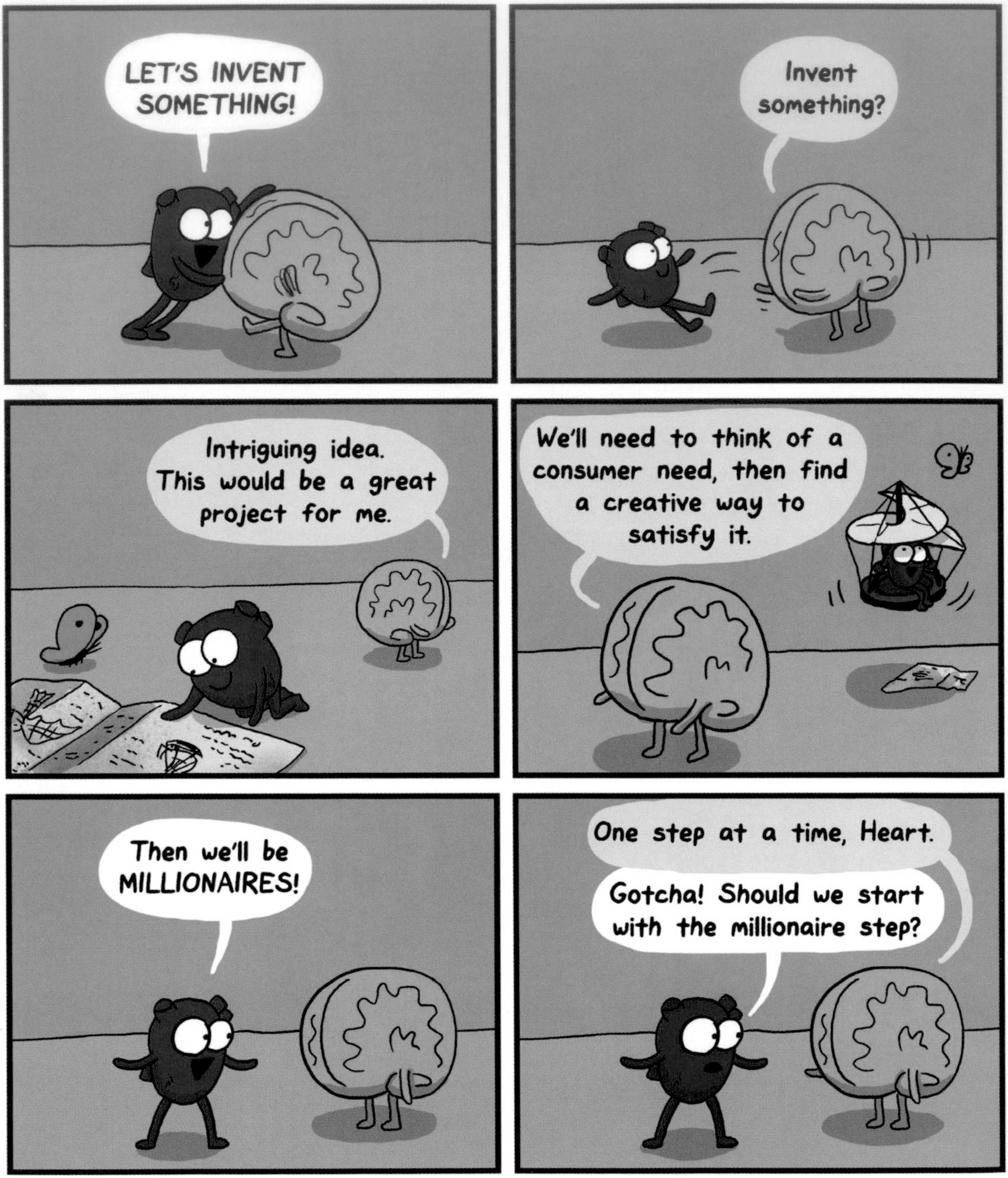
LET'S INVENT SOMETHING!
Invent something?
Intriguing idea. This would be a great project for me.
We'll need to think of a consumer need, then find a creative way to satisfy it.
Then we'll be MILLIONAIRES!
One step at a time, Heart.
Gotcha! Should we start with the millionaire step?

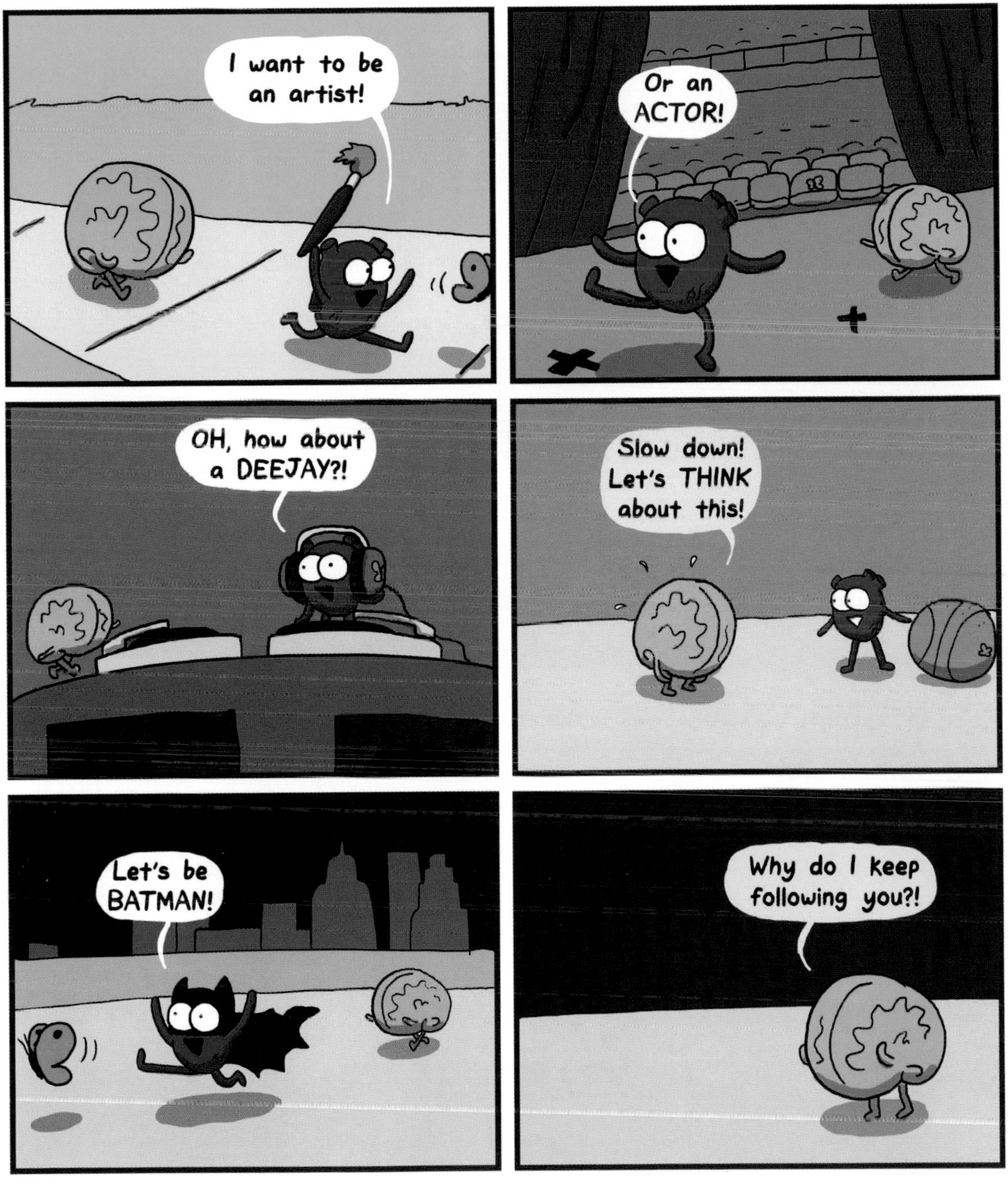
I want to be an artist!
Or an ACTOR!
OH, how about a DEEJAY?!
Slow down! Let's THINK about this!
Let's be BATMAN!
Why do I keep following you?!

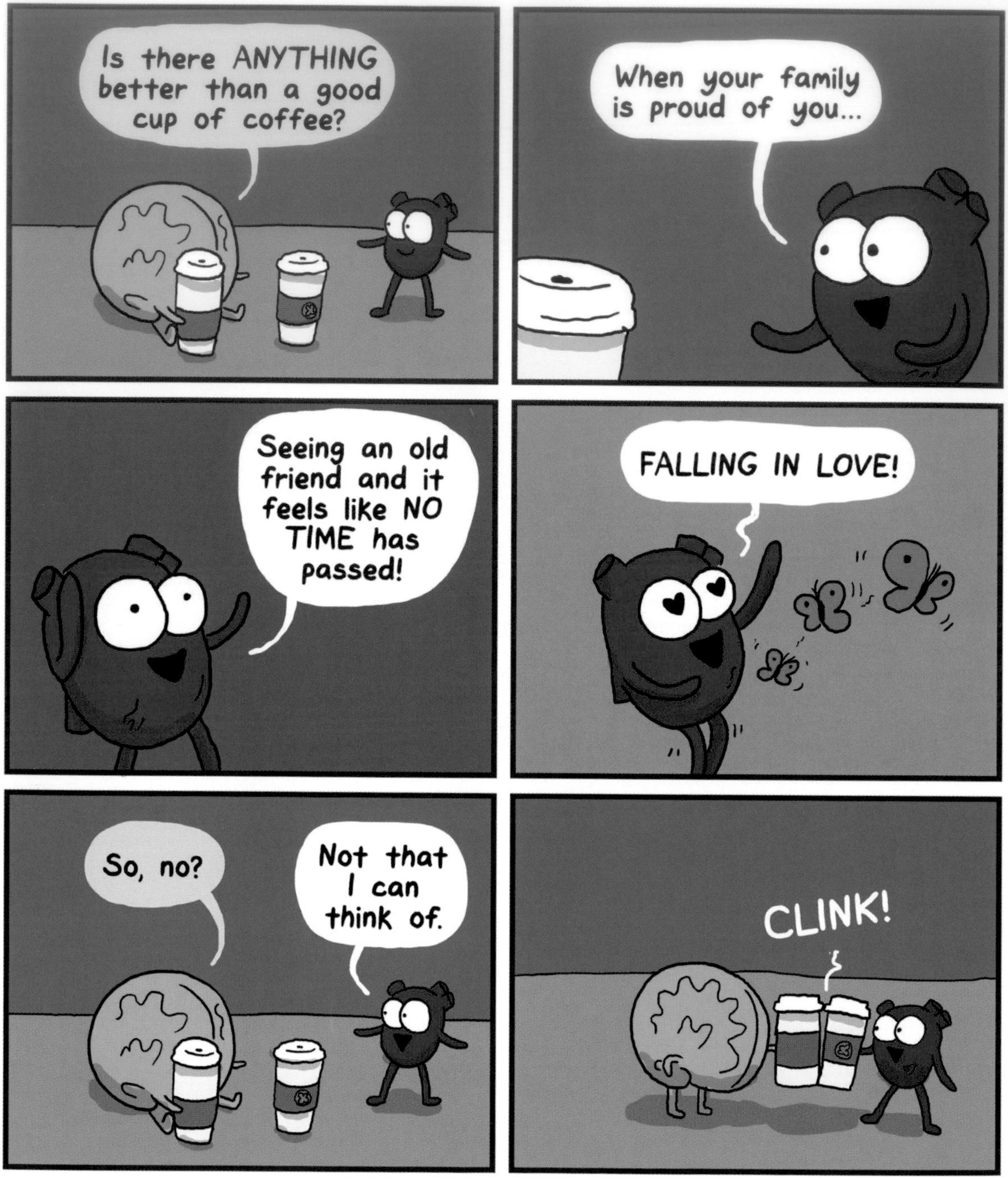
Is there ANYTHING better than a good cup of coffee?
When your family is proud of you...
Seeing an old friend and it feels like NO TIME has passed!
FALLING IN LOVE!
So, no?
Not that I can think of.
CLINK!

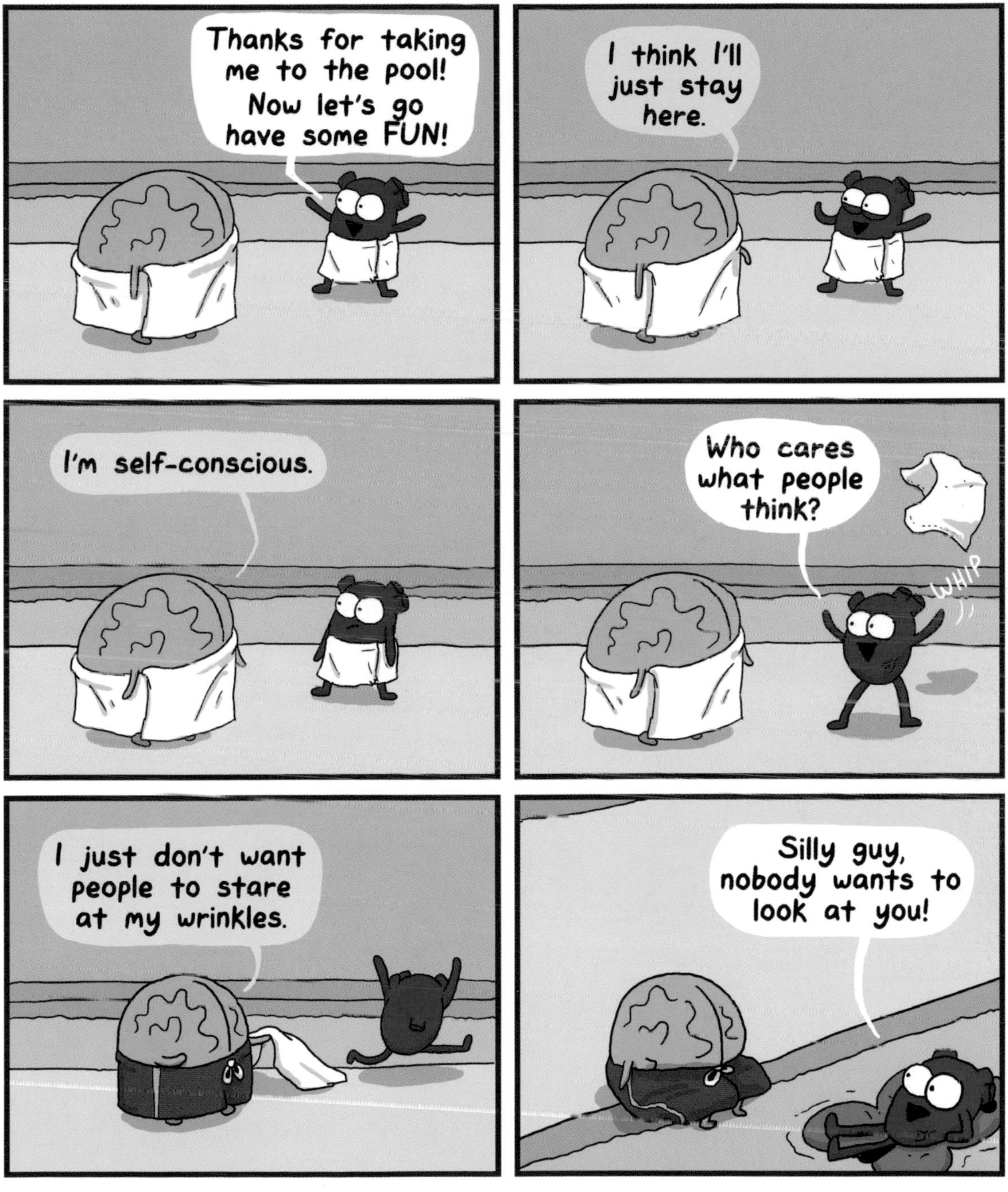
Thanks for taking me to the pool! Now let's go have some FUN!
I think I'll just stay here.
I'm self-conscious.
Who cares what people think?
WHIP
I just don't want people to stare at my wrinkles.
Silly guy, nobody wants to look at you!

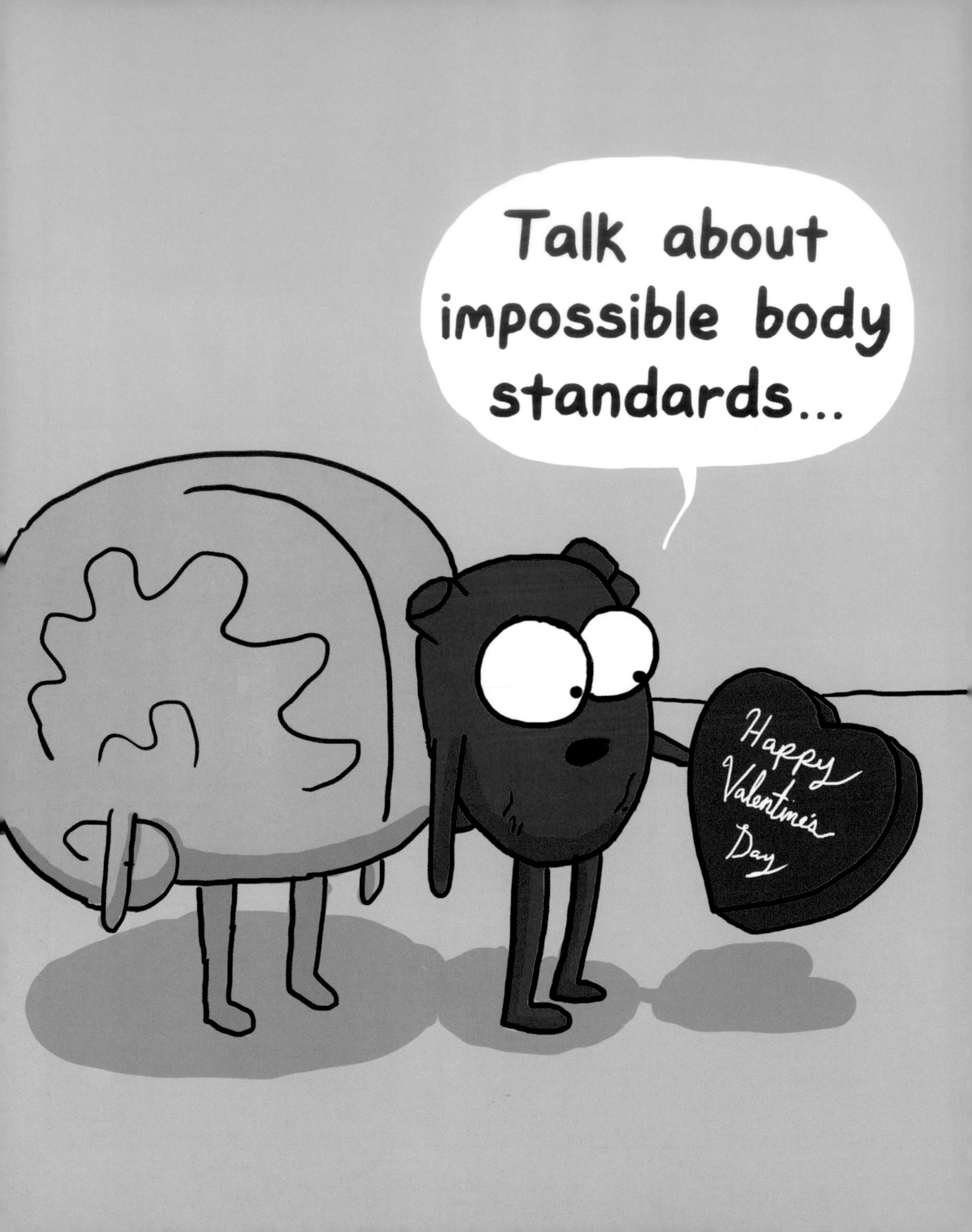
Talk about impossible body standards...
Happy Valentine's Day

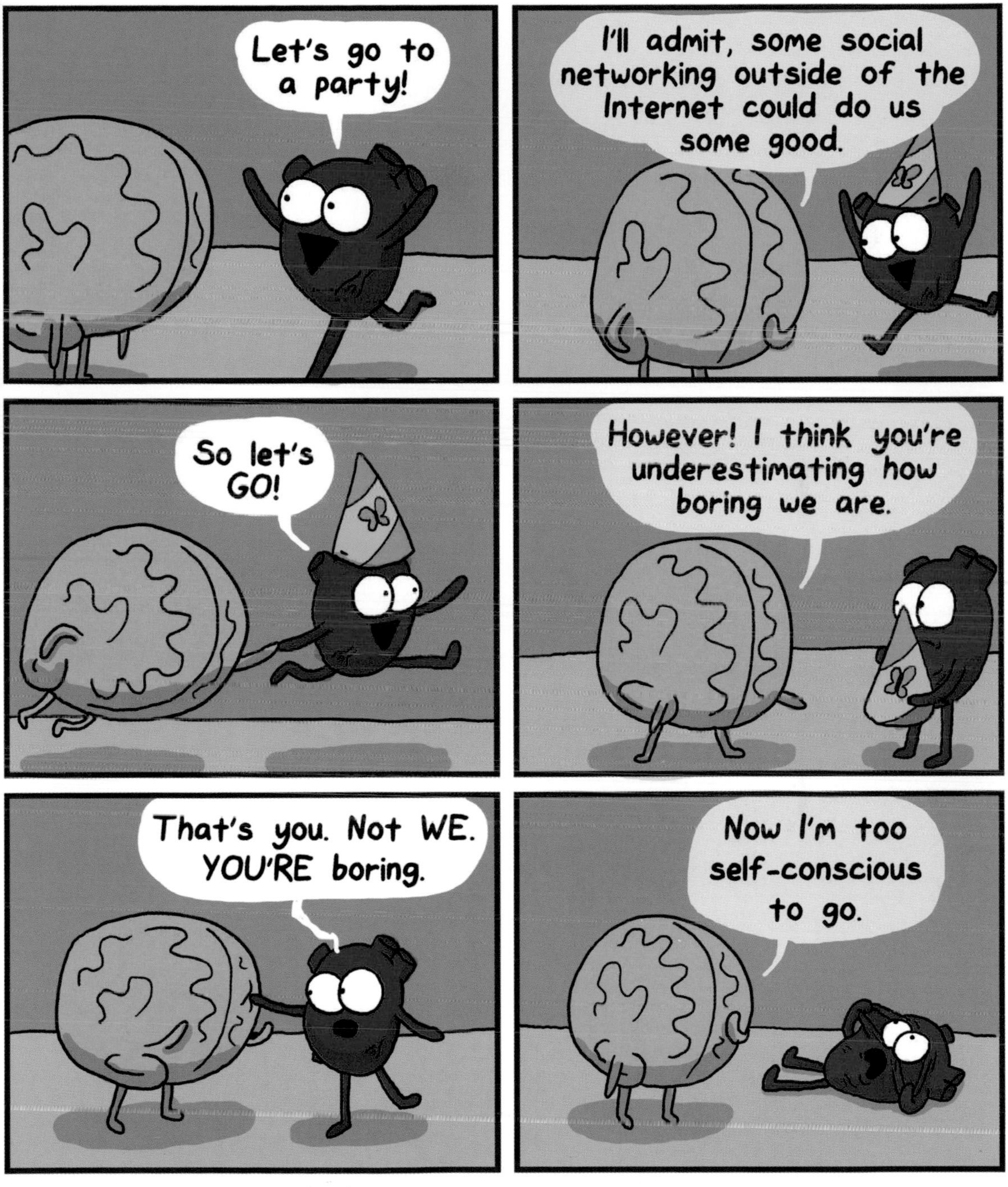
Let's go to a party!
I'll admit, some social networking outside of the Internet could do us some good.
So let's GO!
However! I think you're underestimating how boring we are.
That's you. Not WE. YOU'RE boring.
Now I'm too self-conscious to go.

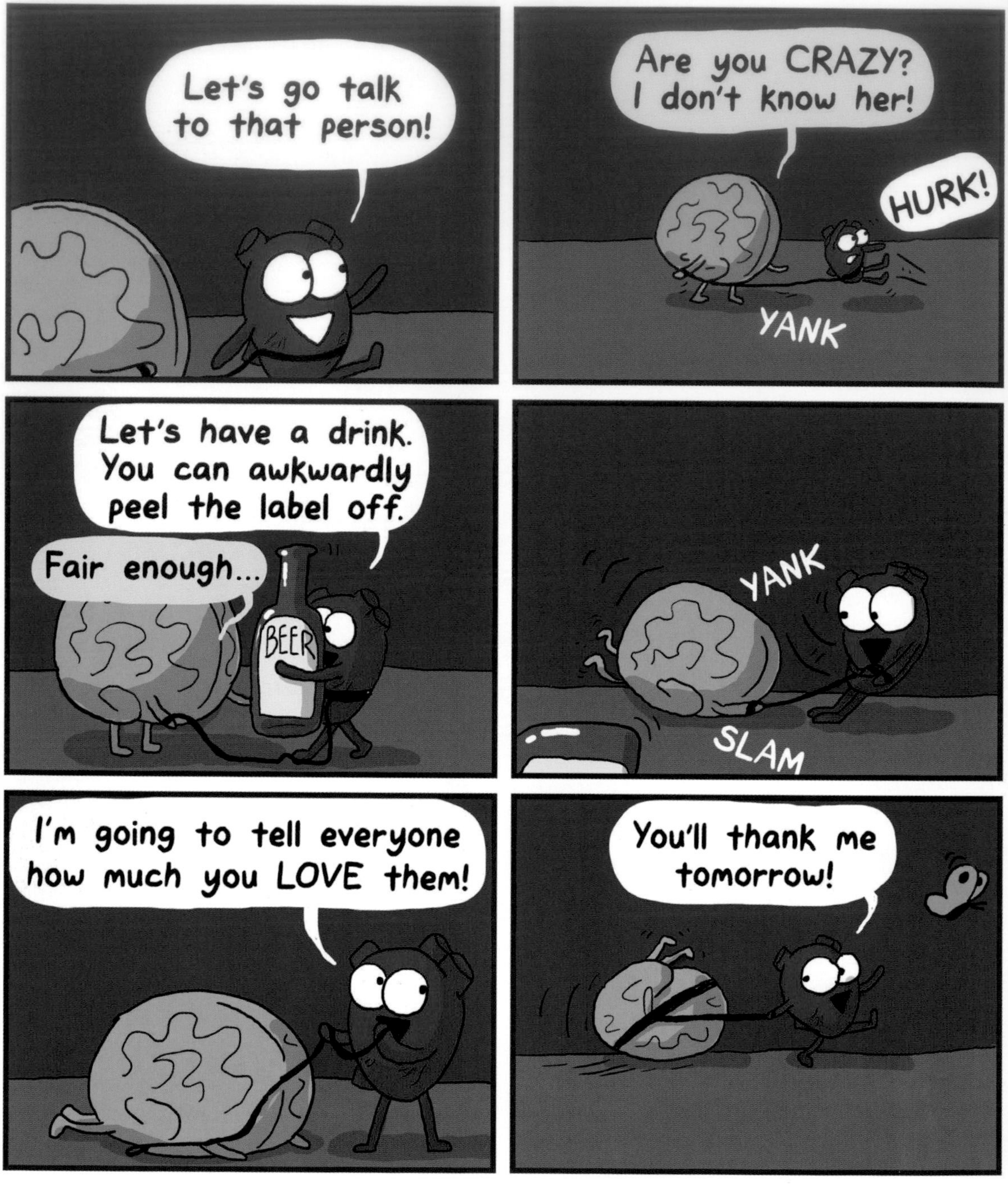
Let's go talk to that person!
Are you CRAZY? I don't know her!
HURK!
YANK
Let's have a drink. You can awkwardly peel the label off.
Fair enough...
BEER
YANK
SLAM
I'm going to tell everyone how much you LOVE them!
You'll thank me tomorrow!

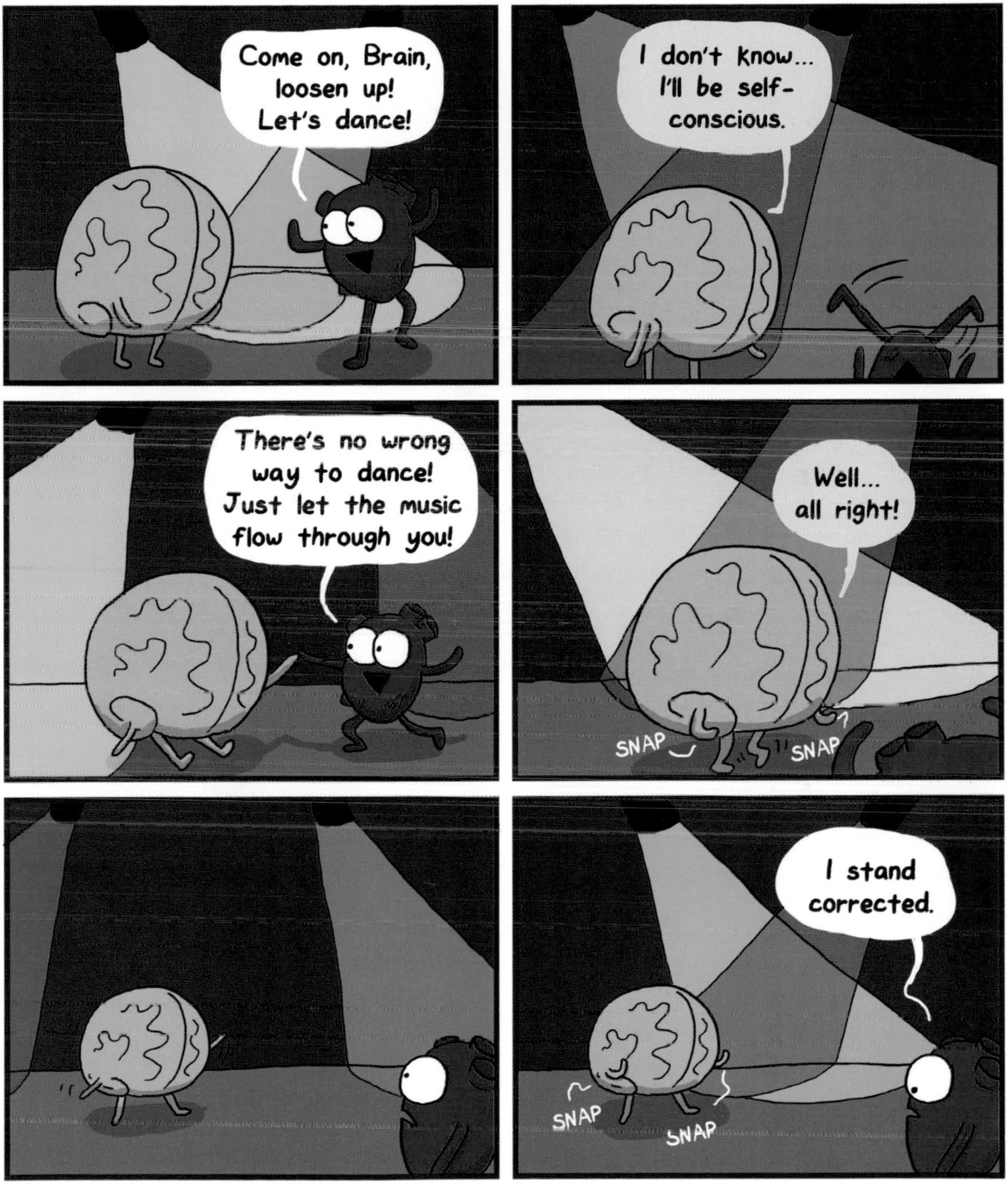
Come on, Brain, loosen up! Let's dance!
I don't know... I'll be self-conscious.
There's no wrong way to dance! Just let the music flow through you!
Well... all right!
SNAP
SNAP
I stand corrected.
SNAP
SNAP

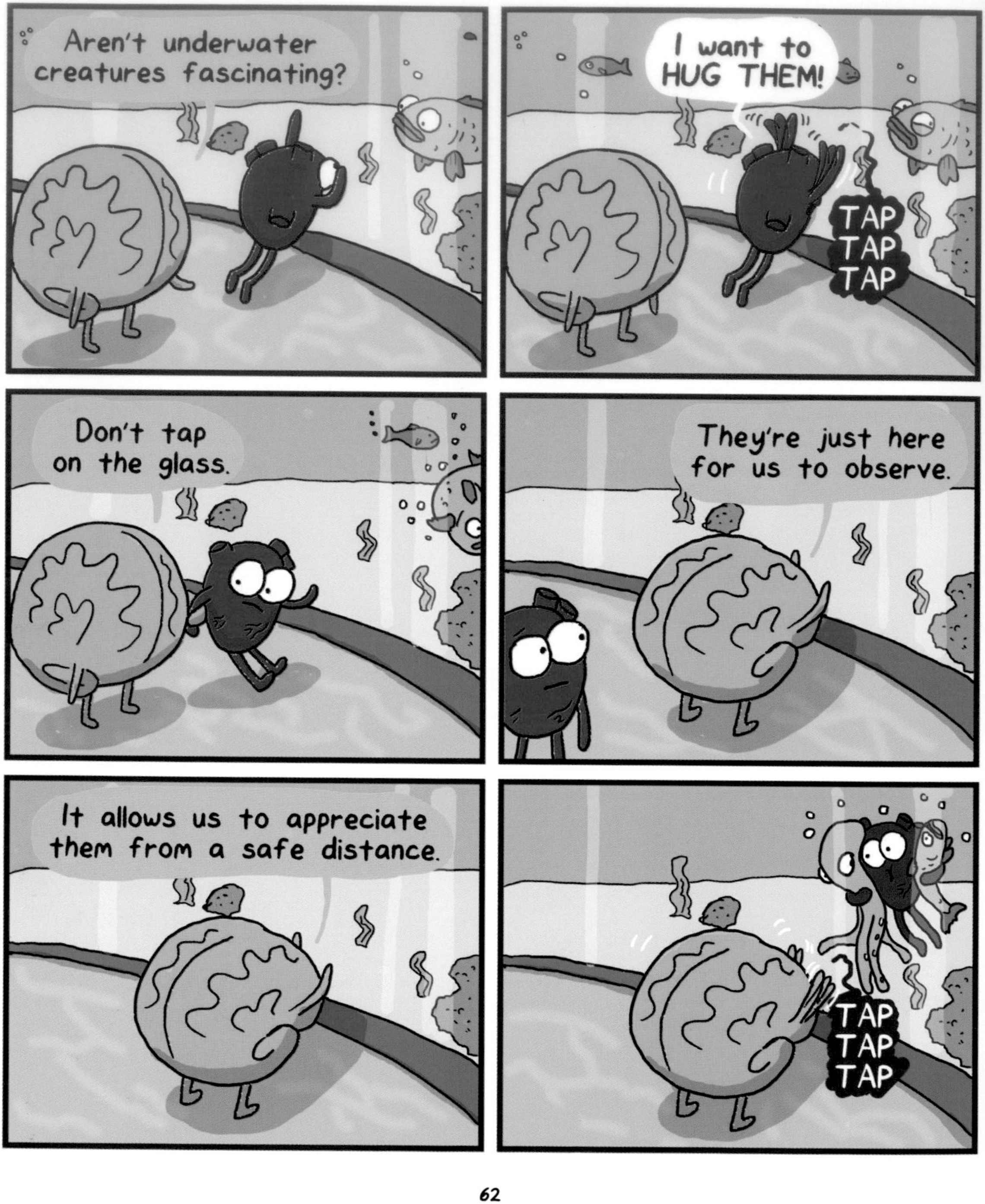
Aren't underwater creatures fascinating?
I want to HUG THEM!
TAP TAP TAP
Don't tap on the glass.
They're just here for us to observe.
It allows us to appreciate them from a safe distance.
TAP TAP TAP

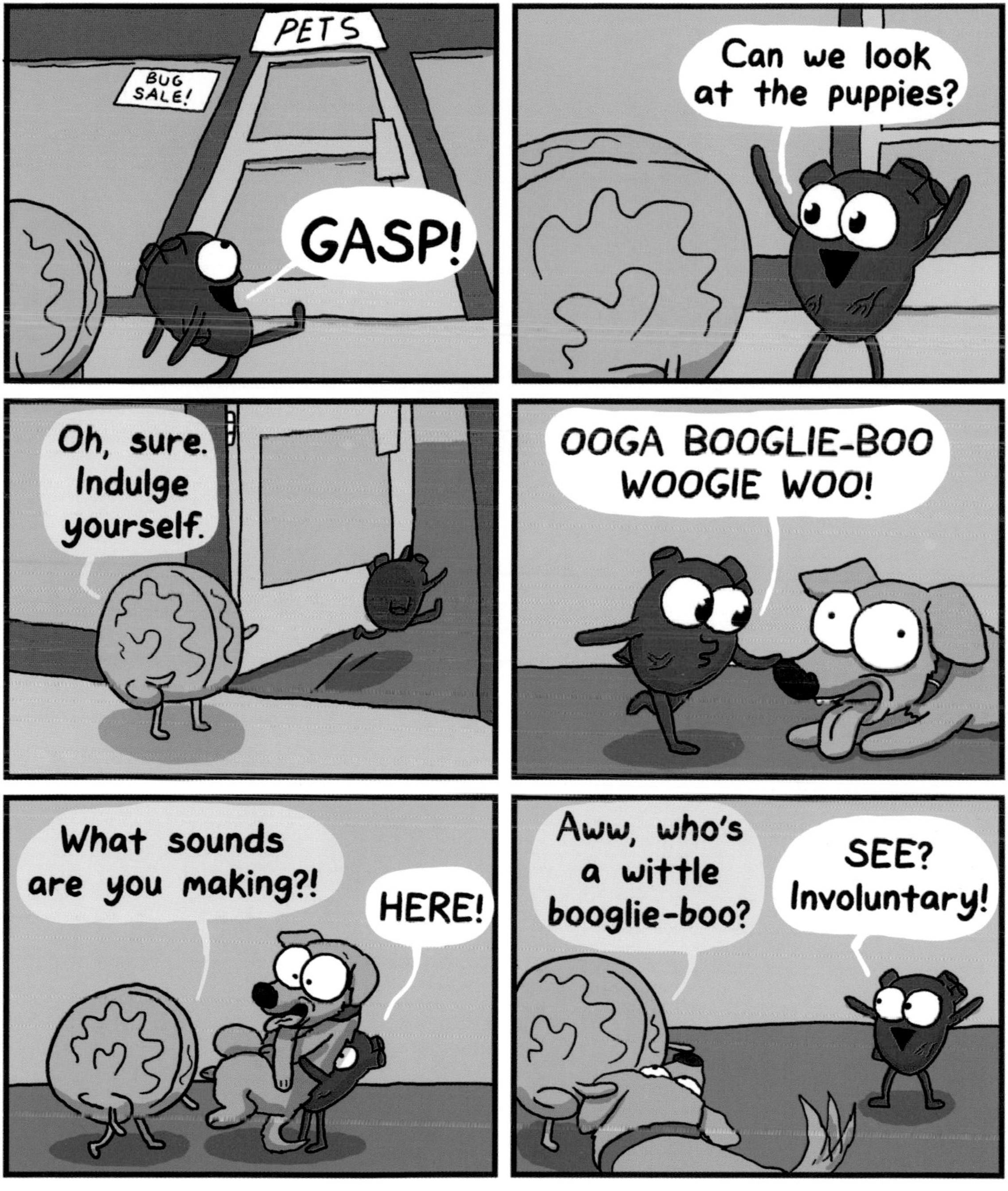
PETS
BUG SALE!
GASP!
Can we look at the puppies?
Oh, sure. Indulge yourself.
OOGA BOOGLIE-BOO WOOGIE WOO!
What sounds are you making?!
HERE!
Aww, who's a wittle booglie-boo?
SEE? Involuntary!

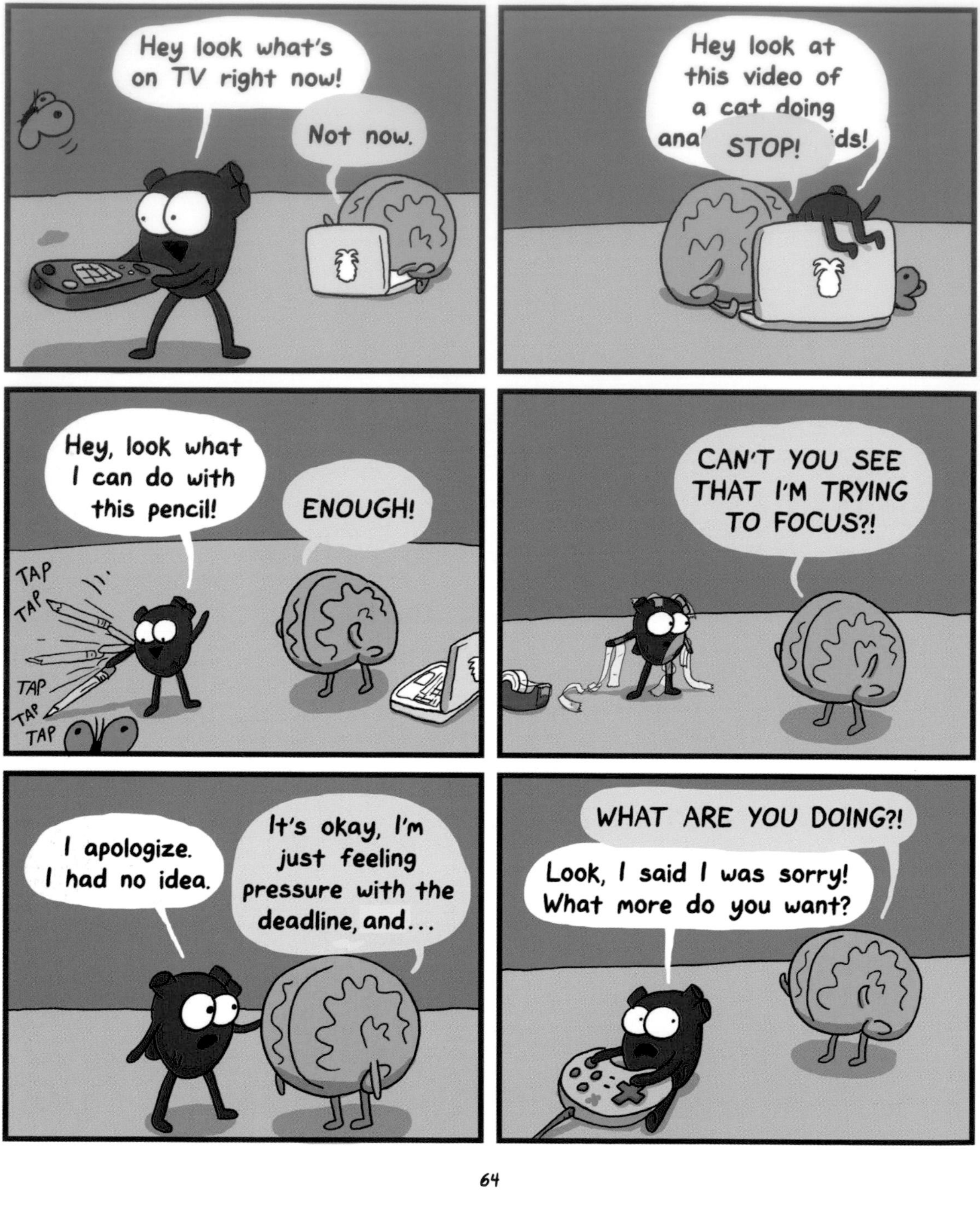
Hey look what's on TV right now!
Not now.
Hey look at this video of a cat doing
STOP!
Hey, look what I can do with this pencil!
TAP
TAP
TAP
TAP
TAP
ENOUGH!
CAN'T YOU SEE THAT I'M TRYING TO FOCUS?!
I apologize. I had no idea.
It's okay, I'm just feeling pressure with the deadline, and...
WHAT ARE YOU DOING?!
Look, I said I was sorry! What more do you want?

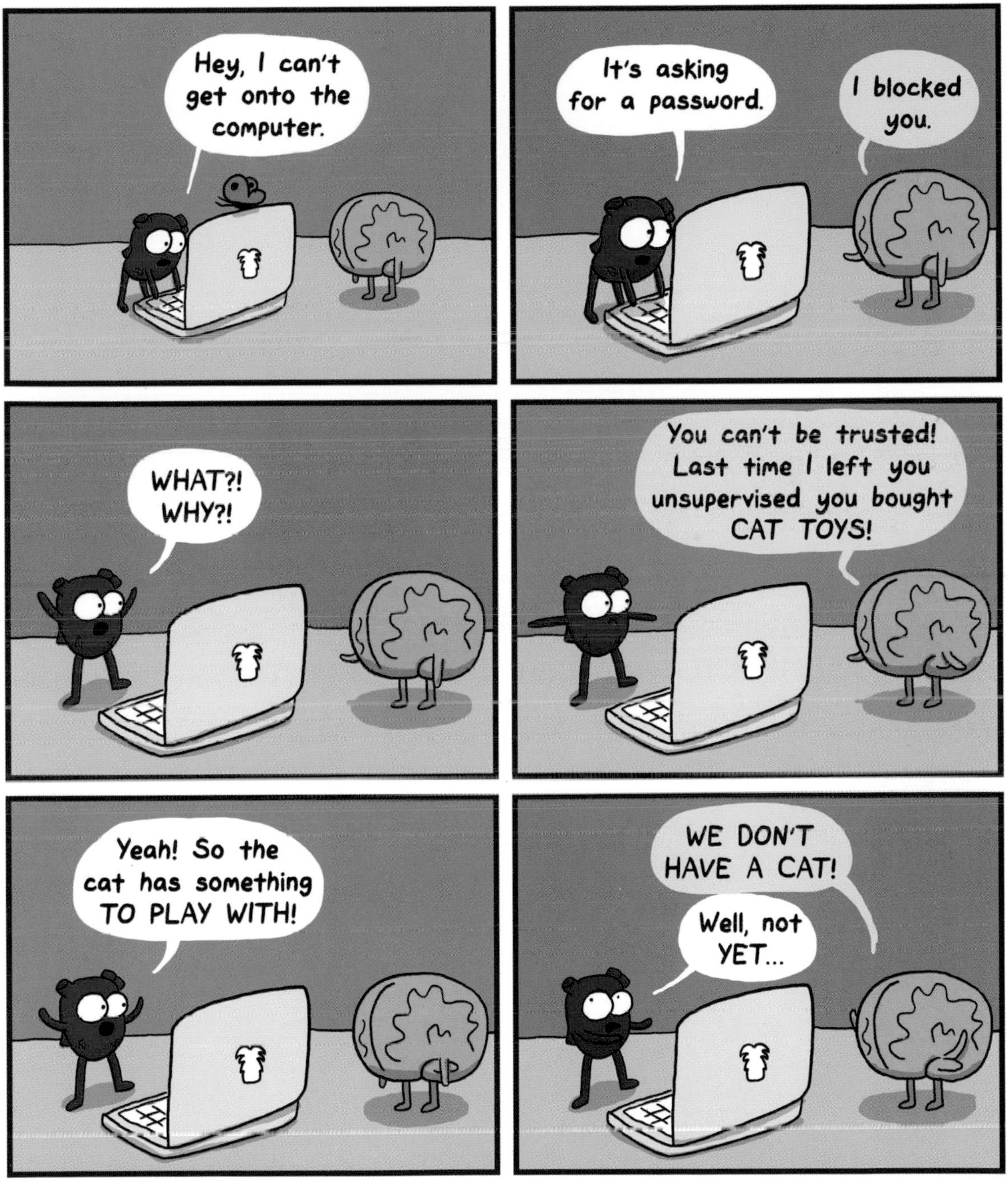
Hey, I can't get onto the computer.
It's asking for a password.
I blocked you.
WHAT?! WHY?!
You can't be trusted! Last time I left you unsupervised you bought CAT TOYS!
Yeah! So the cat has something TO PLAY WITH!
WE DON'T HAVE A CAT!
Well, not YET...

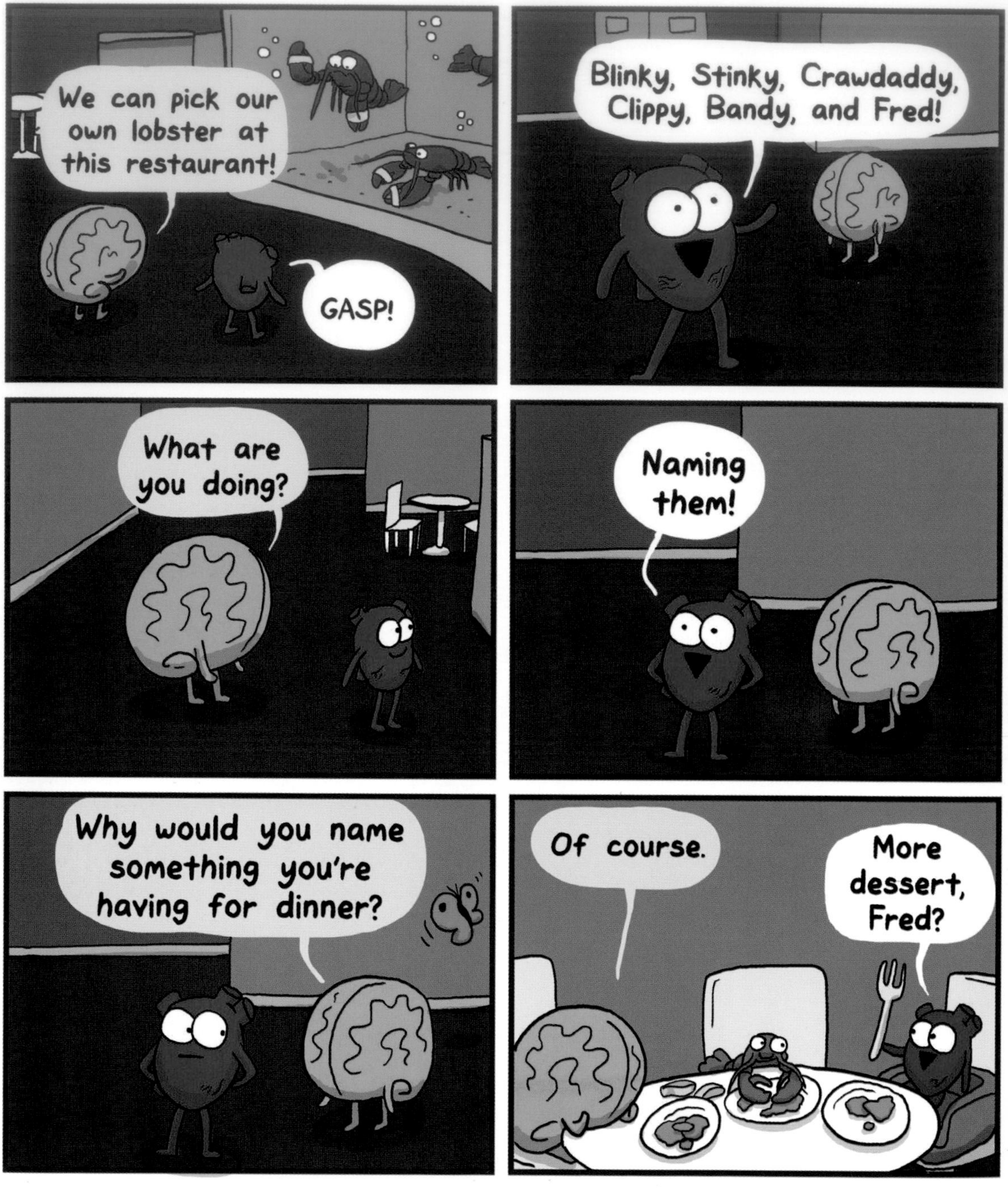
We can pick our own lobster at this restaurant!
GASP!
Blinky, Stinky, Crawdaddy, Clippy, Bandy, and Fred!
What are you doing?
Naming them!
Why would you name something you're having for dinner?
Of course.
More dessert, Fred?

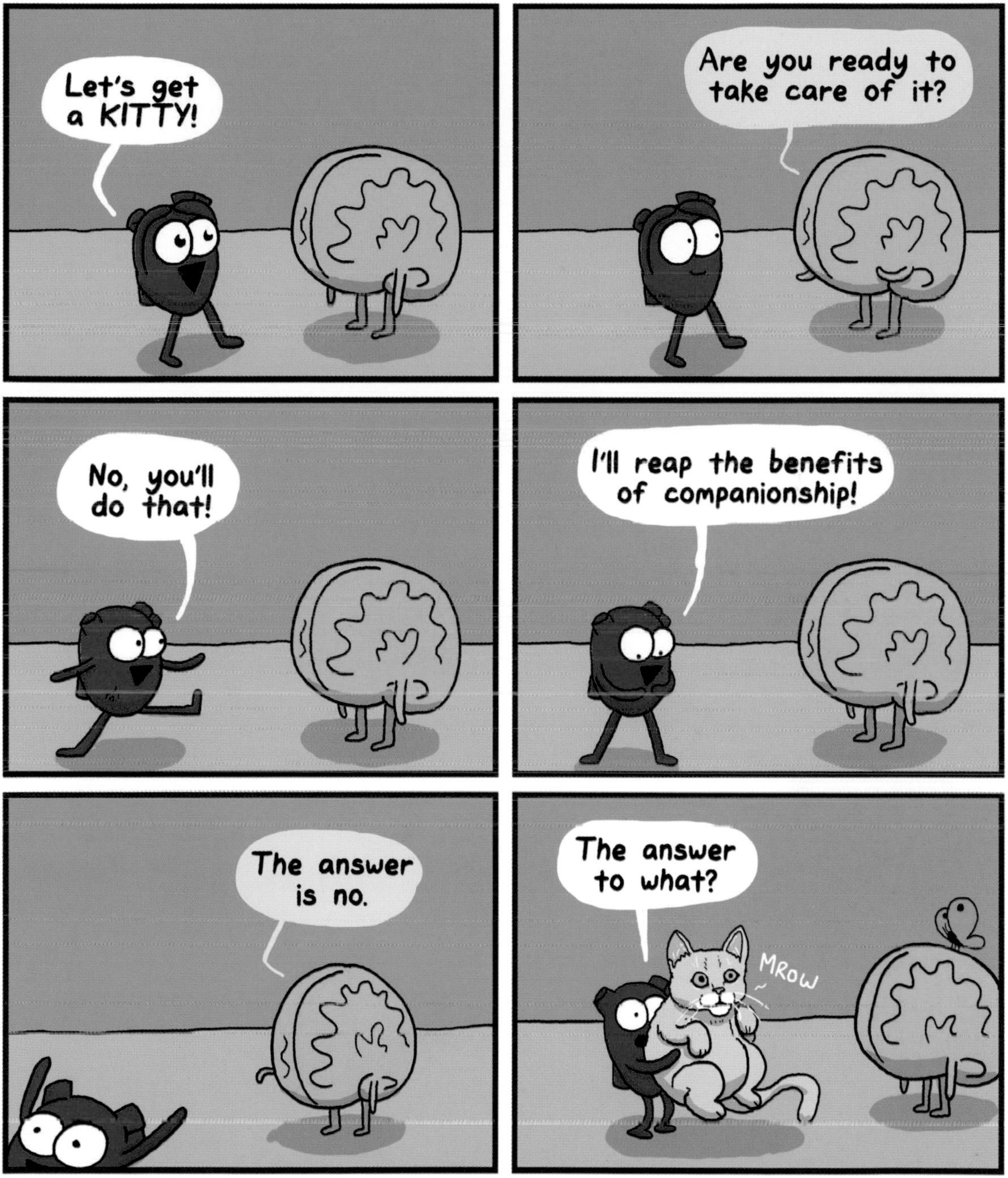
Let's get a KITTY!
Are you ready to take care of it?
No, you'll do that!
I'll reap the benefits of companionship!
The answer is no.
The answer to what?
MROW

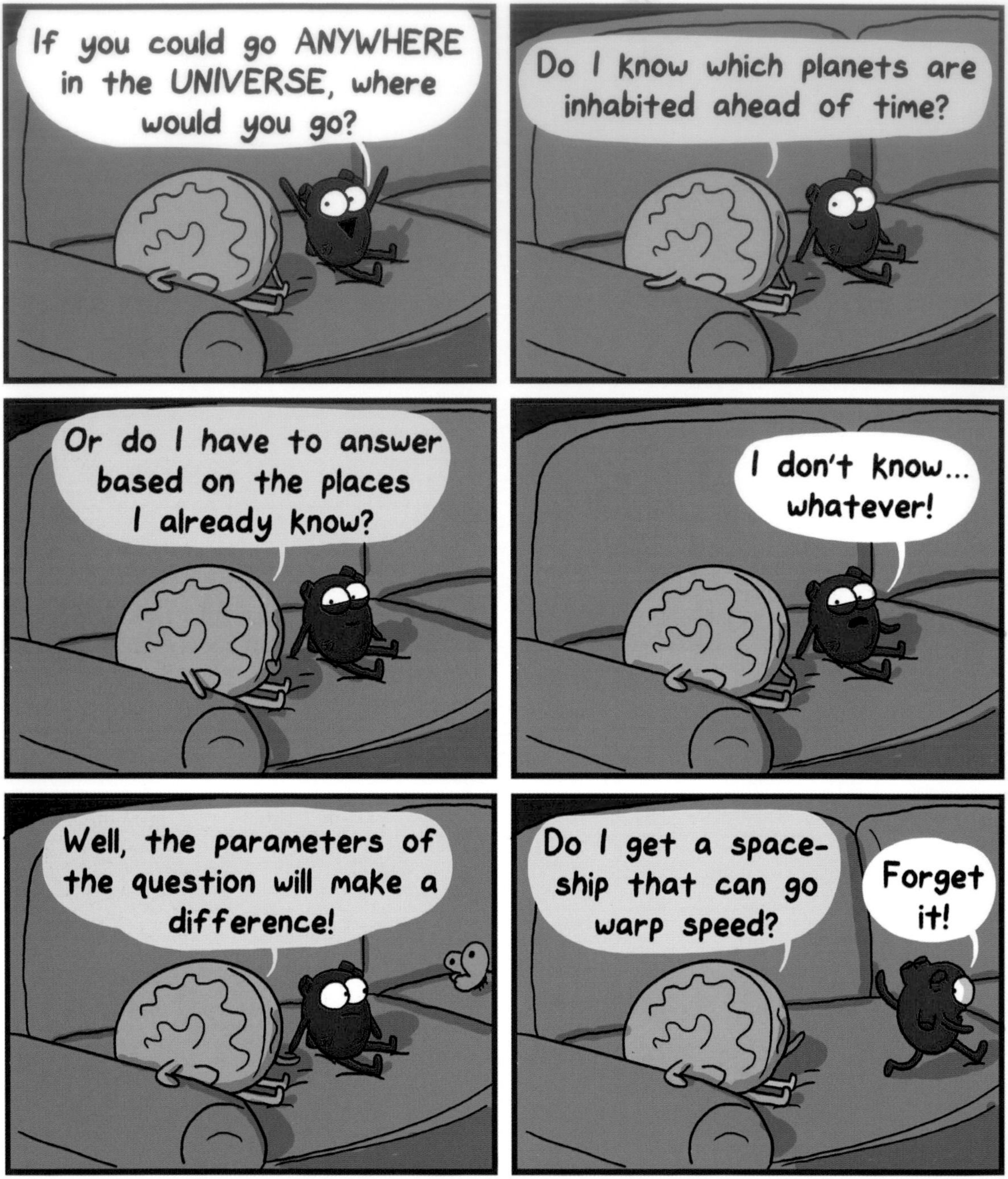
If you could go ANYWHERE in the UNIVERSE, where would you go?
Do I know which planets are inhabited ahead of time?
Or do I have to answer based on the places I already know?
I don't know... whatever!
Well, the parameters of the question will make a difference!
Do I get a space-ship that can go warp speed?
Forget it!

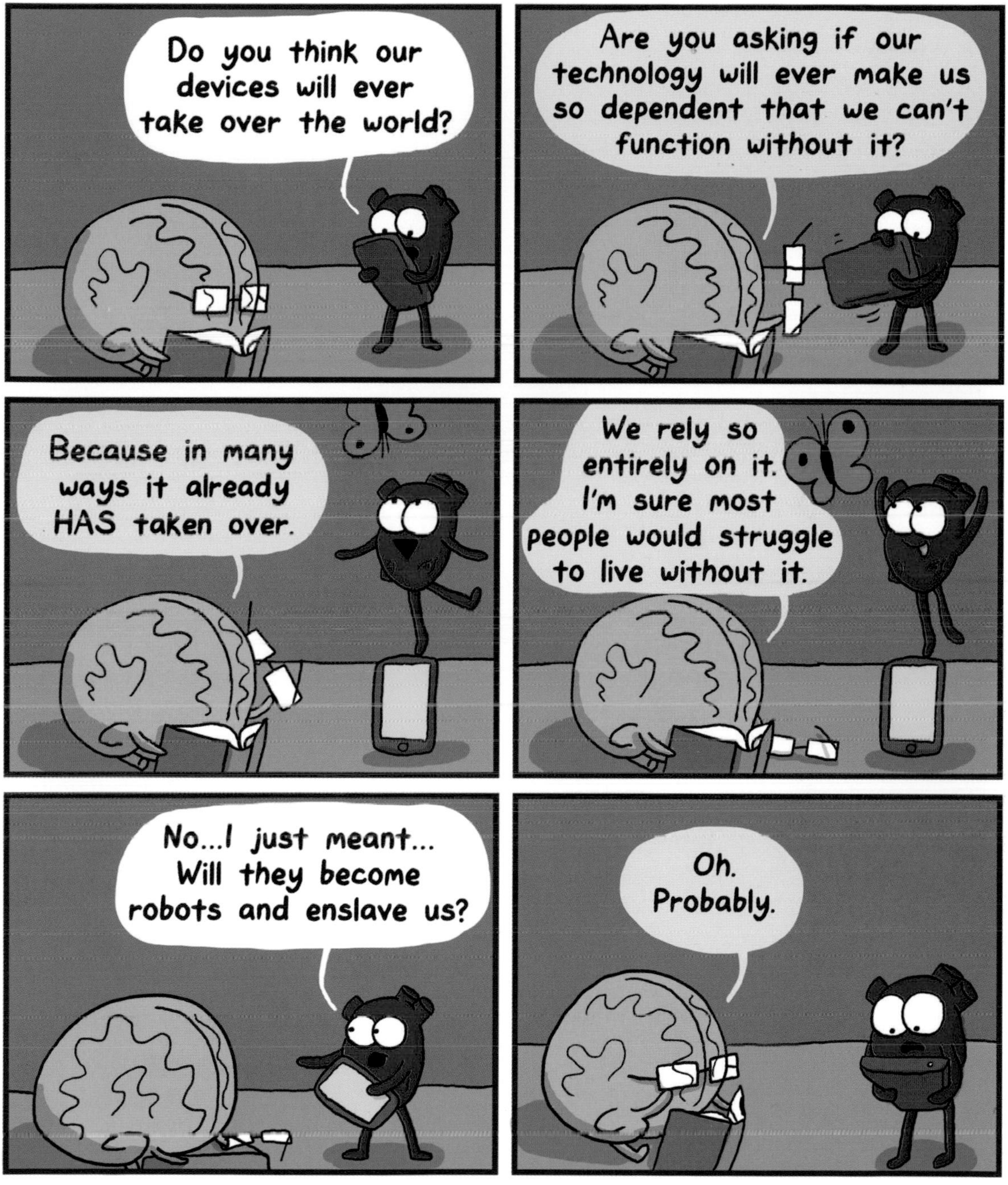
Do you think our devices will ever take over the world?
Are you asking if our technology will ever make us so dependent that we can't function without it?
Because in many ways it already HAS taken over.
We rely so entirely on it. I'm sure most people would struggle to live without it.
No...I just meant... Will they become robots and enslave us?
Oh. Probably.

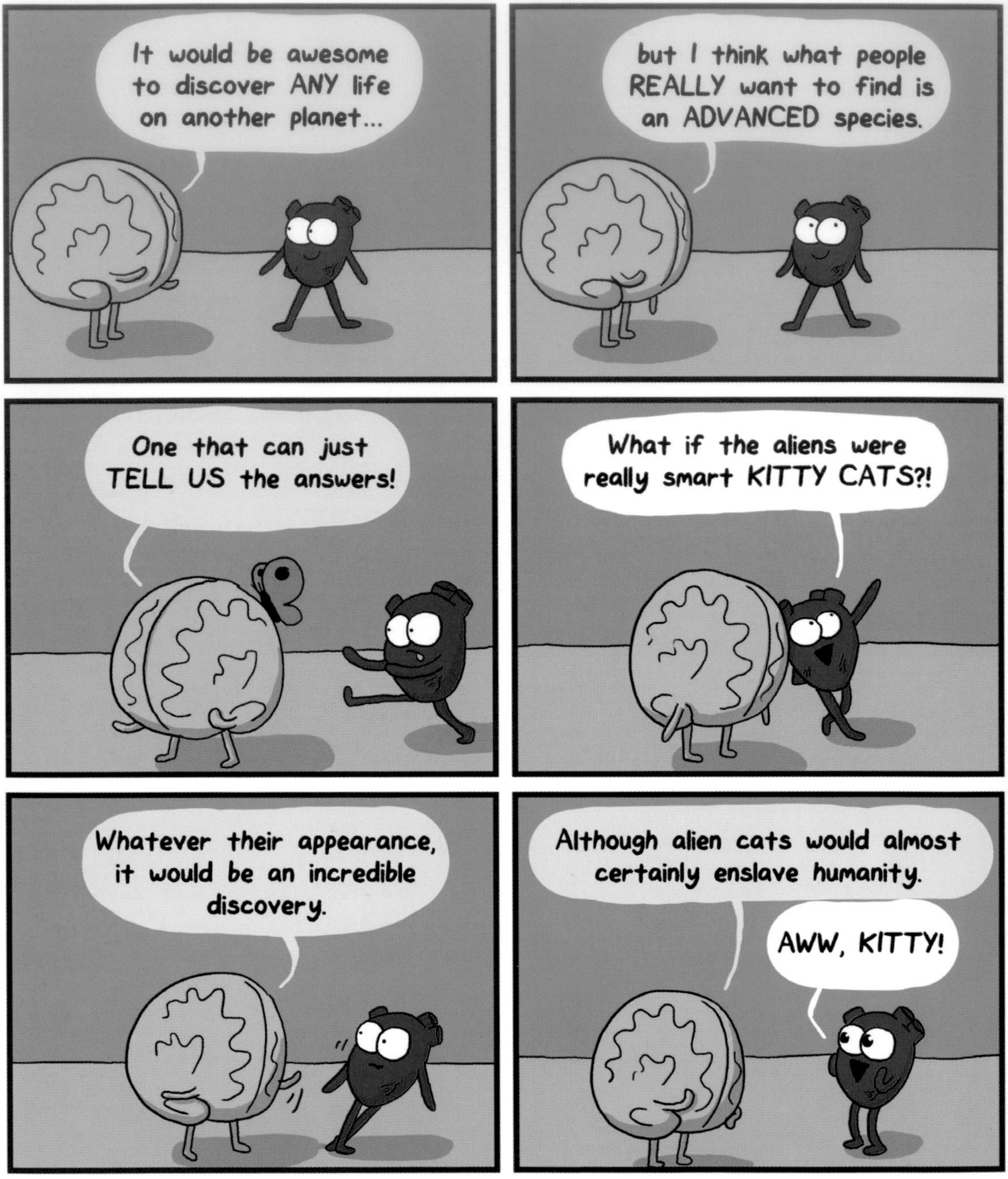
It would be awesome to discover ANY life on another planet...
but I think what people REALLY want to find is an ADVANCED species.
One that can just TELL US the answers!
What if the aliens were really smart KITTY CATS?!
Whatever their appearance, it would be an incredible discovery.
Although alien cats would almost certainly enslave humanity.
AWW, KITTY!

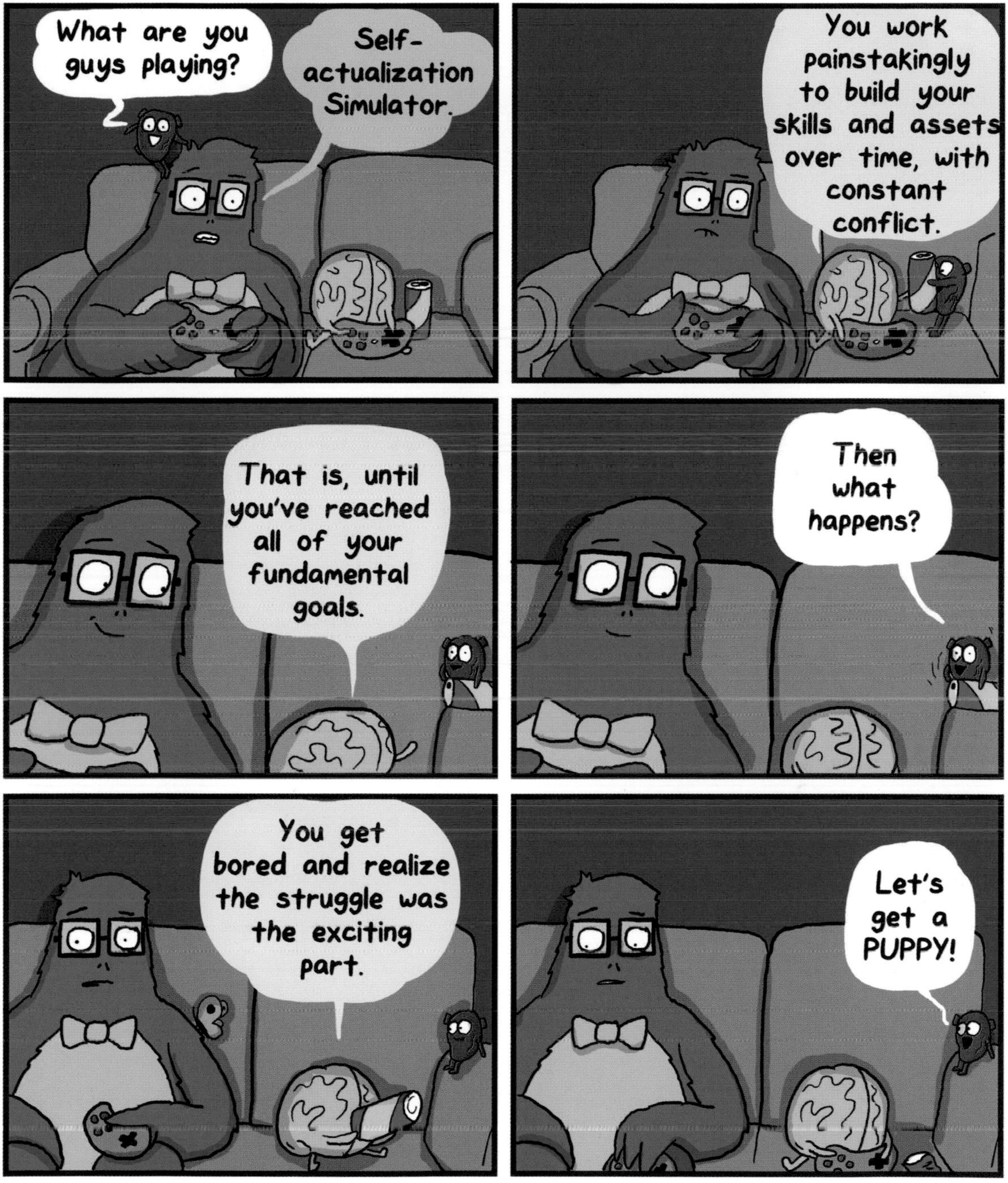
What are you guys playing?
Self-actualization Simulator.
You work painstakingly to build your skills and assets over time, with constant conflict.
That is, until you've reached all of your fundamental goals.
Then what happens?
You get bored and realize the struggle was the exciting part.
Let's get a PUPPY!

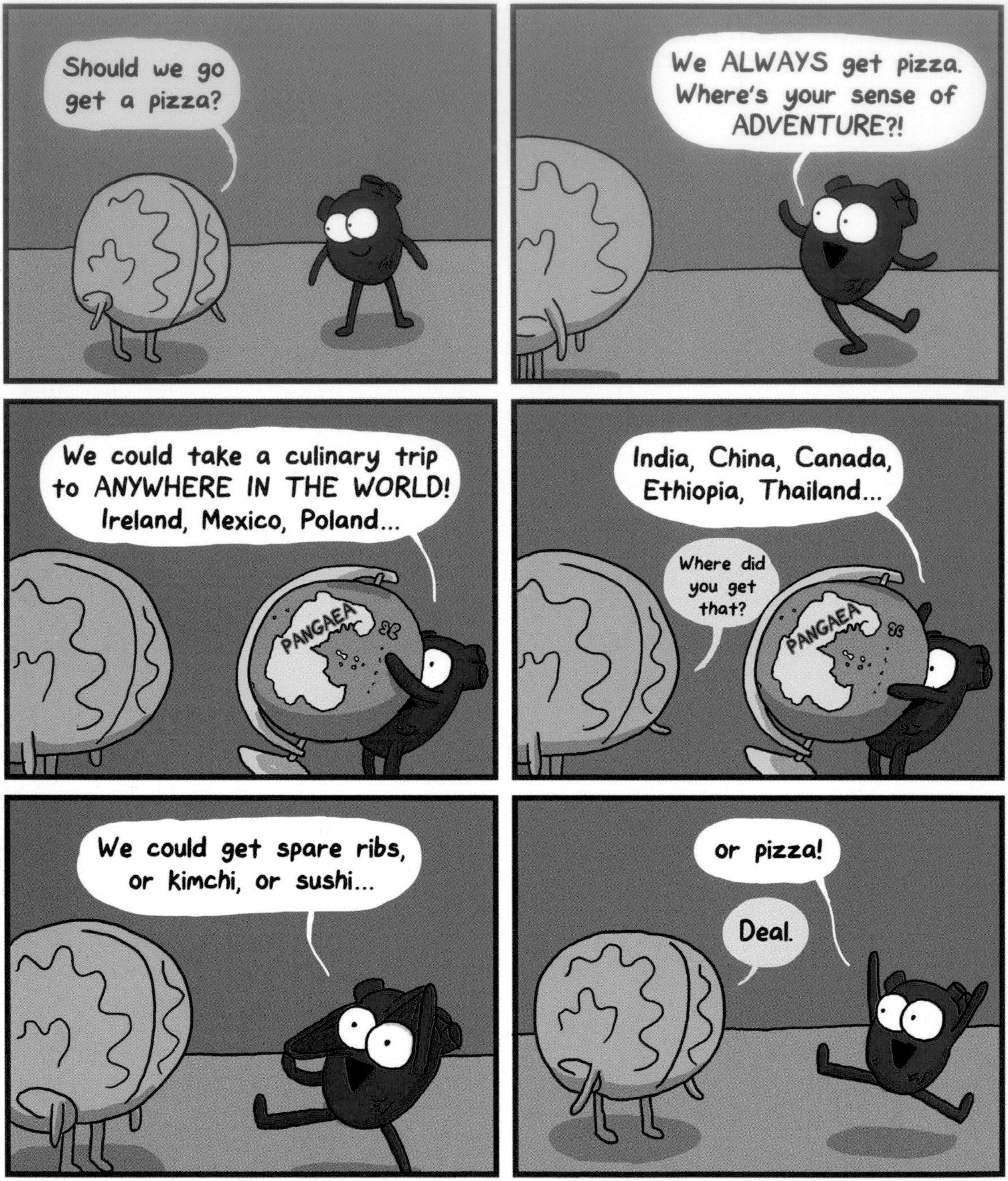
Should we go get a pizza?
We ALWAYS get pizza. Where's your sense of ADVENTURE?!
We could take a culinary trip to ANYWHERE IN THE WORLD! Ireland, Mexico, Poland...
PANGAEA
India, China, Canada, Ethiopia, Thailand...
Where did you get that?
PANGAEA
We could get spare ribs, or kimchi, or sushi...
or pizza!
Deal.

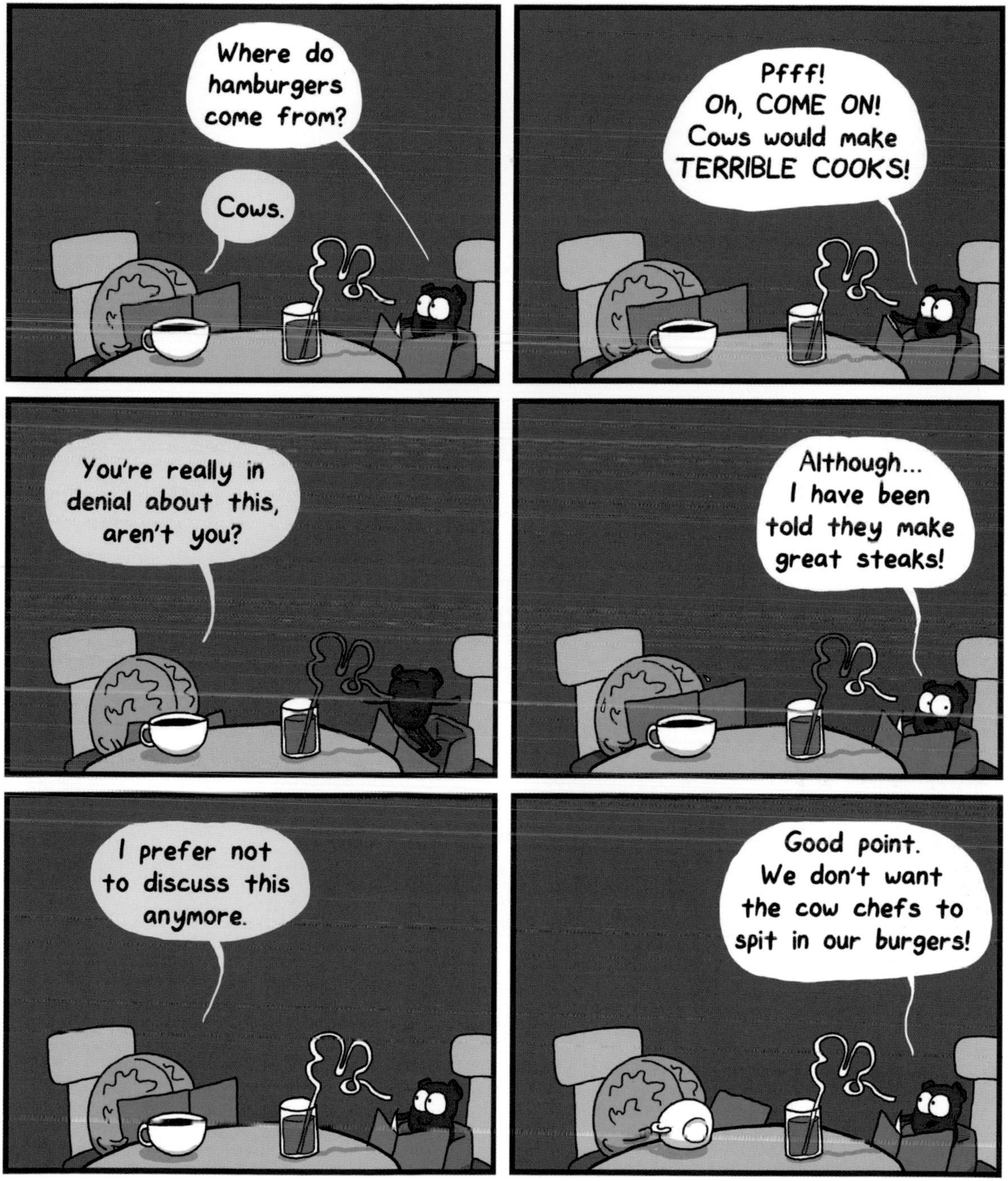
Where do hamburgers come from?
Cows.
Pfff! Oh, COME ON! Cows would make TERRIBLE COOKS!
You're really in denial about this, aren't you?
Although... I have been told they make great steaks!
I prefer not to discuss this anymore.
Good point. We don't want the cow chefs to spit in our burgers!

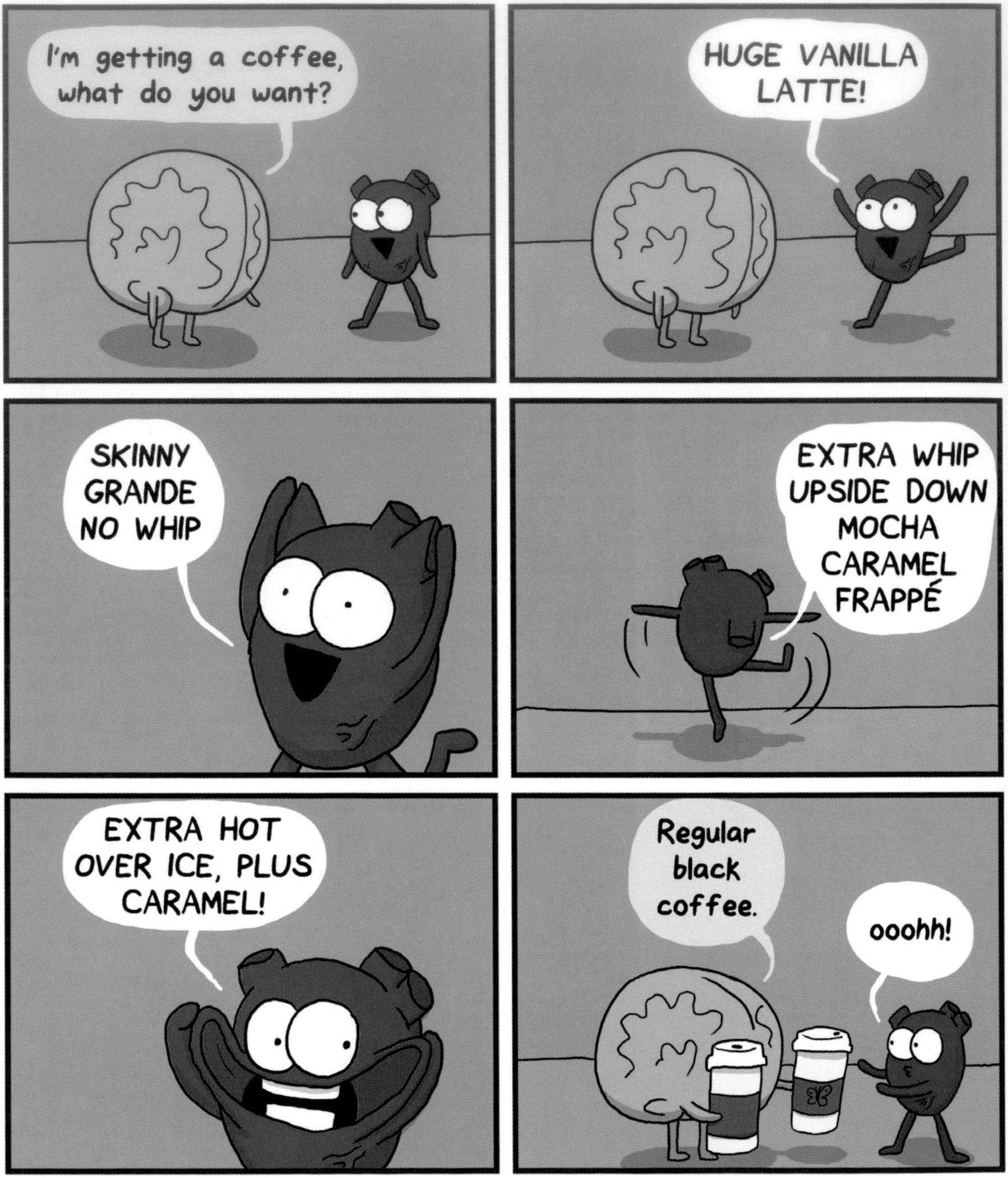
I'm getting a coffee, what do you want?
HUGE VANILLA LATTE!
SKINNY GRANDE NO WHIP
EXTRA WHIP UPSIDE DOWN MOCHA CARAMEL FRAPPÉ
EXTRA HOT OVER ICE, PLUS CARAMEL!
Regular black coffee.
ooohh!

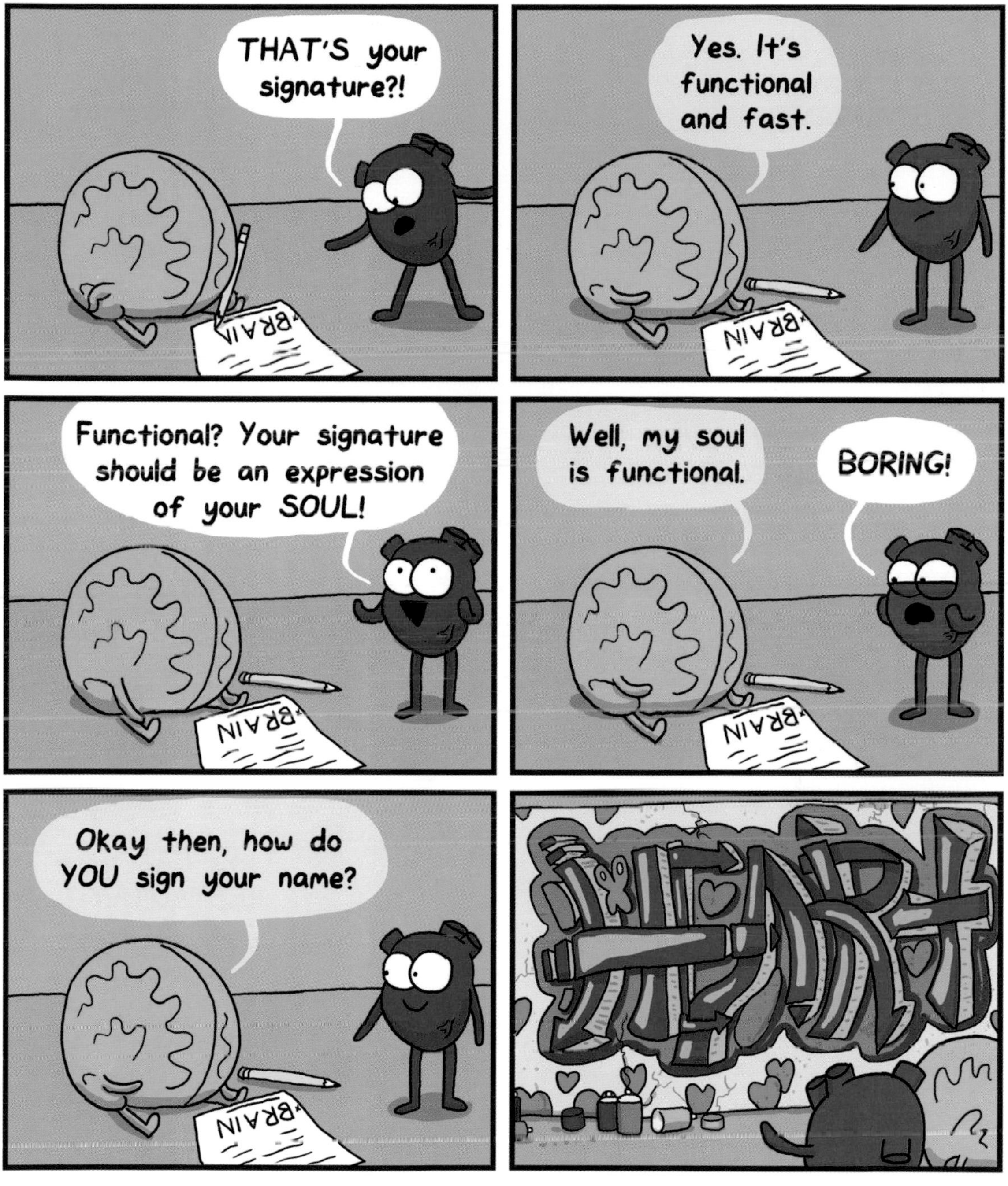
THAT'S your signature?!
Yes. It's functional and fast.
Functional? Your signature should be an expression of your SOUL!
Well, my soul is functional.
BORING!
Okay then, how do YOU sign your name?

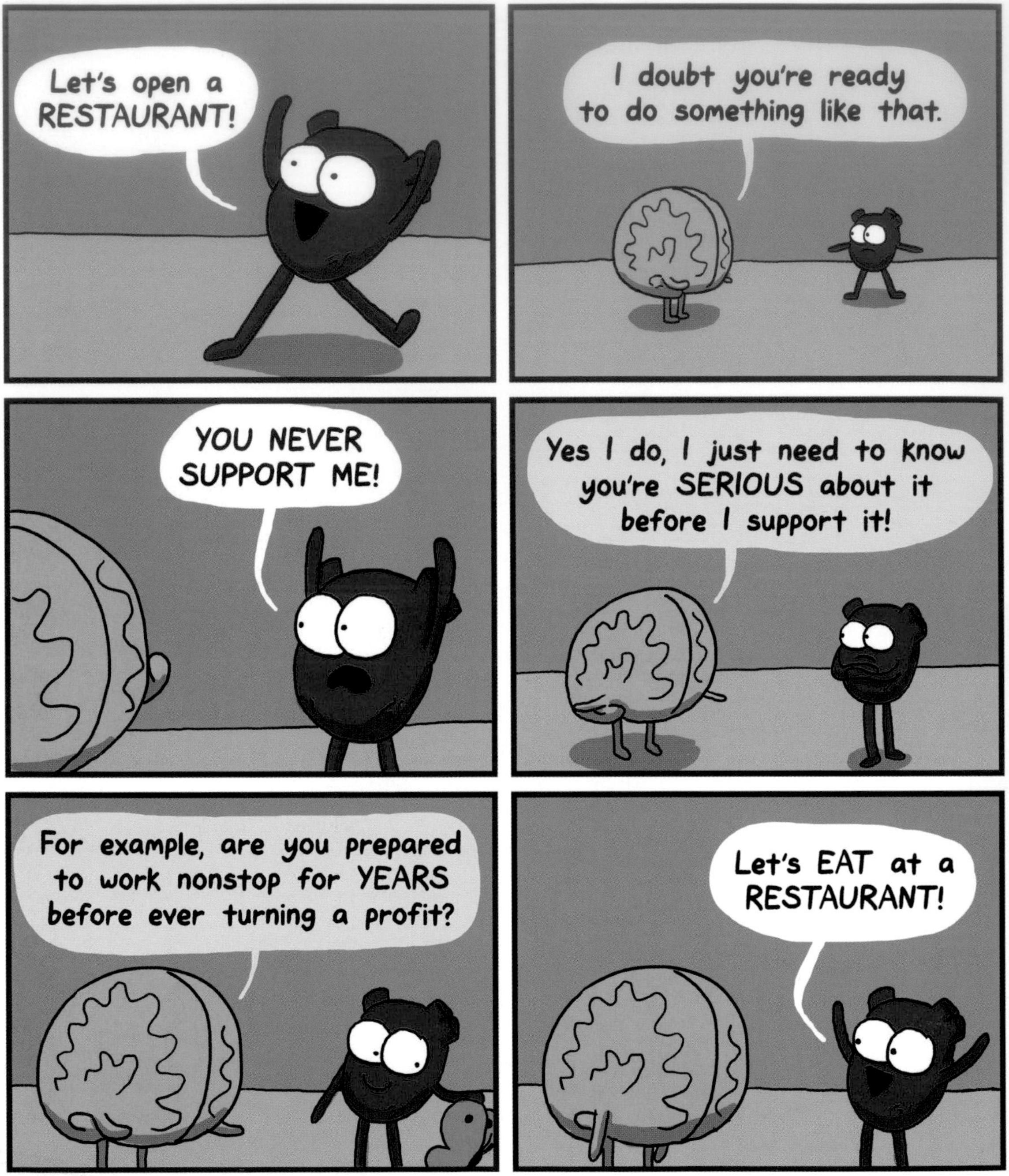
Let's open a RESTAURANT!
I doubt you're ready to do something like that.
YOU NEVER SUPPORT ME!
Yes I do, I just need to know you're SERIOUS about it before I support it!
For example, are you prepared to work nonstop for YEARS before ever turning a profit?
Let's EAT at a RESTAURANT!

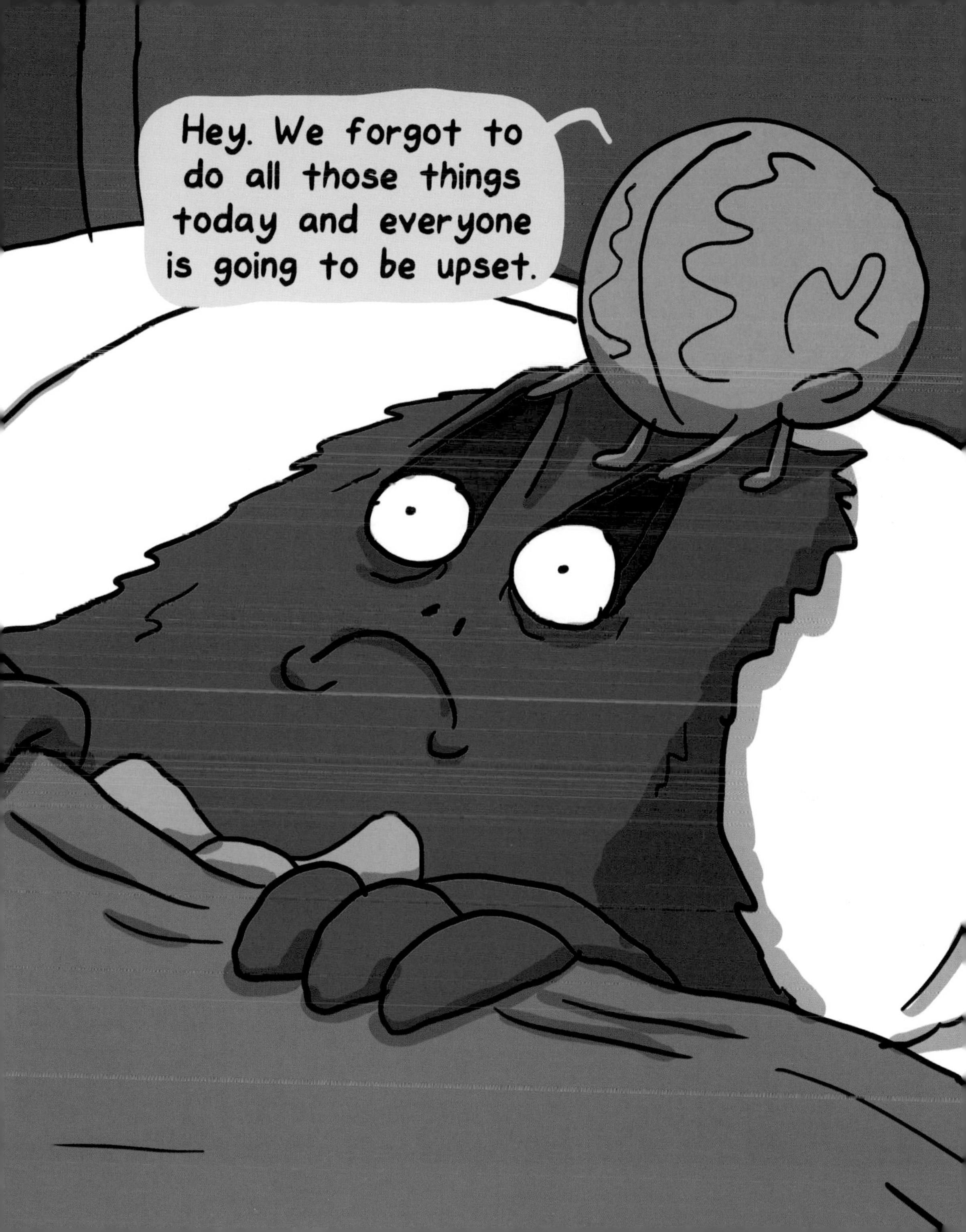
Hey. We forgot to do all those things today and everyone is going to be upset.

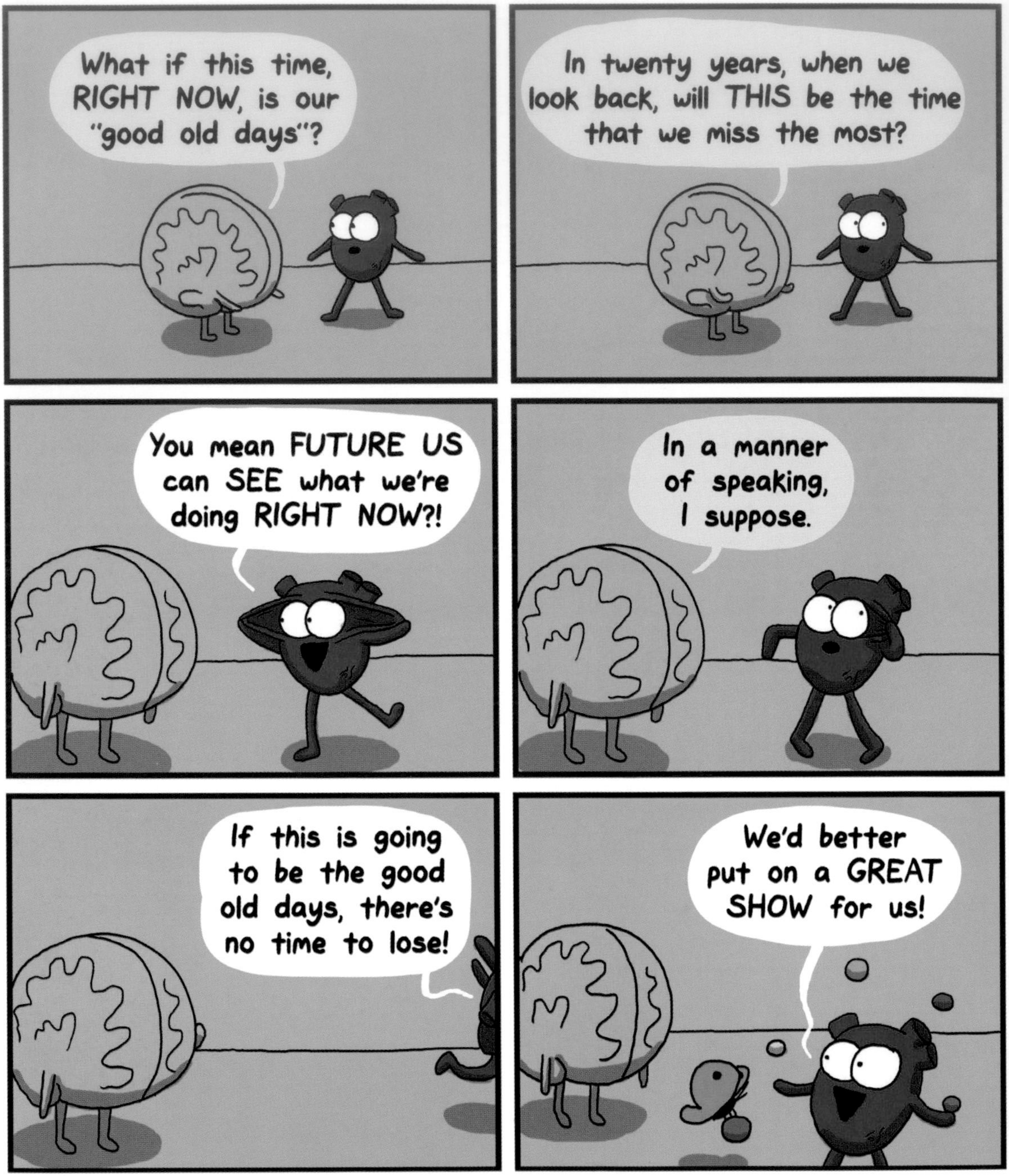
What if this time, RIGHT NOW, is our "good old days"?
In twenty years, when we look back, will THIS be the time that we miss the most?
You mean FUTURE US can SEE what we're doing RIGHT NOW?!
In a manner of speaking, I suppose.
If this is going to be the good old days, there's no time to lose!
We'd better put on a GREAT SHOW for us!

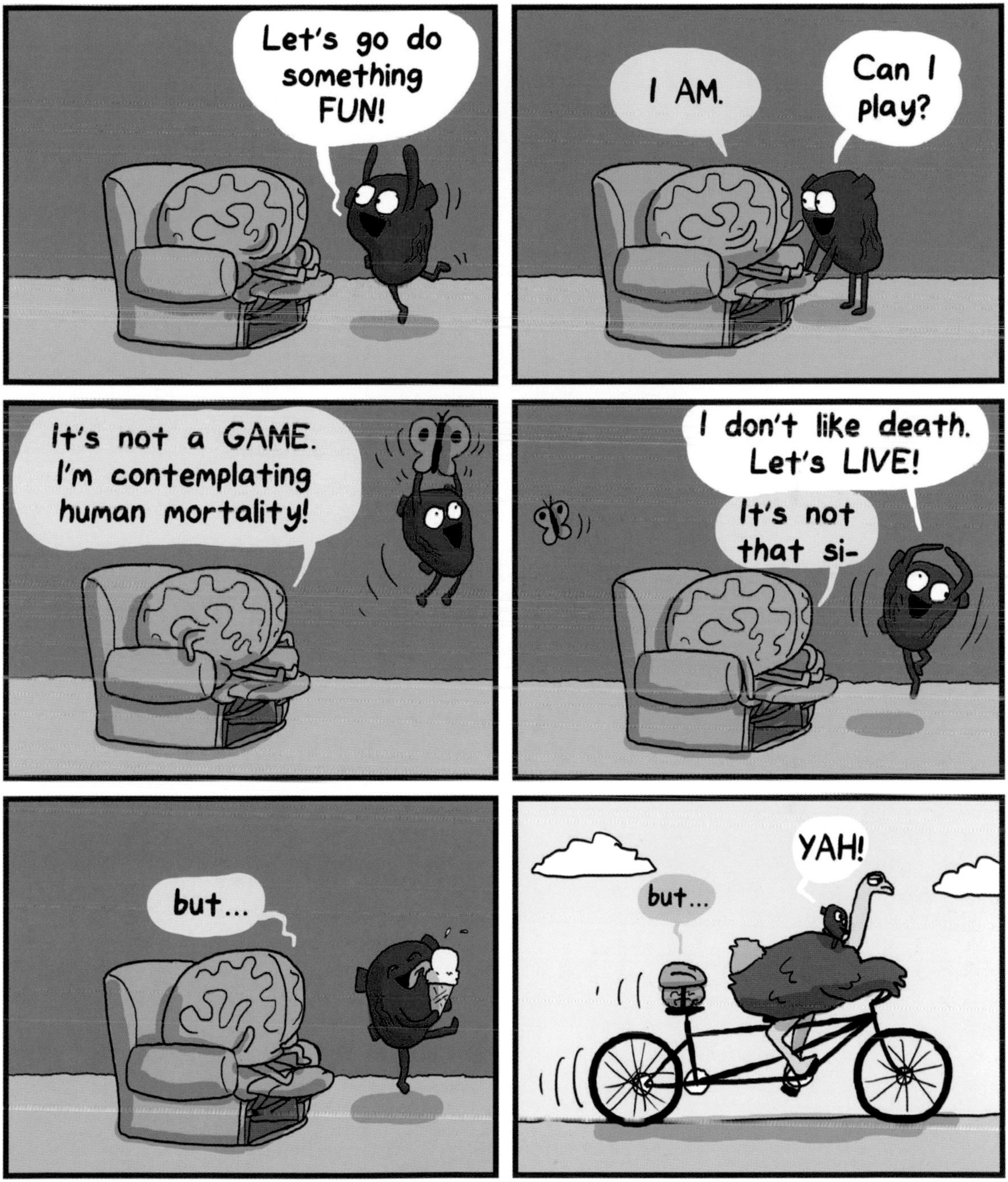
Let's go do something FUN!
I AM.
Can I play?
It's not a GAME. I'm contemplating human mortality!
I don't like death. Let's LIVE!
It's not that si-
but...
YAH!
but...

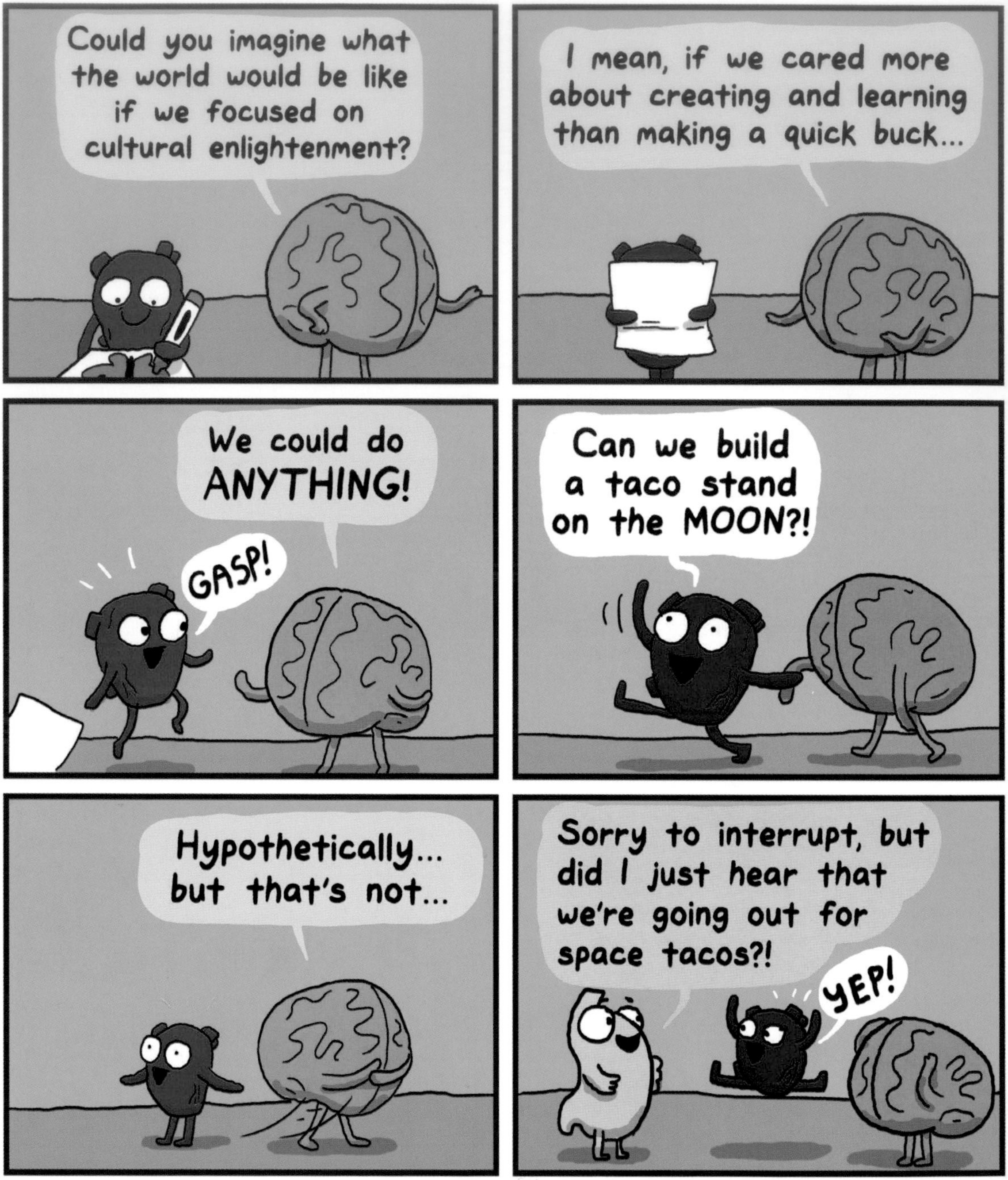
Could you imagine what the world would be like if we focused on cultural enlightenment?
I mean, if we cared more about creating and learning than making a quick buck...
We could do ANYTHING!
GASP!
Can we build a taco stand on the MOON?!
Hypothetically... but that's not...
Sorry to interrupt, but did I just hear that we're going out for space tacos?!
YEP!

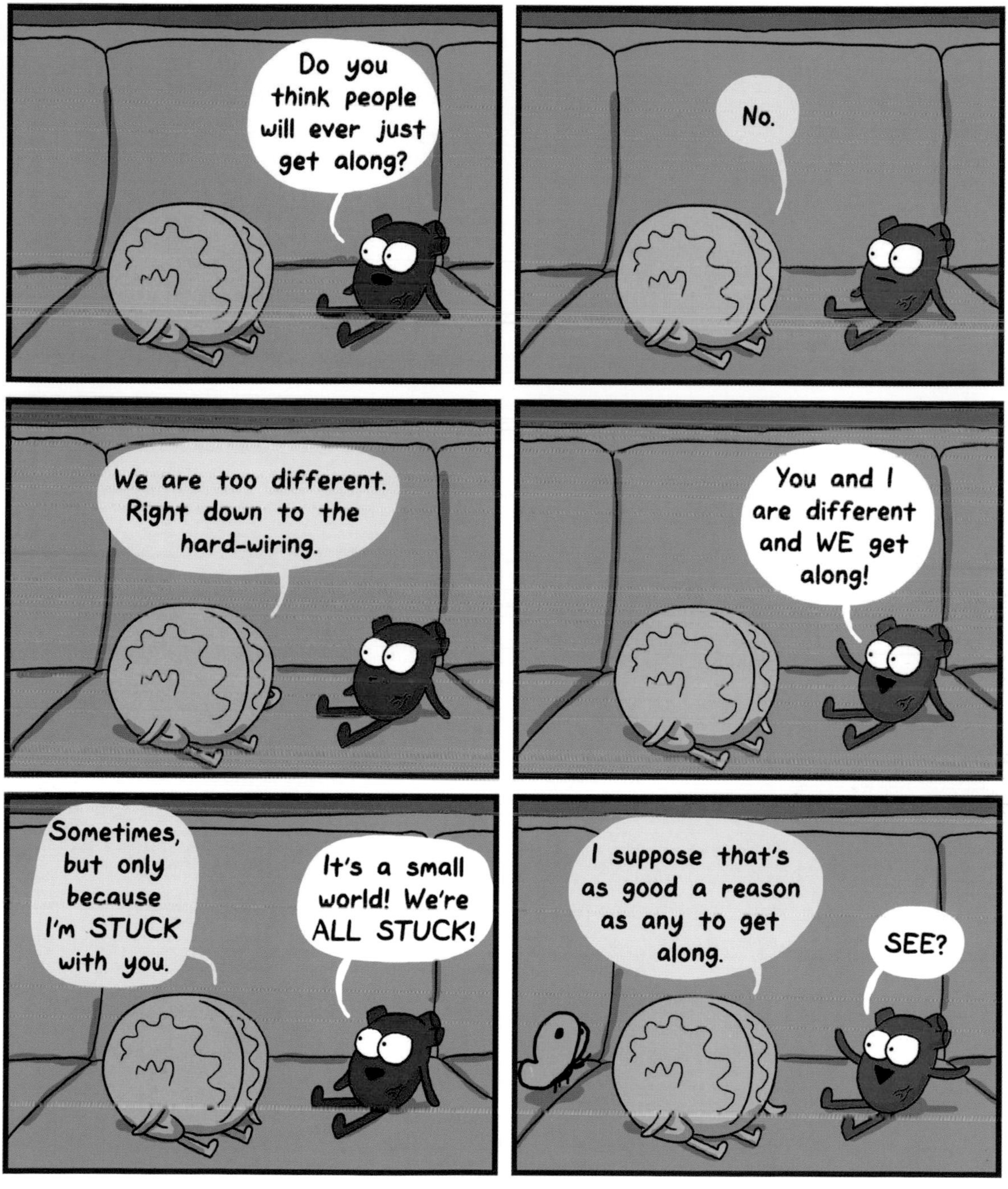
Do you think people will ever just get along?
No.
We are too different. Right down to the hard-wiring.
You and I are different and WE get along!
Sometimes, but only because I'm STUCK with you.
It's a small world! We're ALL STUCK!
I suppose that's as good a reason as any to get along.
SEE?

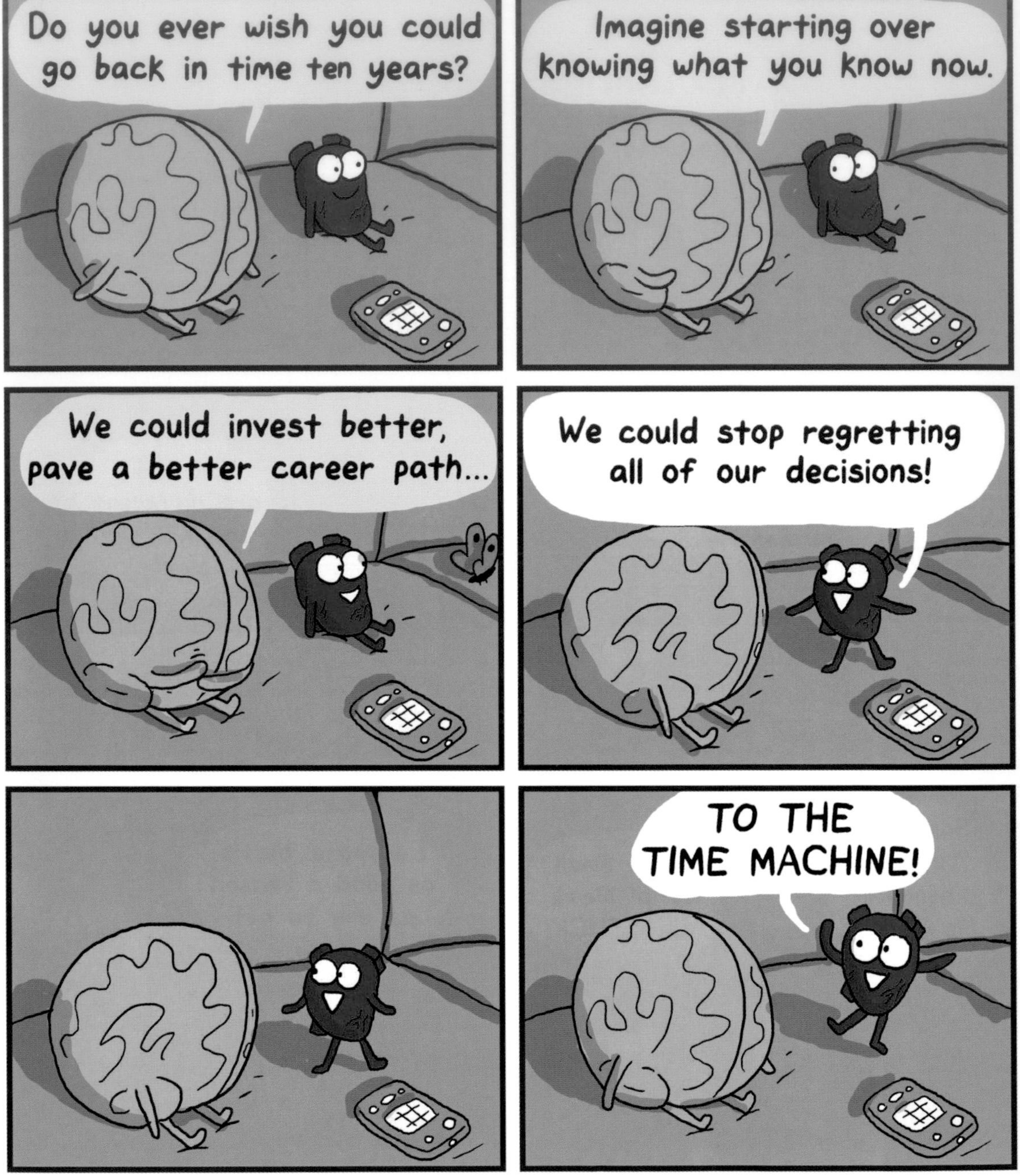
Do you ever wish you could go back in time ten years?
Imagine starting over knowing what you know now.
We could invest better, pave a better career path...
We could stop regretting all of our decisions!
TO THE TIME MACHINE!

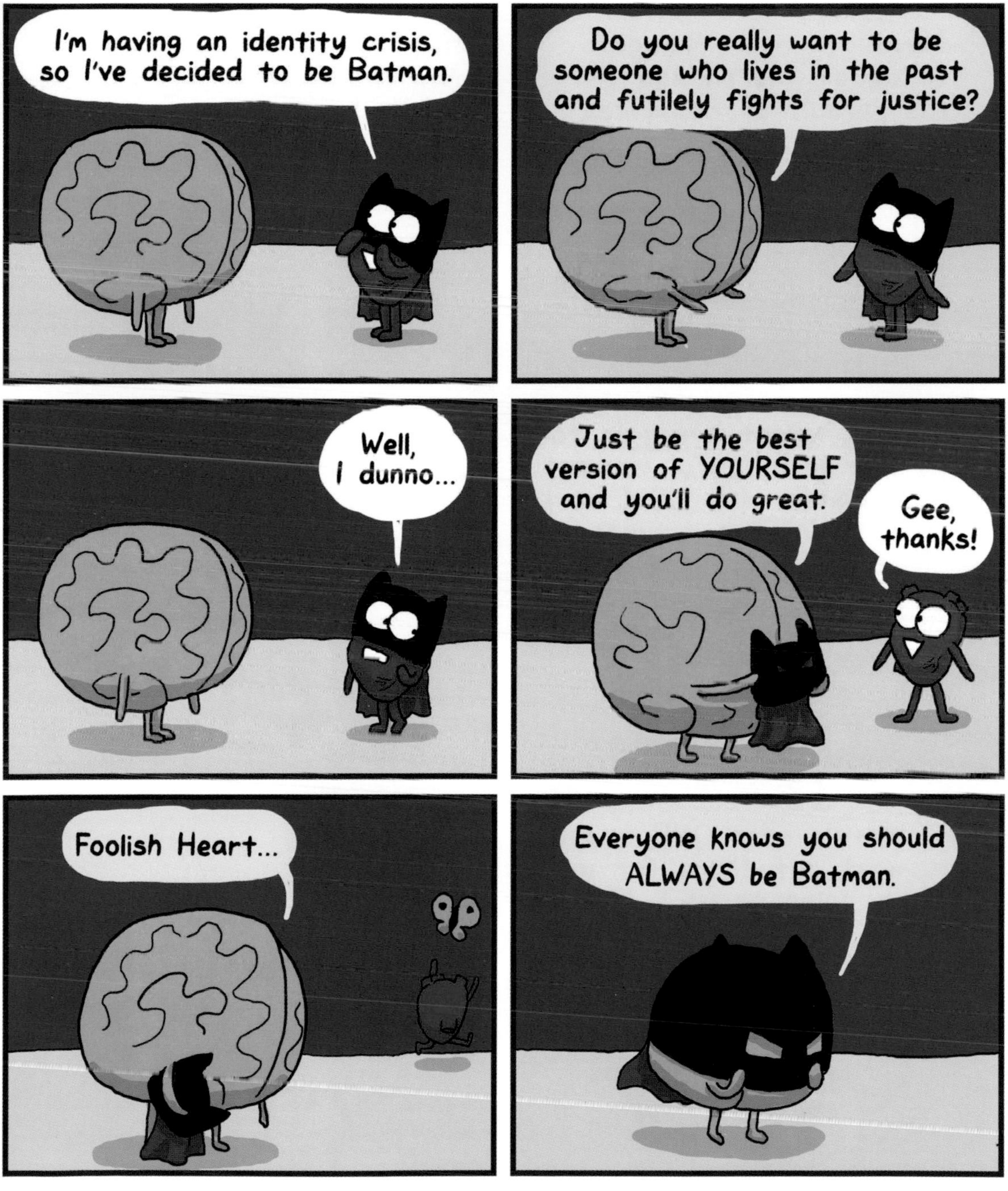
I'm having an identity crisis, so I've decided to be Batman.
Do you really want to be someone who lives in the past and futilely fights for justice?
Well, I dunno...
Just be the best version of YOURSELF and you'll do great.
Gee, thanks!
Foolish Heart...
Everyone knows you should ALWAYS be Batman.

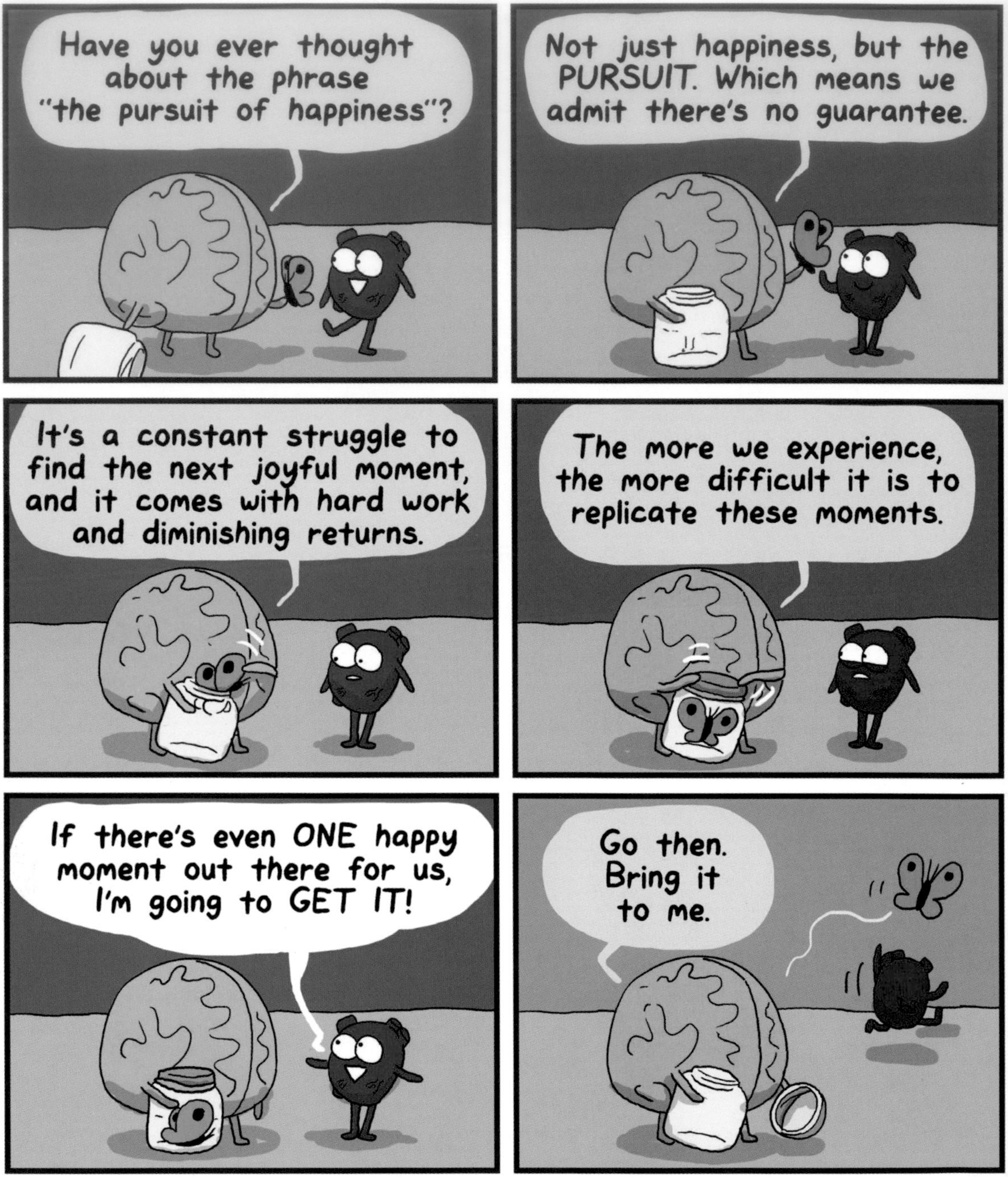
Have you ever thought about the phrase "the pursuit of happiness"?
Not just happiness, but the PURSUIT. Which means we admit there's no guarantee.
It's a constant struggle to find the next joyful moment, and it comes with hard work and diminishing returns.
The more we experience, the more difficult it is to replicate these moments.
If there's even ONE happy moment out there for us, I'm going to GET IT!
Go then. Bring it to me.

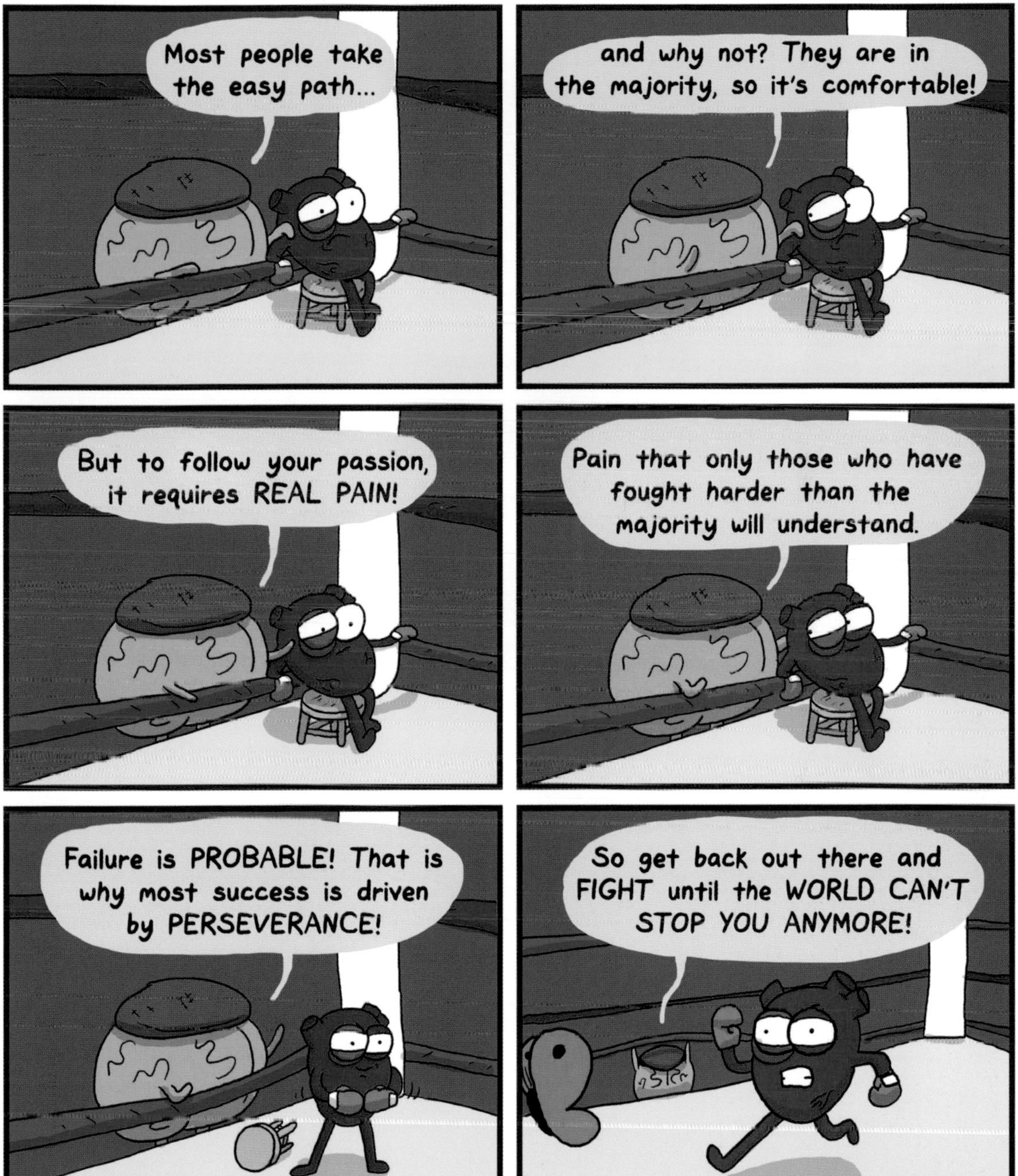
Most people take the easy path...
and why not? They are in the majority, so it's comfortable!
But to follow your passion, it requires REAL PAIN!
Pain that only those who have fought harder than the majority will understand.
Failure is PROBABLE! That is why most success is driven by PERSEVERANCE!
So get back out there and FIGHT until the WORLD CAN'T STOP YOU ANYMORE!

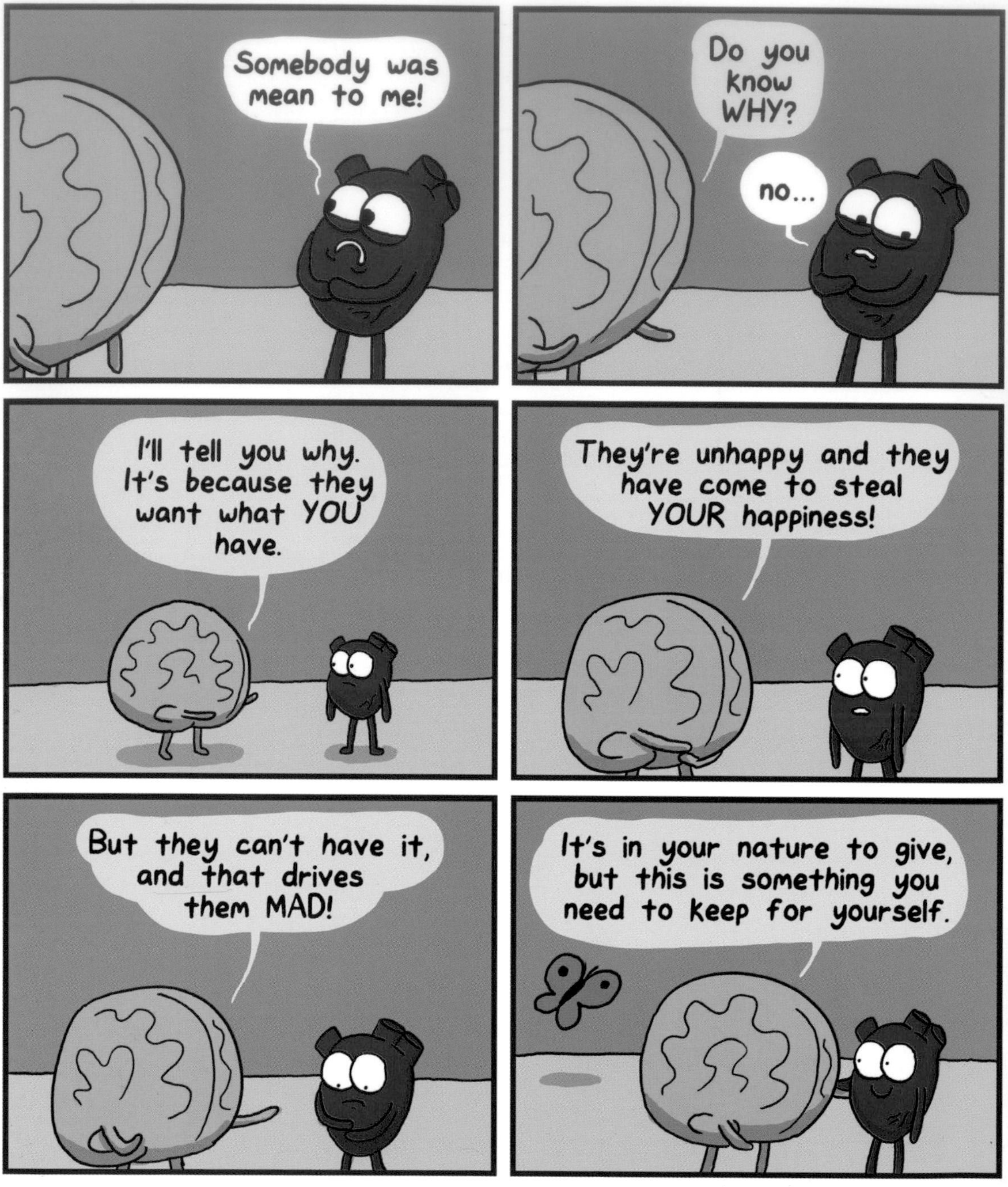
Somebody was mean to me!
Do you know WHY?
no...
I'll tell you why. It's because they want what YOU have.
They're unhappy and they have come to steal YOUR happiness!
But they can't have it, and that drives them MAD!
It's in your nature to give, but this is something you need to keep for yourself.

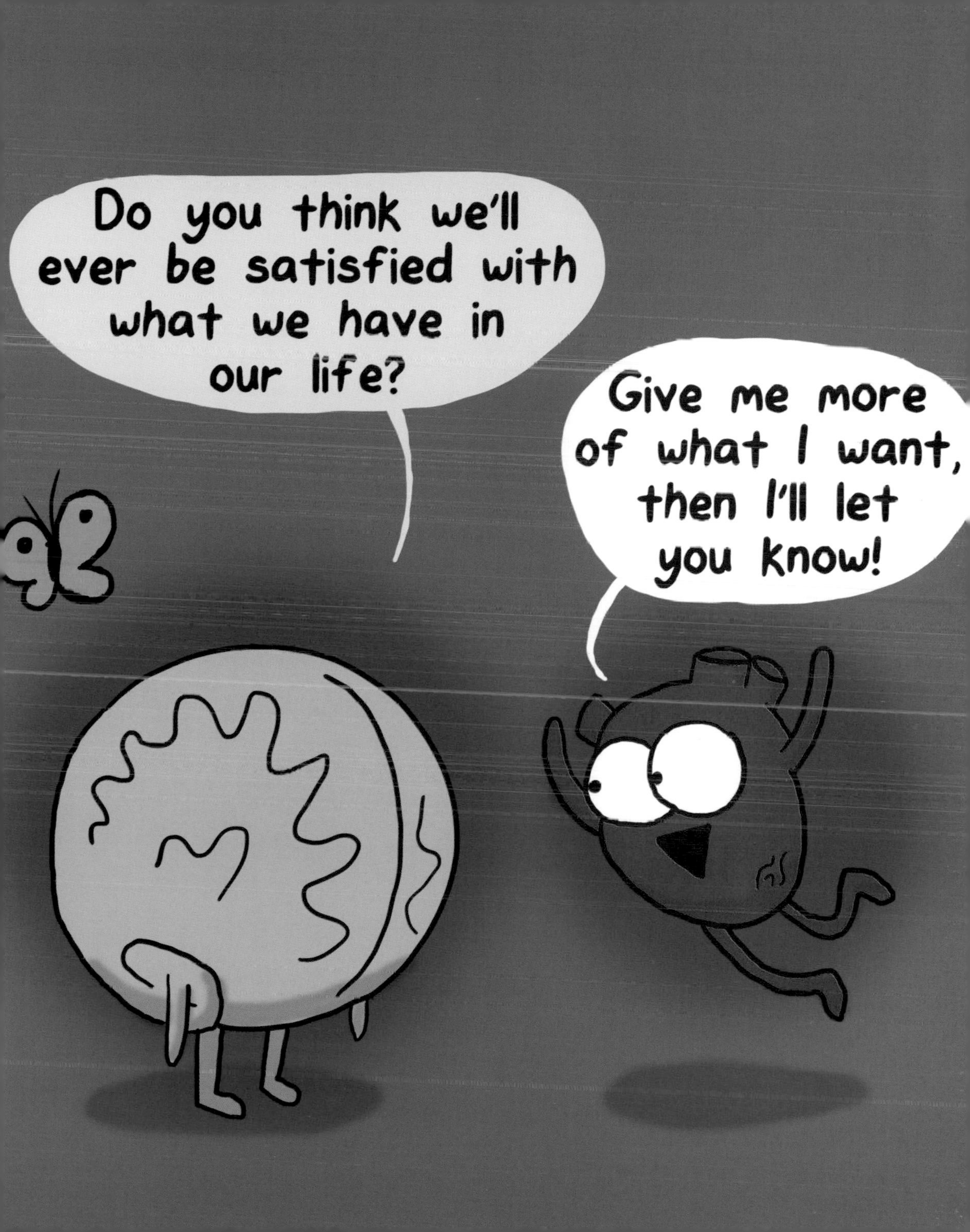
Do you think we'll ever be satisfied with what we have in our life?
Give me more of what I want, then I'll let you know!

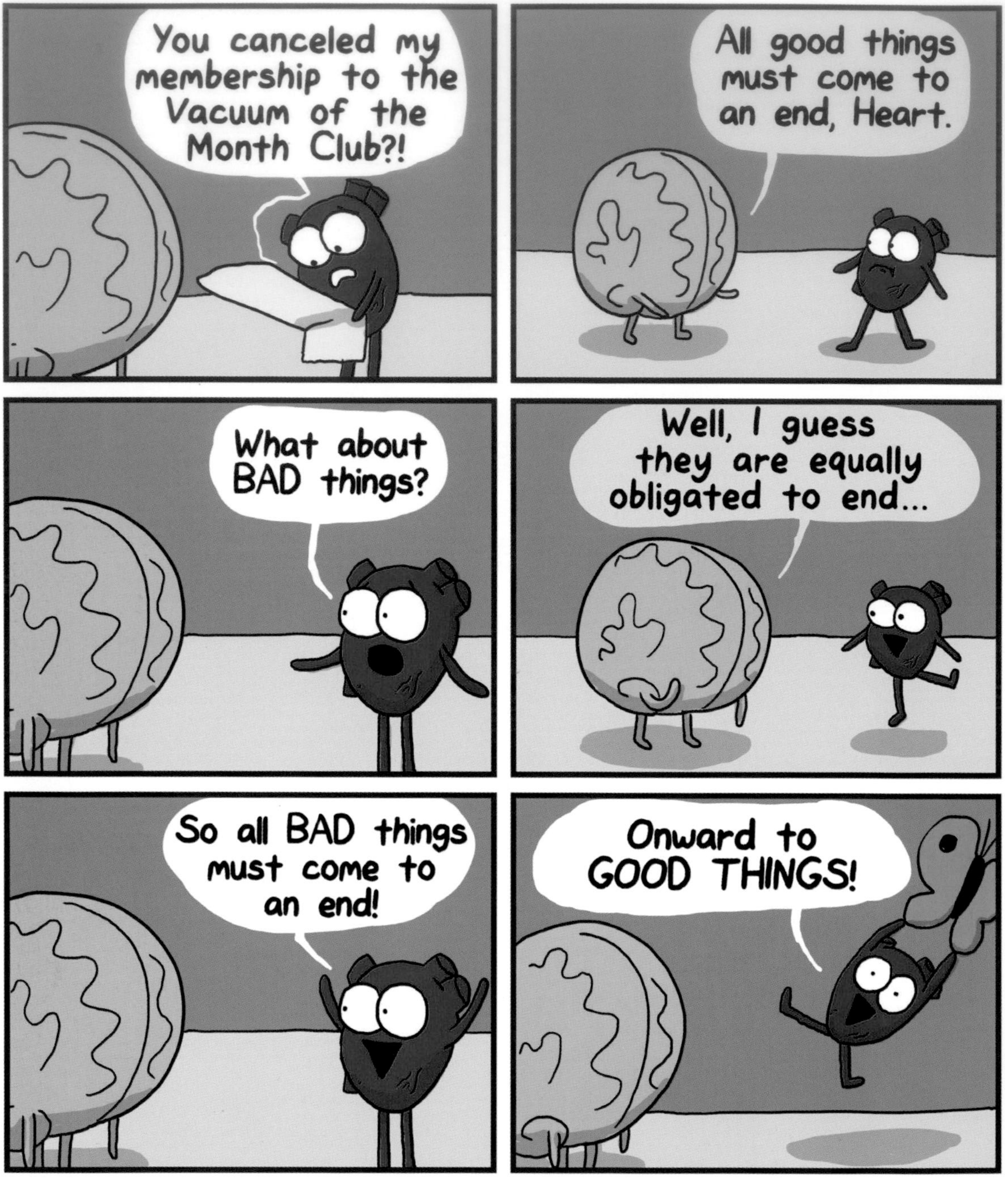
You canceled my membership to the Vacuum of the Month Club?!
All good things must come to an end, Heart.
What about BAD things?
Well, I guess they are equally obligated to end...
So all BAD things must come to an end!
Onward to GOOD THINGS!

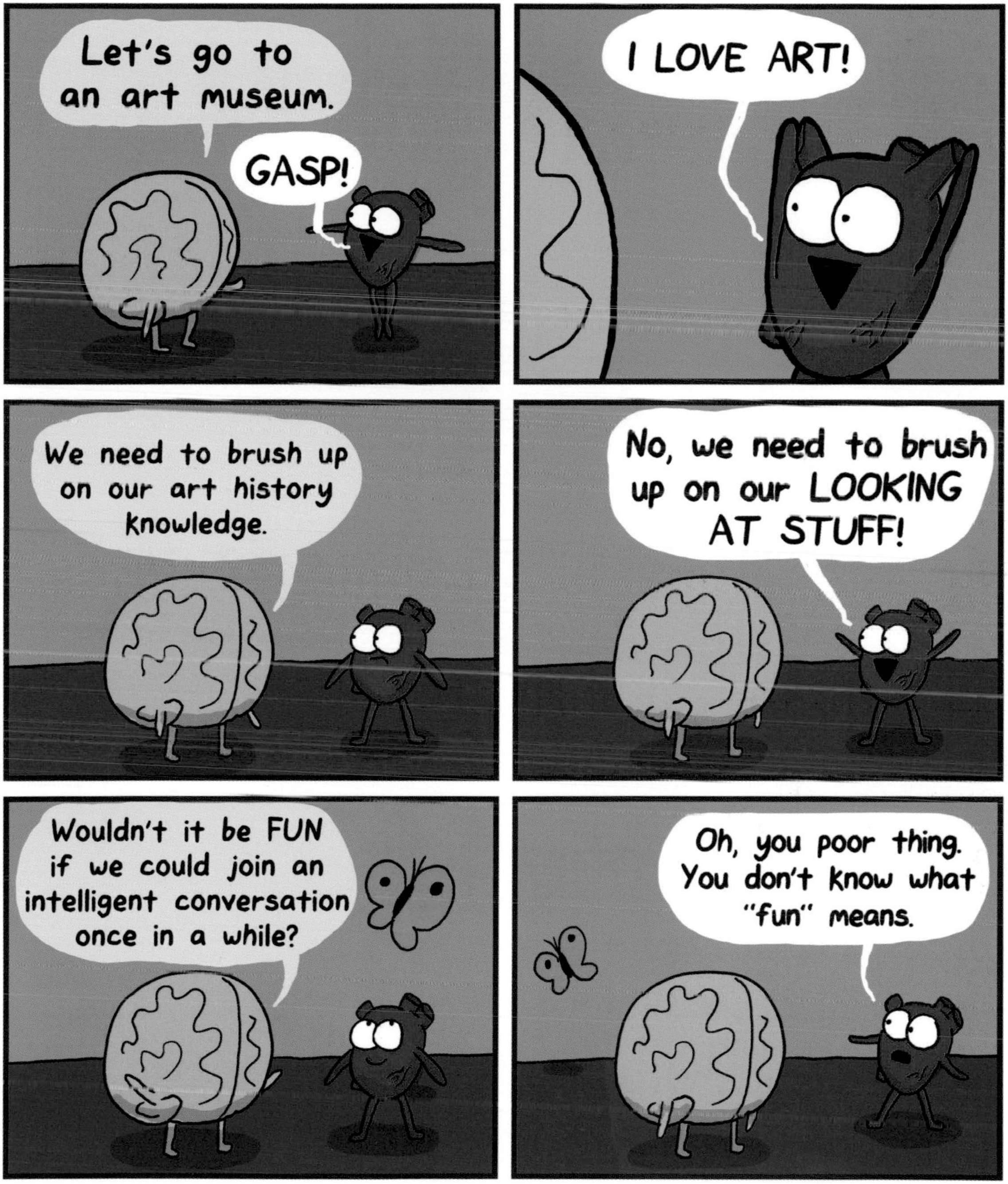
Let's go to an art museum.
GASP!
I LOVE ART!
We need to brush up on our art history knowledge.
No, we need to brush up on our LOOKING AT STUFF!
Wouldn't it be FUN if we could join an intelligent conversation once in a while?
Oh, you poor thing. You don't know what "fun" means.

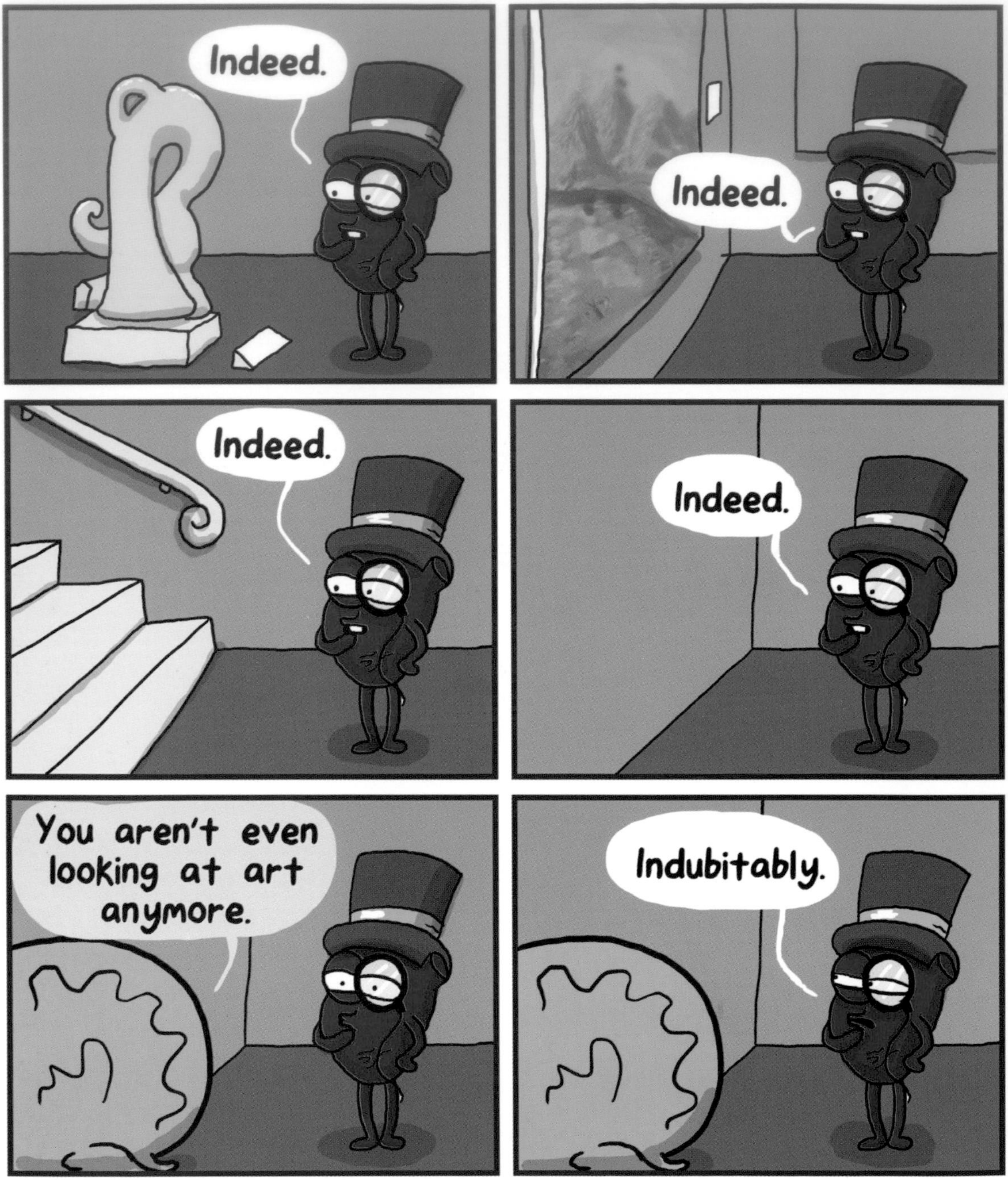
Indeed.
Indeed.
Indeed.
Indeed.
You aren't even looking at art anymore.
Indubitably.

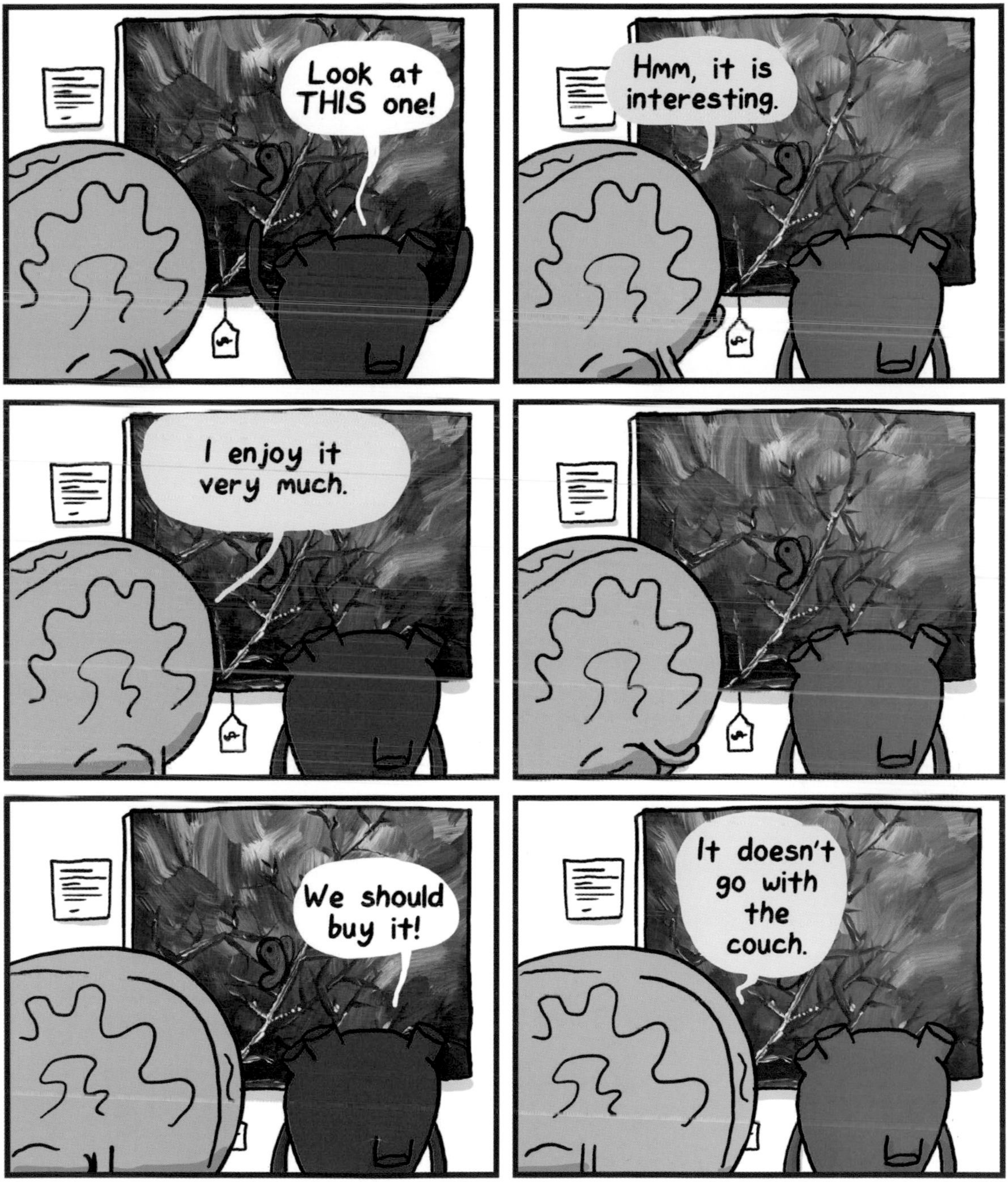
Look at THIS one!
Hmm, it is interesting.
I enjoy it very much.
We should buy it!
It doesn't go with the couch.

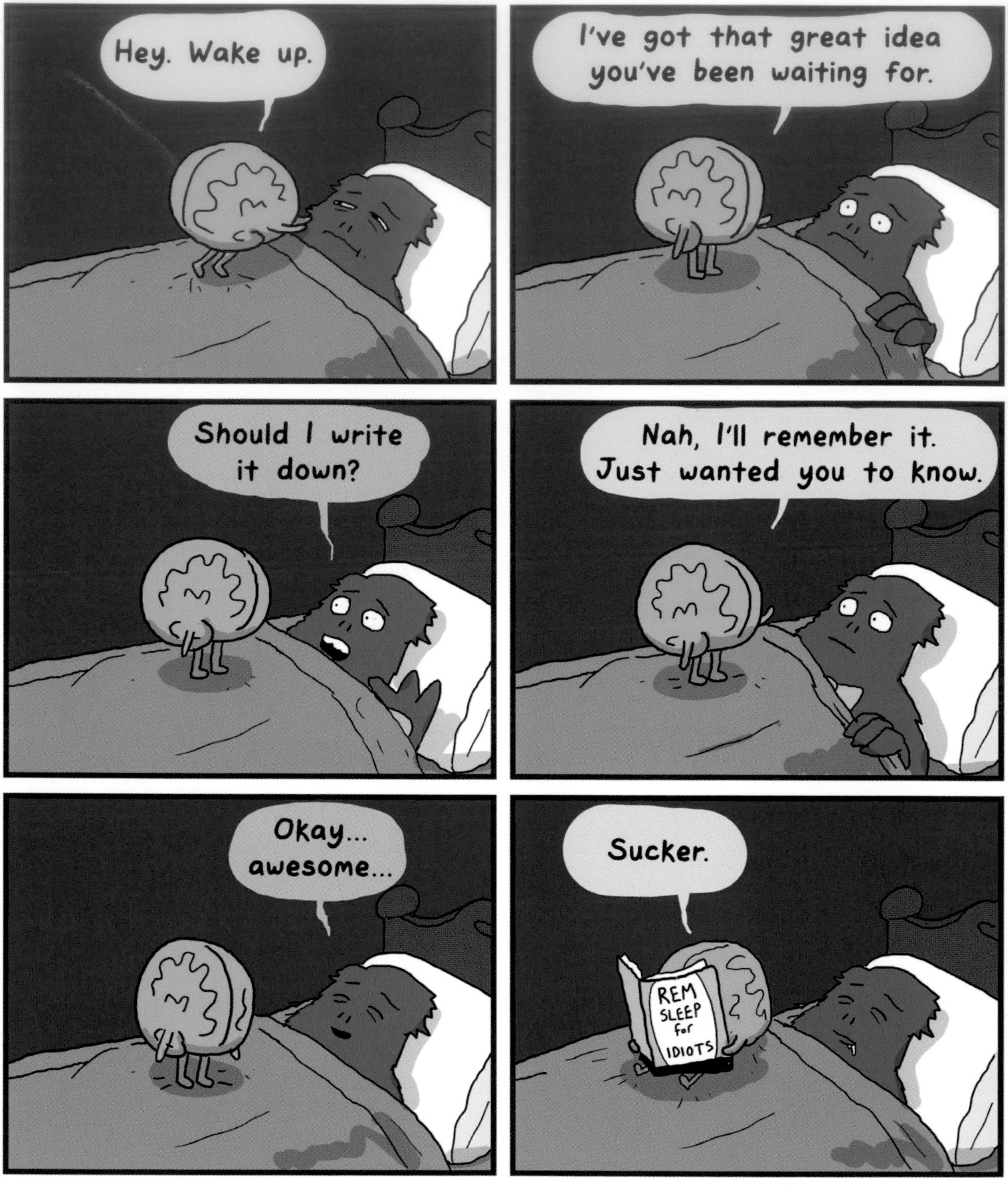
Hey. Wake up.
I've got that great idea you've been waiting for.
Should I write it down?
Nah, I'll remember it. Just wanted you to know.
Okay... awesome...
Sucker.
REM SLEEP for IDIOTS

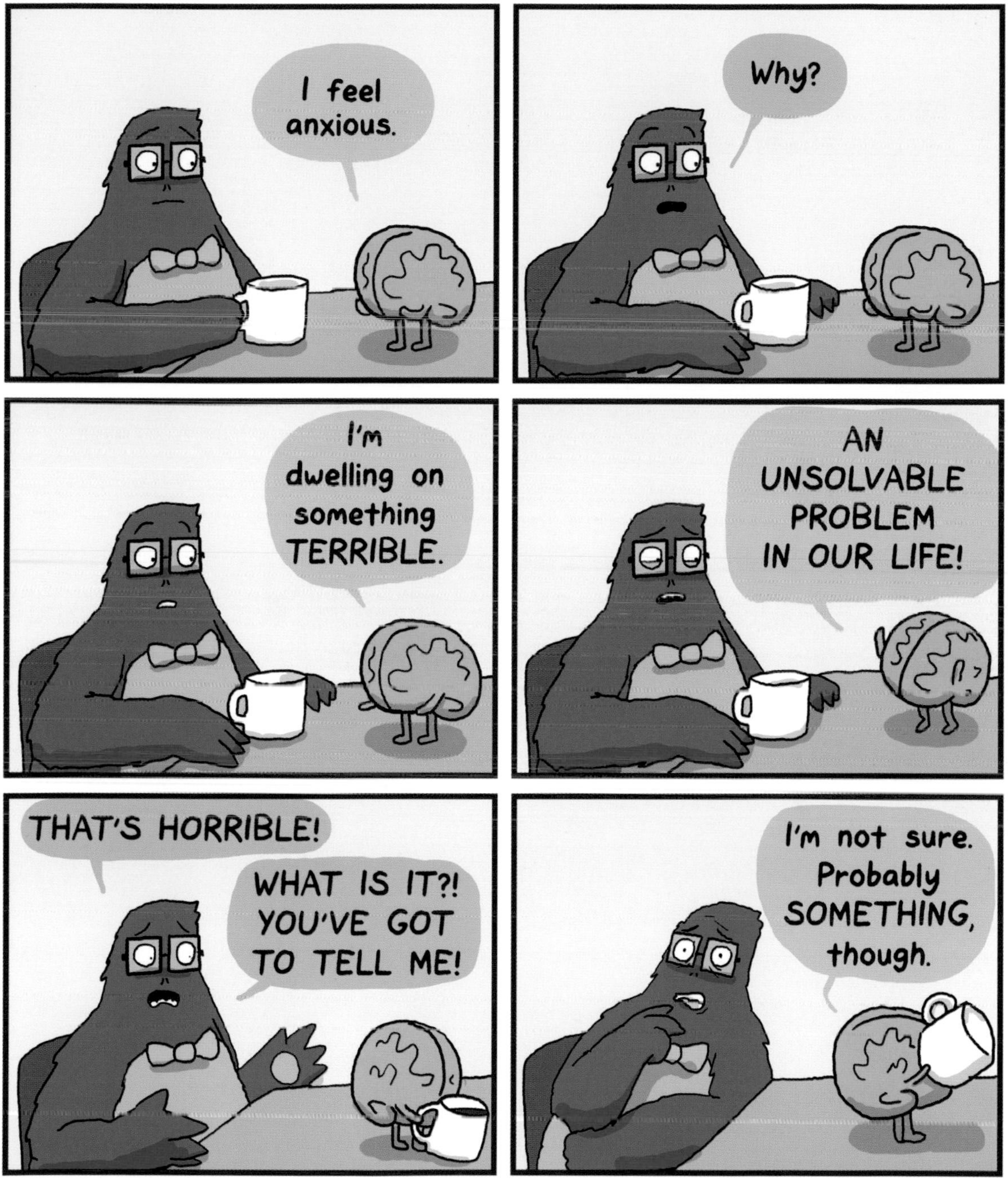
I feel anxious.
Why?
I'm dwelling on something TERRIBLE.
AN UNSOLVABLE PROBLEM IN OUR LIFE!
THAT'S HORRIBLE!
WHAT IS IT?! YOU'VE GOT TO TELL ME!
I'm not sure. Probably SOMETHING, though.

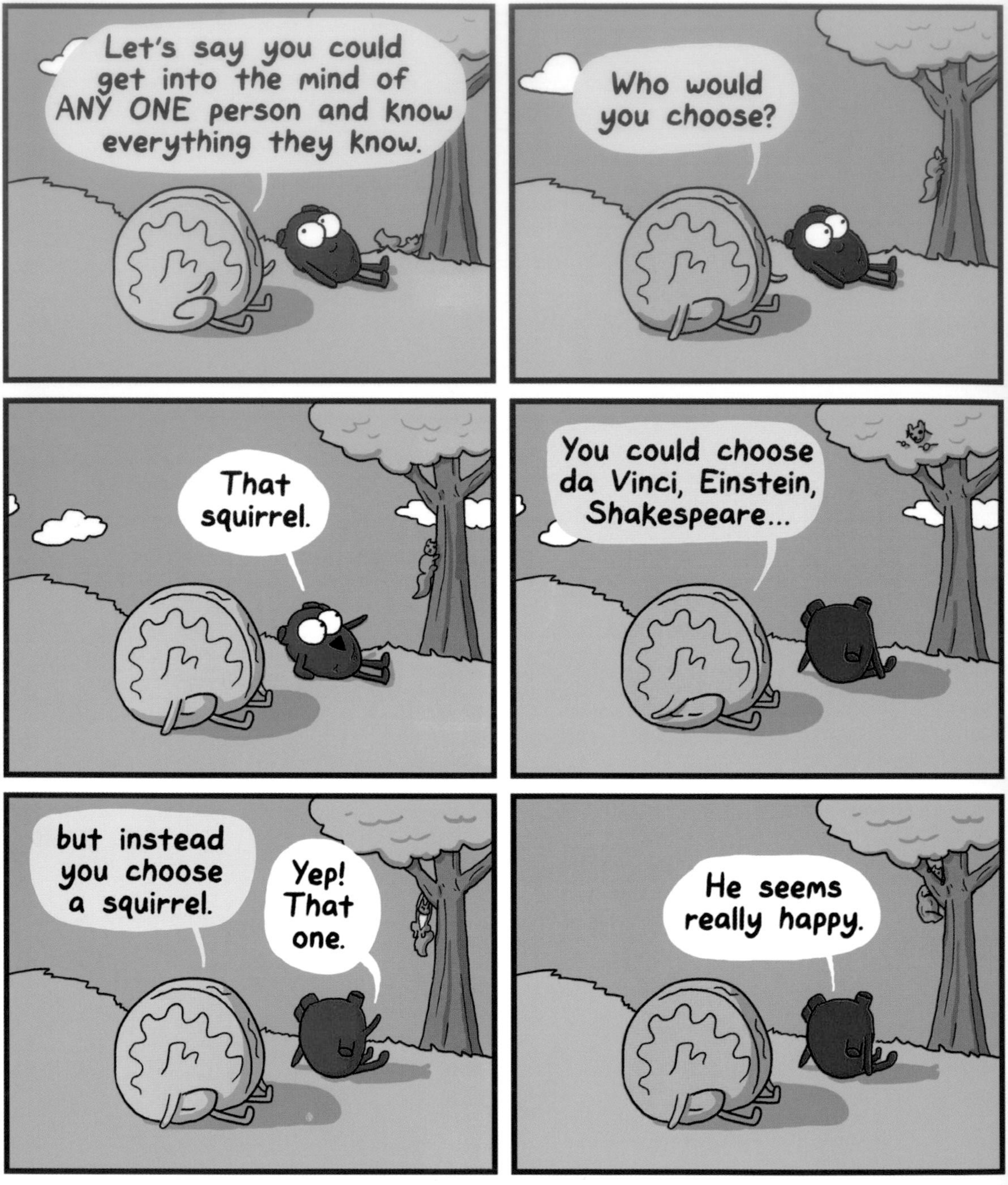
Let's say you could get into the mind of ANY ONE person and know everything they know.
Who would you choose?
That squirrel.
You could choose da Vinci, Einstein, Shakespeare...
but instead you choose a squirrel.
Yep! That one.
He seems really happy.

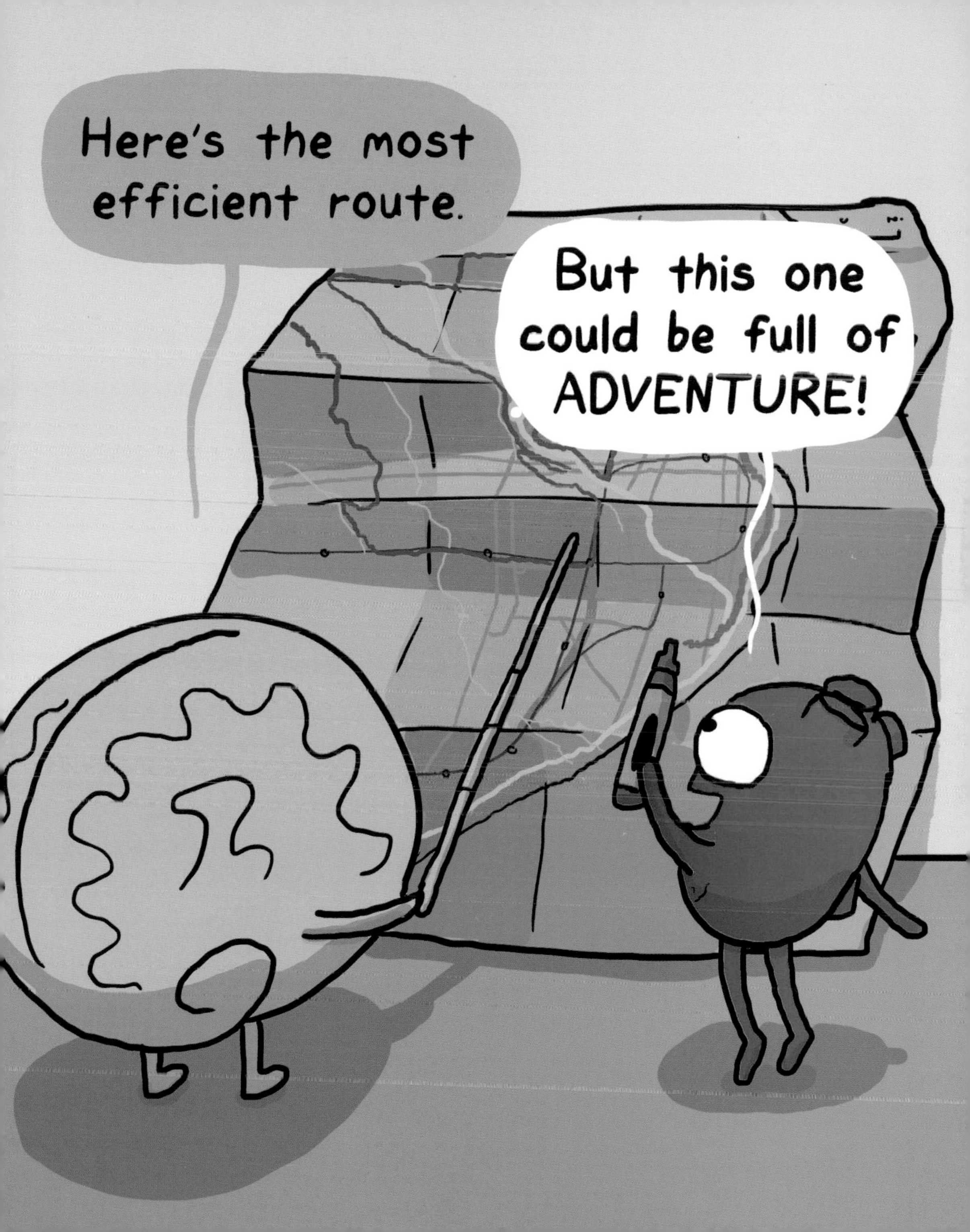
Here's the most efficient route.
But this one could be full of ADVENTURE!

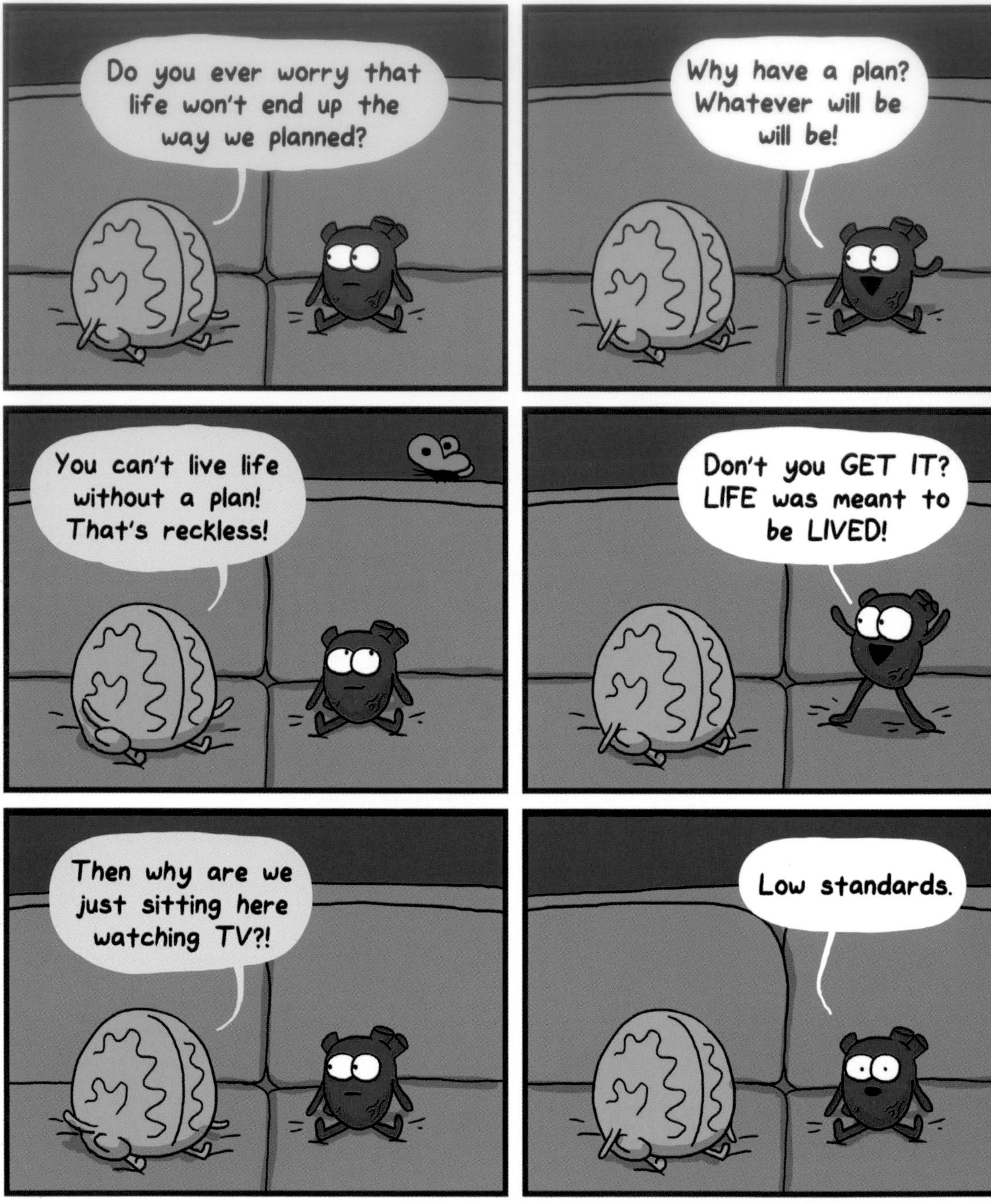
Do you ever worry that life won't end up the way we planned?
Why have a plan? Whatever will be will be!
You can't live life without a plan! That's reckless!
Don't you GET IT? LIFE was meant to be LIVED!
Then why are we just sitting here watching TV?!
Low standards.

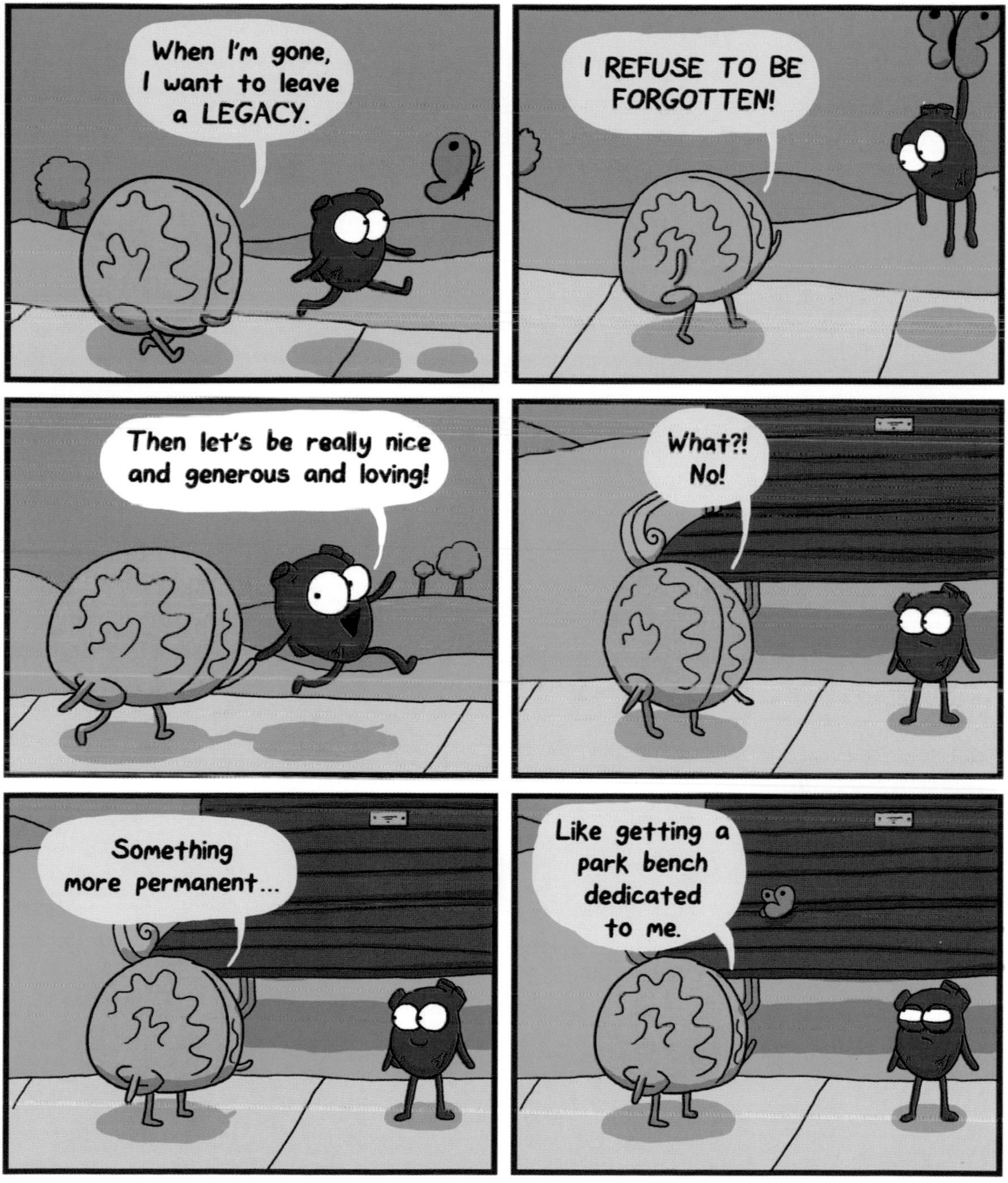
When I'm gone, I want to leave a LEGACY.
I REFUSE TO BE FORGOTTEN!
Then let's be really nice and generous and loving!
What?! No!
Something more permanent...
Like getting a park bench dedicated to me.

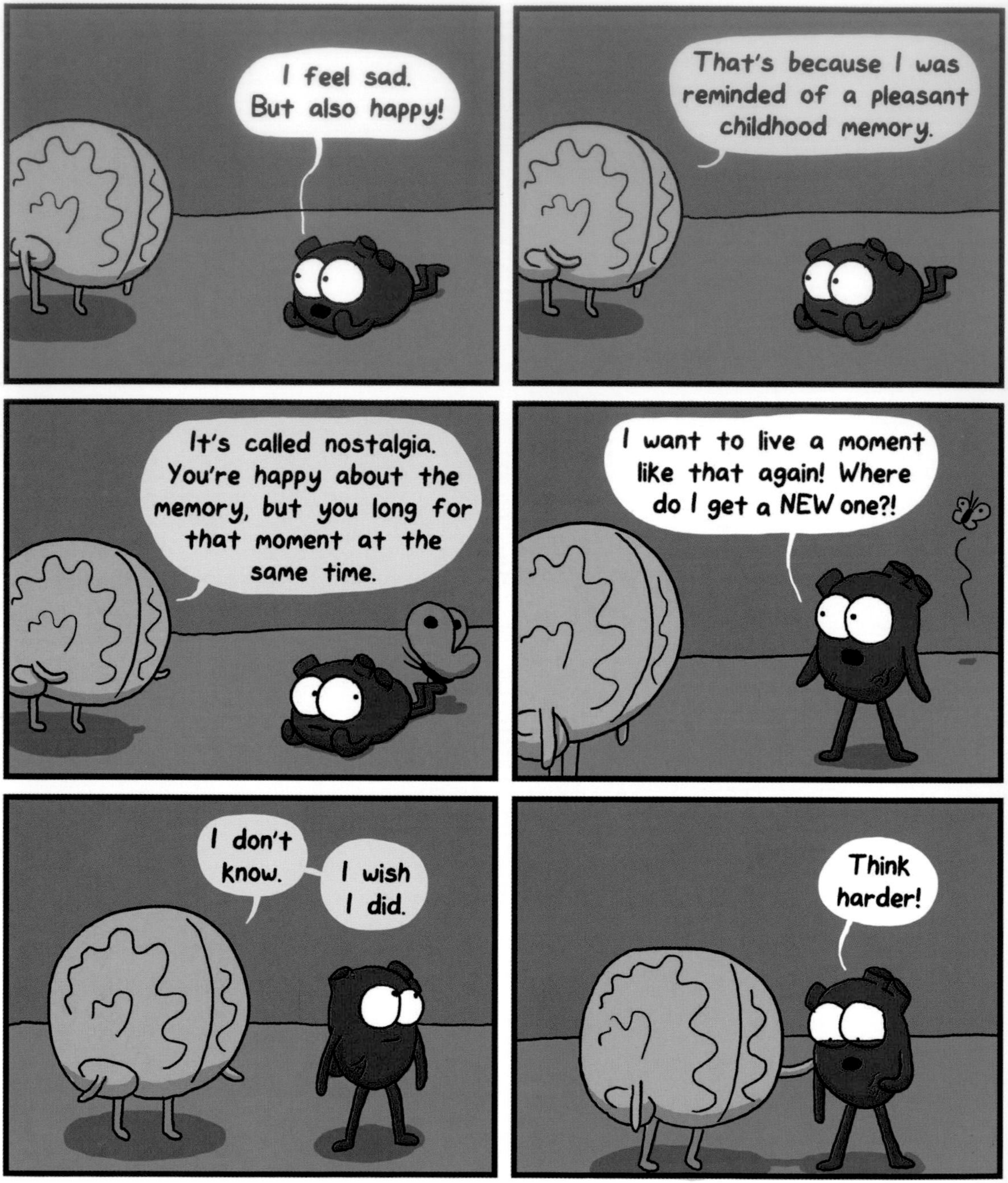
I feel sad. But also happy!
That's because I was reminded of a pleasant childhood memory.
It's called nostalgia. You're happy about the memory, but you long for that moment at the same time.
I want to live a moment like that again! Where do I get a NEW one?!
I don't know.
I wish I did.
Think harder!

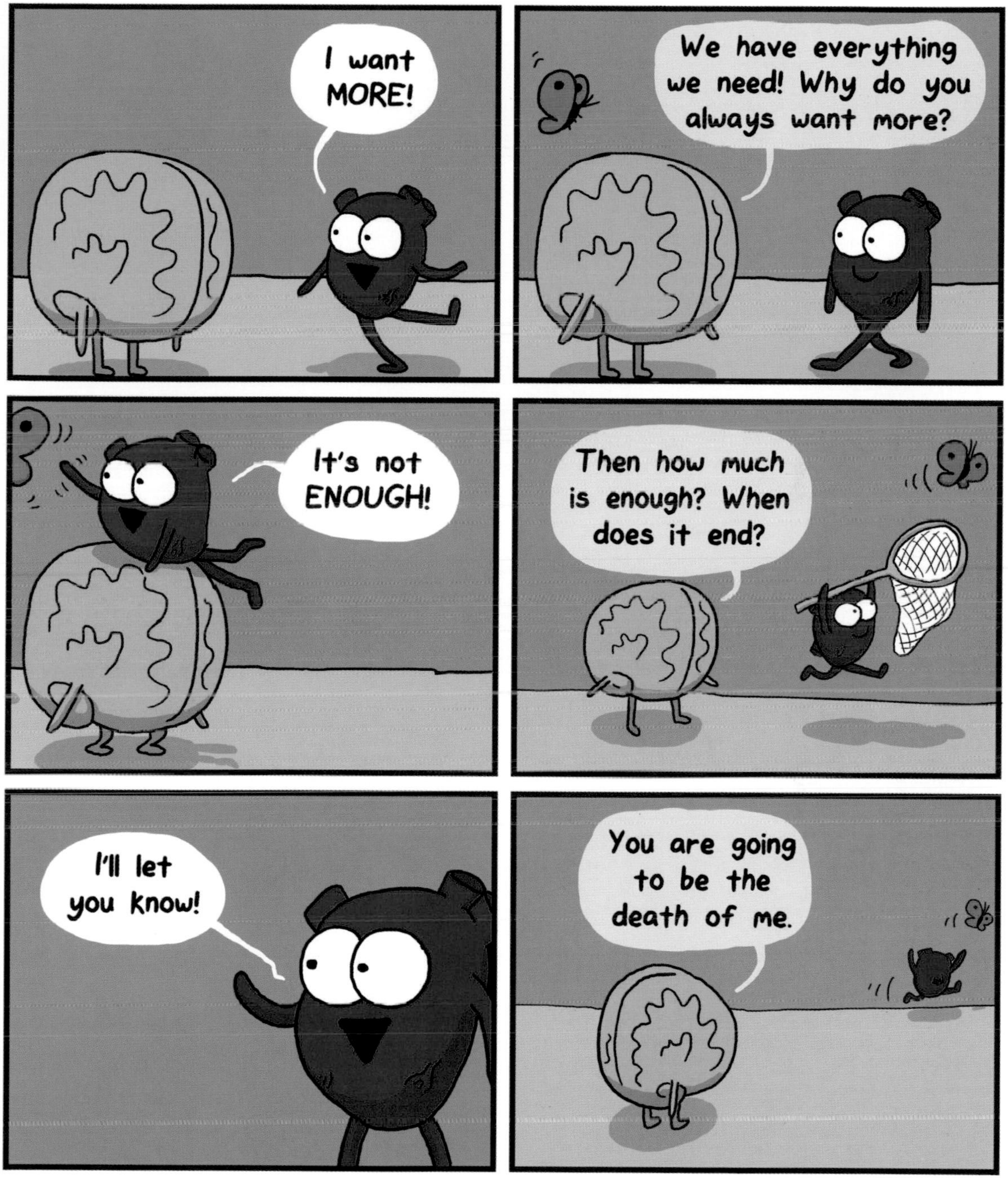
I want MORE!
We have everything we need! Why do you always want more?
It's not ENOUGH!
Then how much is enough? When does it end?
I'll let you know!
You are going to be the death of me.

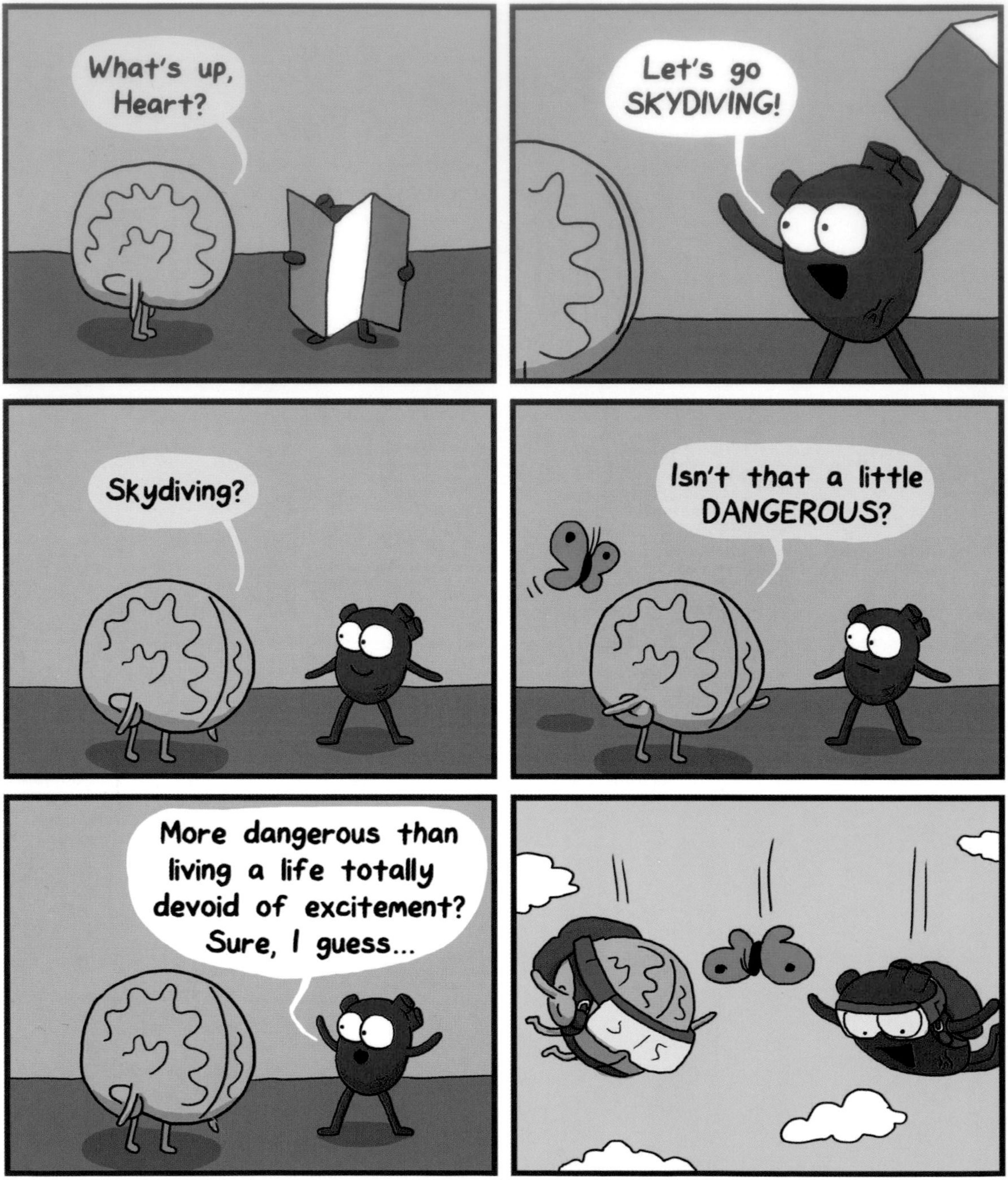
What's up, Heart?
Let's go SKYDIVING!
Skydiving?
Isn't that a little DANGEROUS?
More dangerous than living a life totally devoid of excitement? Sure, I guess...

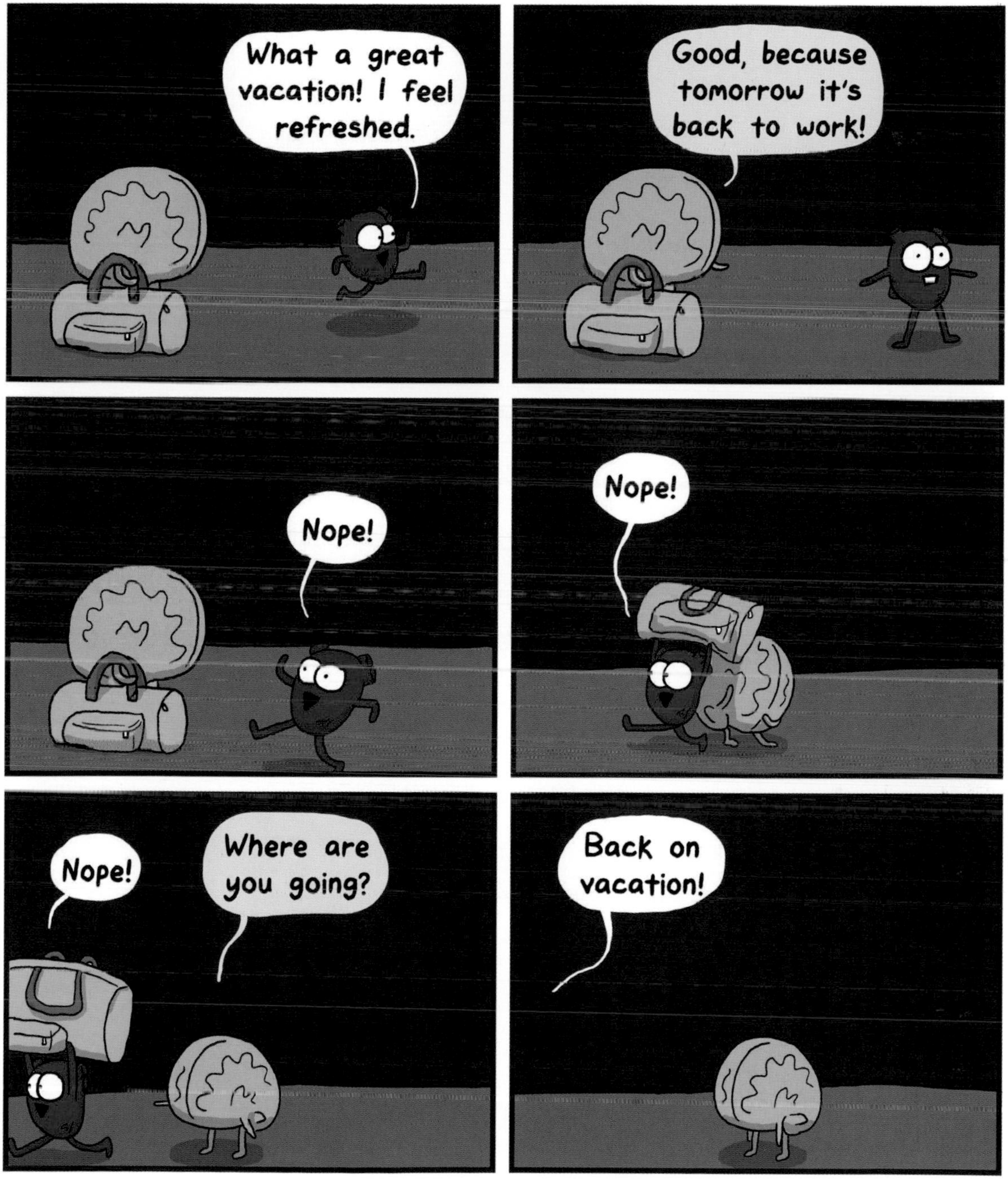
What a great vacation! I feel refreshed.
Good, because tomorrow it's back to work!
Nope!
Nope!
Nope!
Where are you going?
Back on vacation!

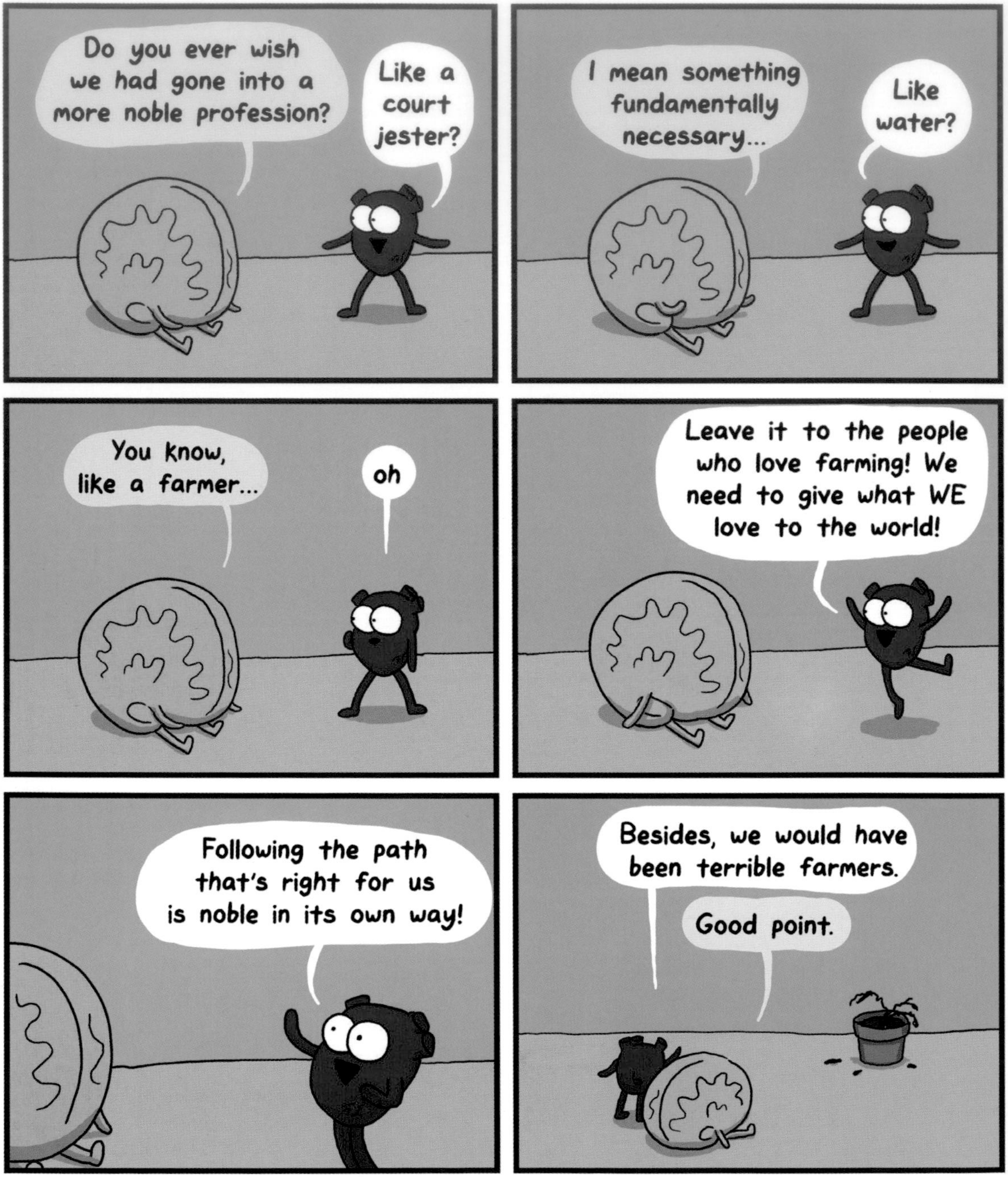
Do you ever wish we had gone into a more noble profession?
Like a court jester?
I mean something fundamentally necessary...
Like water?
You know, like a farmer...
oh
Leave it to the people who love farming! We need to give what WE love to the world!
Following the path that's right for us is noble in its own way!
Besides, we would have been terrible farmers.
Good point.

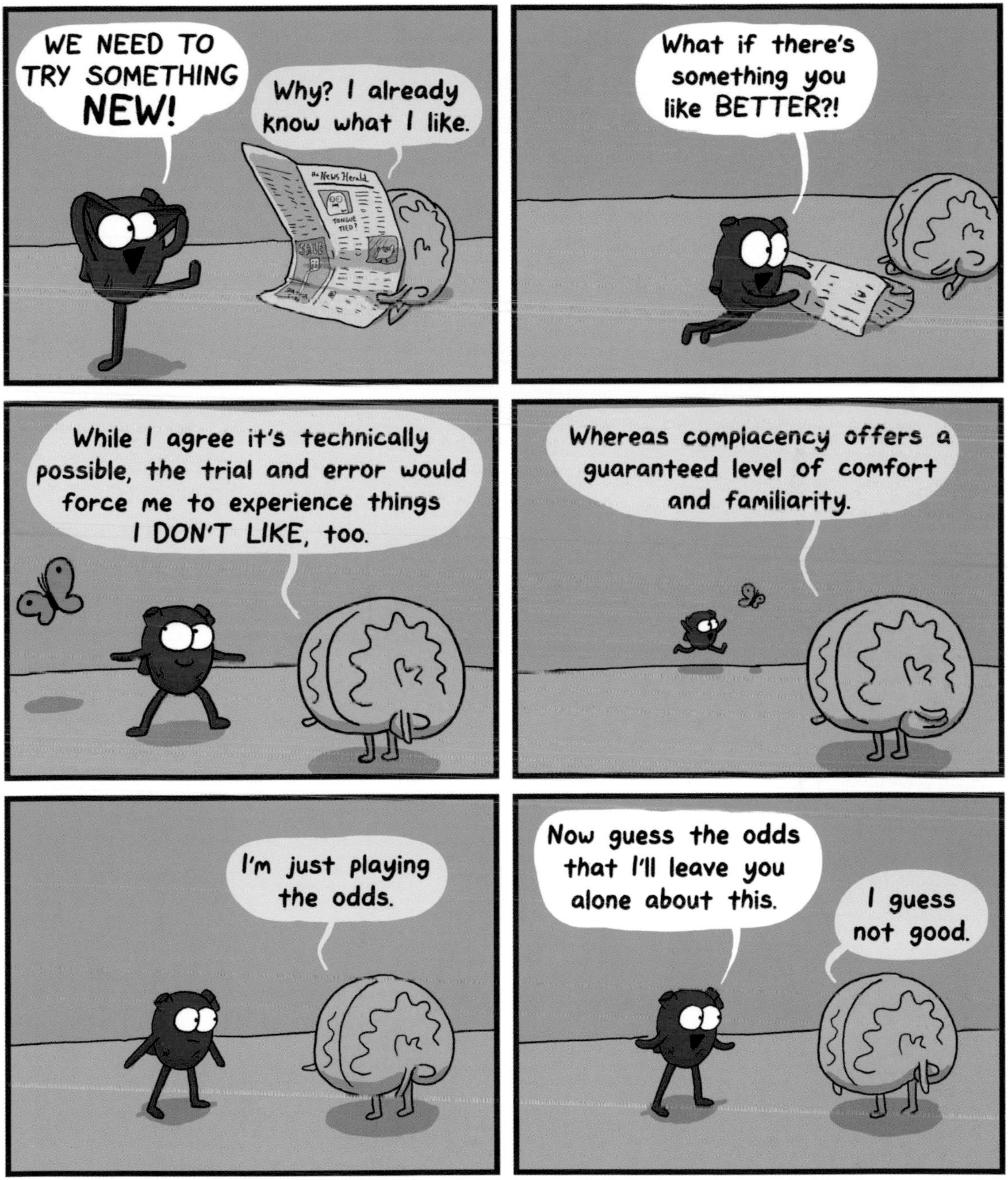
WE NEED TO TRY SOMETHING NEW!
Why? I already know what I like.
What if there's something you like BETTER?!
While I agree it's technically possible, the trial and error would force me to experience things I DON'T LIKE, too.
Whereas complacency offers a guaranteed level of comfort and familiarity.
I'm just playing the odds.
Now guess the odds that I'll leave you alone about this.
I guess not good.

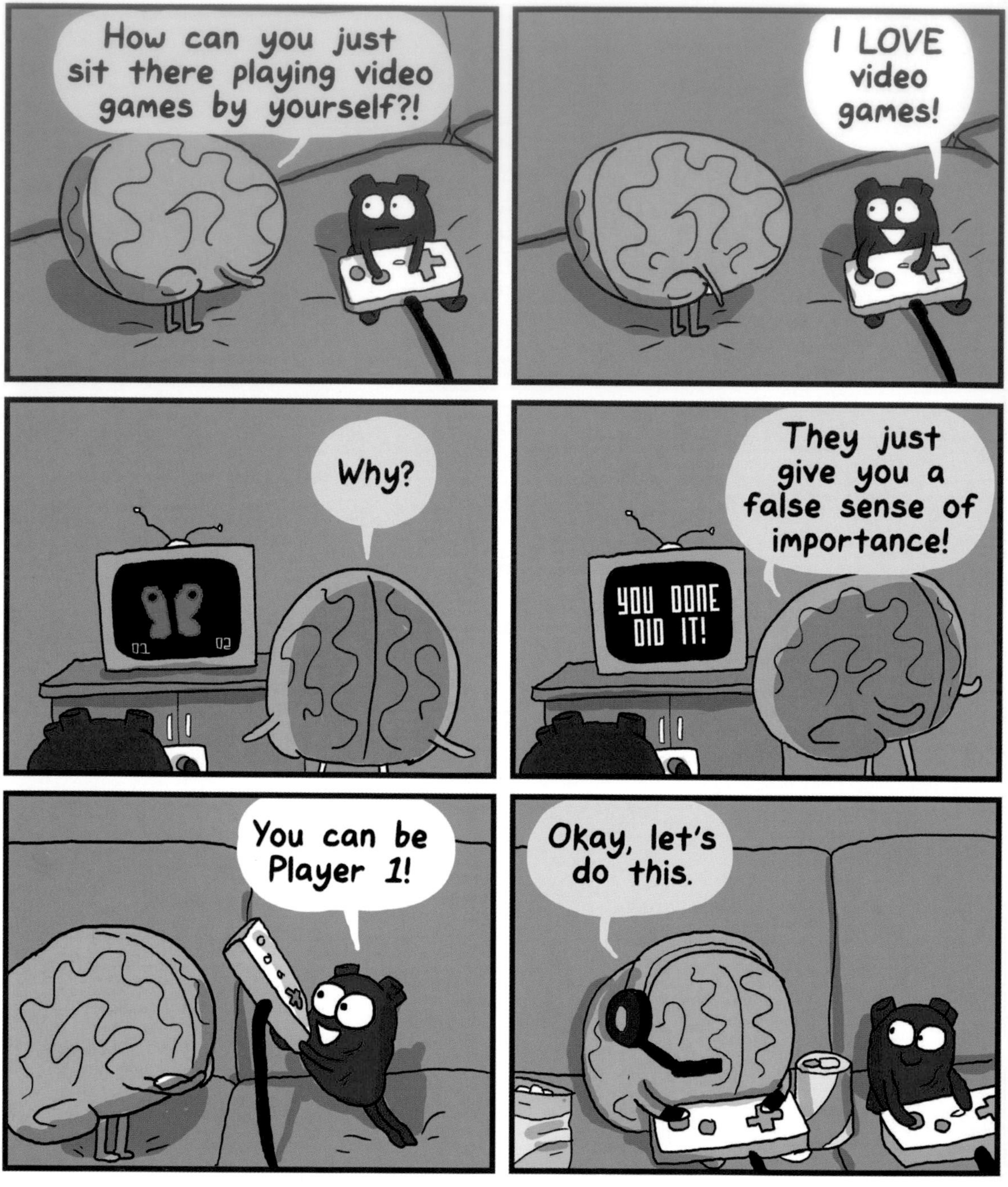
How can you just sit there playing video games by yourself?!
I LOVE video games!
Why?
YOU DONE DID IT!
They just give you a false sense of importance!
You can be Player 1!
Okay, let's do this.

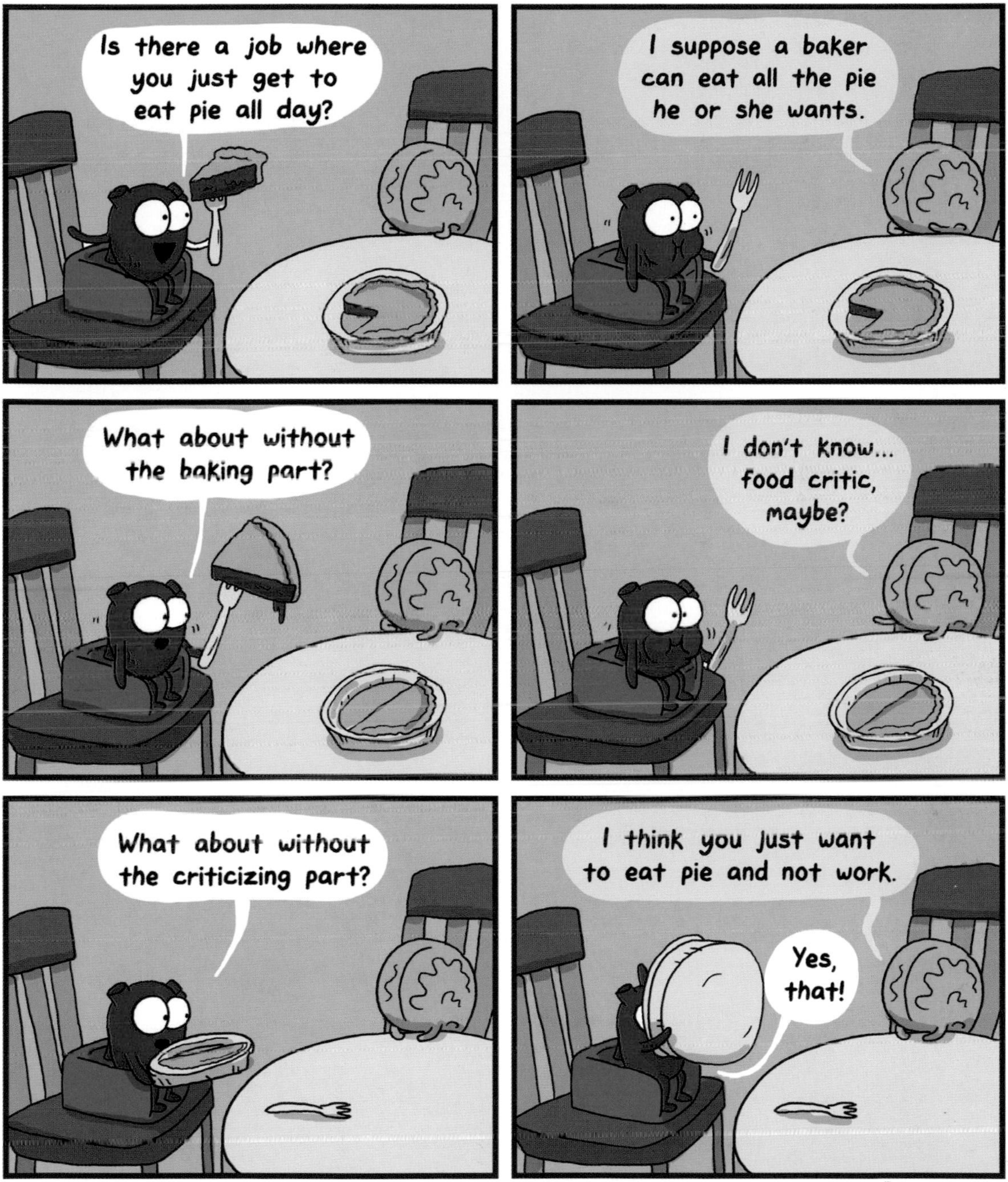
Is there a job where you just get to eat pie all day?
I suppose a baker can eat all the pie he or she wants.
What about without the baking part?
I don't know... food critic, maybe?
What about without the criticizing part?
I think you just want to eat pie and not work.
Yes, that!

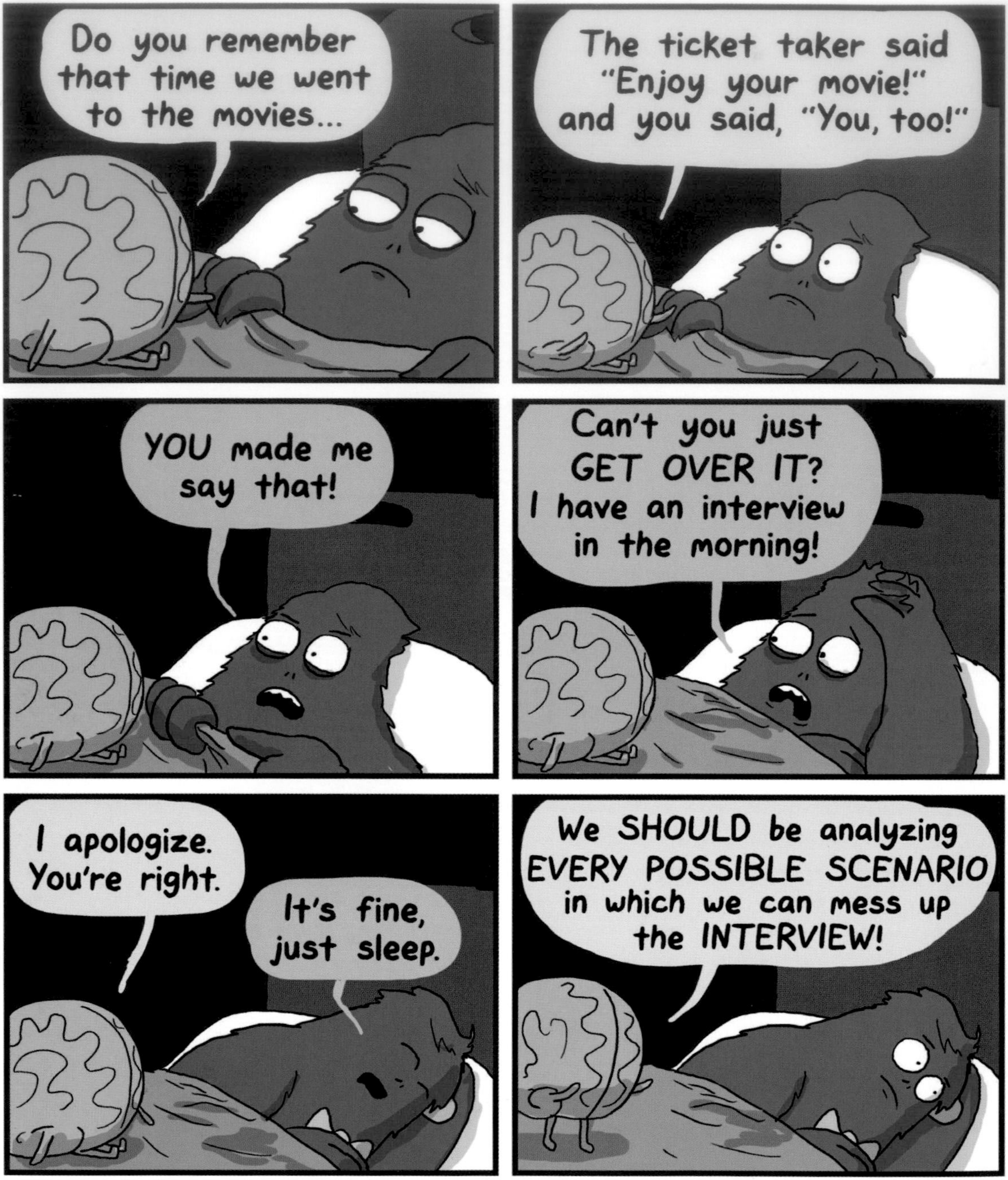
Do you remember that time we went to the movies...
The ticket taker said "Enjoy your movie!" and you said, "You, too!"
YOU made me say that!
Can't you just GET OVER IT? I have an interview in the morning!
I apologize. You're right.
It's fine, just sleep.
We SHOULD be analyzing EVERY POSSIBLE SCENARIO in which we can mess up the INTERVIEW!

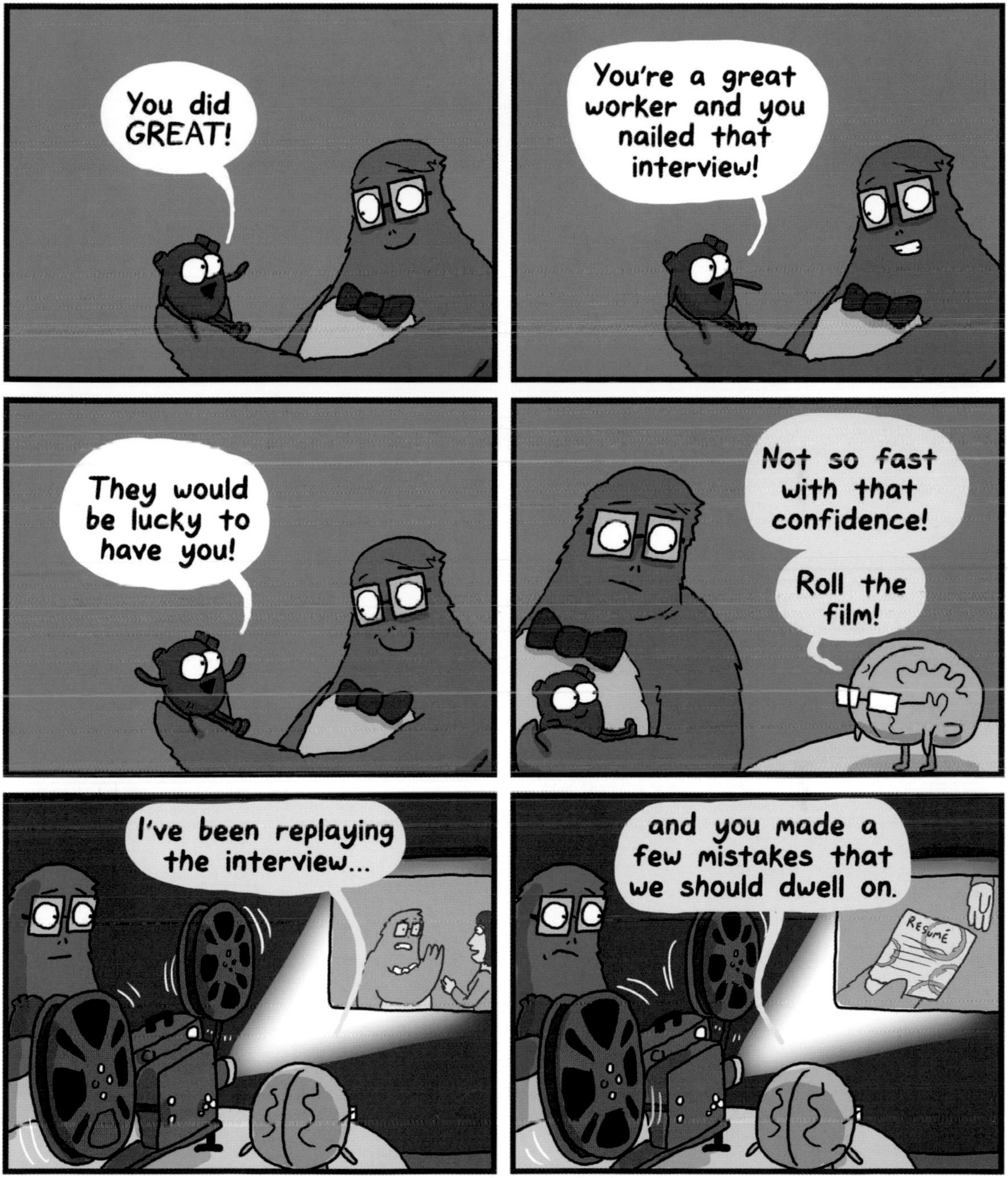
You did GREAT!
You're a great worker and you nailed that interview!
They would be lucky to have you!
Not so fast with that confidence!
Roll the film!
I've been replaying the interview...
and you made a few mistakes that we should dwell on.
RESUMÉ

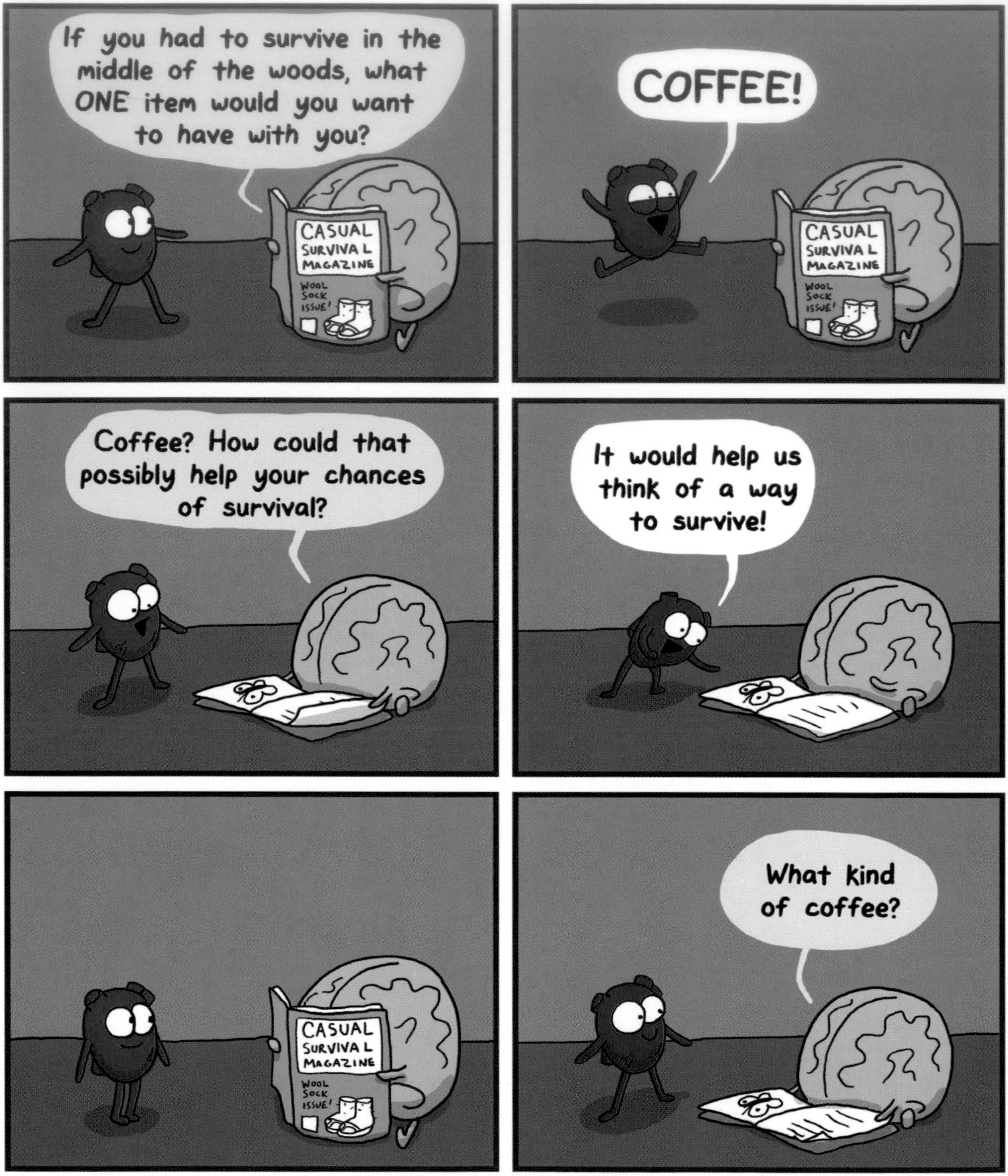
If you had to survive in the middle of the woods, what ONE item would you want to have with you?
CASUAL SURVIVAL MAGAZINE
WOOL SOCK ISSUE!
COFFEE!
CASUAL SURVIVAL MAGAZINE
WOOL SOCK ISSUE!
Coffee? How could that possibly help your chances of survival?
It would help us think of a way to survive!
CASUAL SURVIVAL MAGAZINE
WOOL SOCK ISSUE!
What kind of coffee?

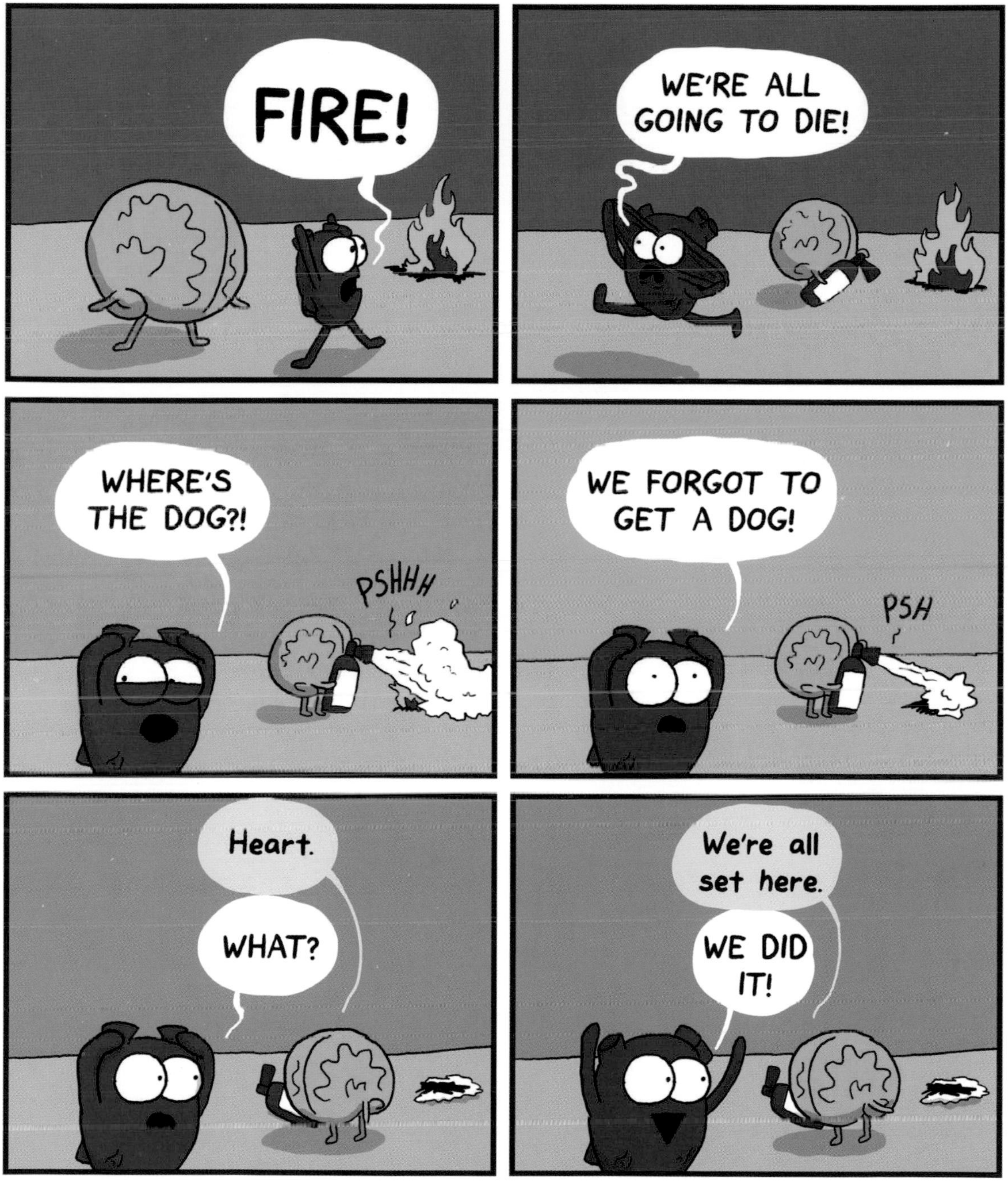

FIRE!
WE'RE ALL GOING TO DIE!
WHERE'S THE DOG?!
PSHHH
WE FORGOT TO GET A DOG!
PSH
Heart.
WHAT?
We're all set here.
WE DID IT!

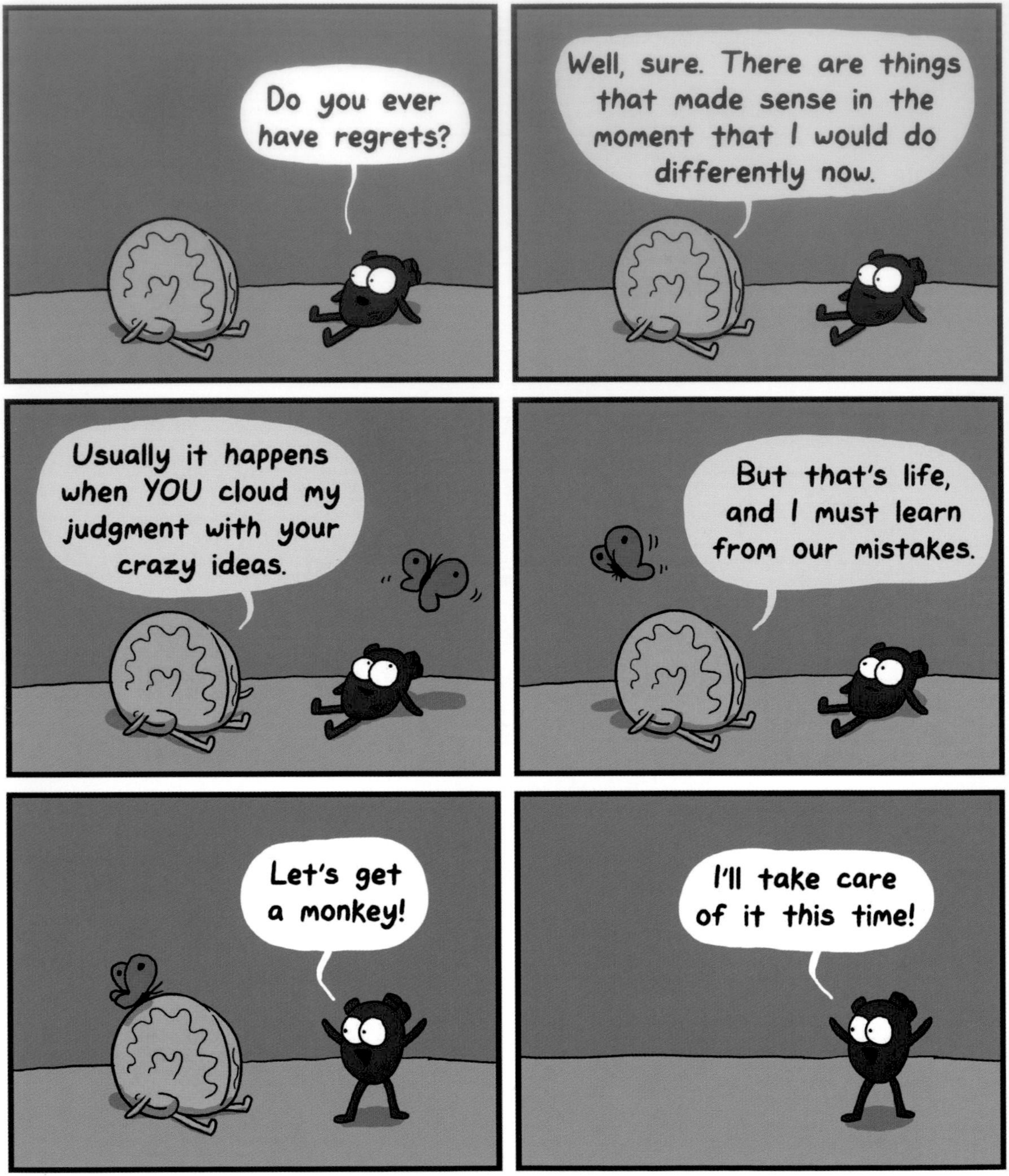
Do you ever have regrets?
Well, sure. There are things that made sense in the moment that I would do differently now.
Usually it happens when YOU cloud my judgment with your crazy ideas.
But that's life, and I must learn from our mistakes.
Let's get a monkey!
I'll take care of it this time!

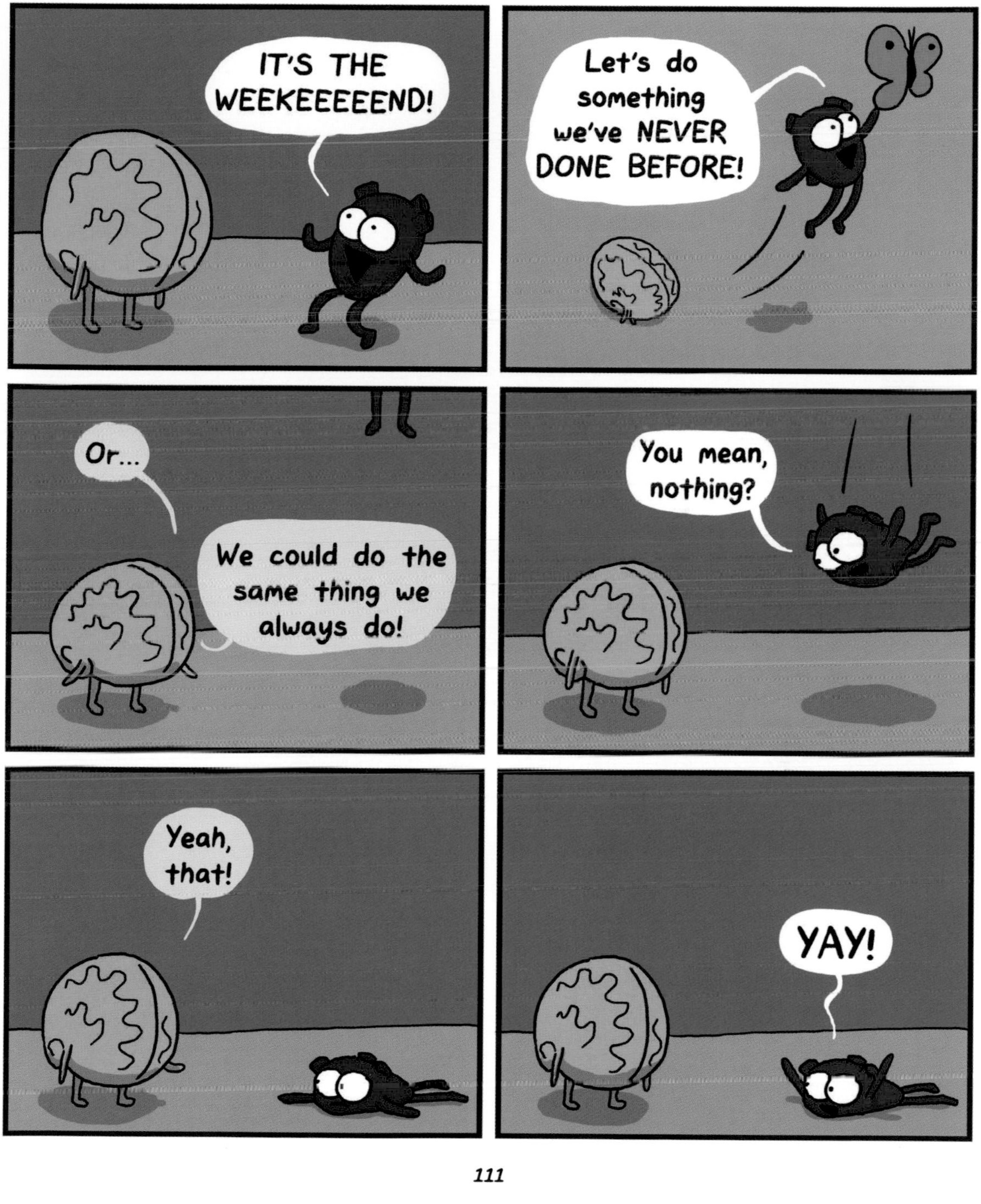
IT'S THE WEEKEEEEEND!
Let's do something we've NEVER DONE BEFORE!
Or...
We could do the same thing we always do!
You mean, nothing?
Yeah, that!
YAY!

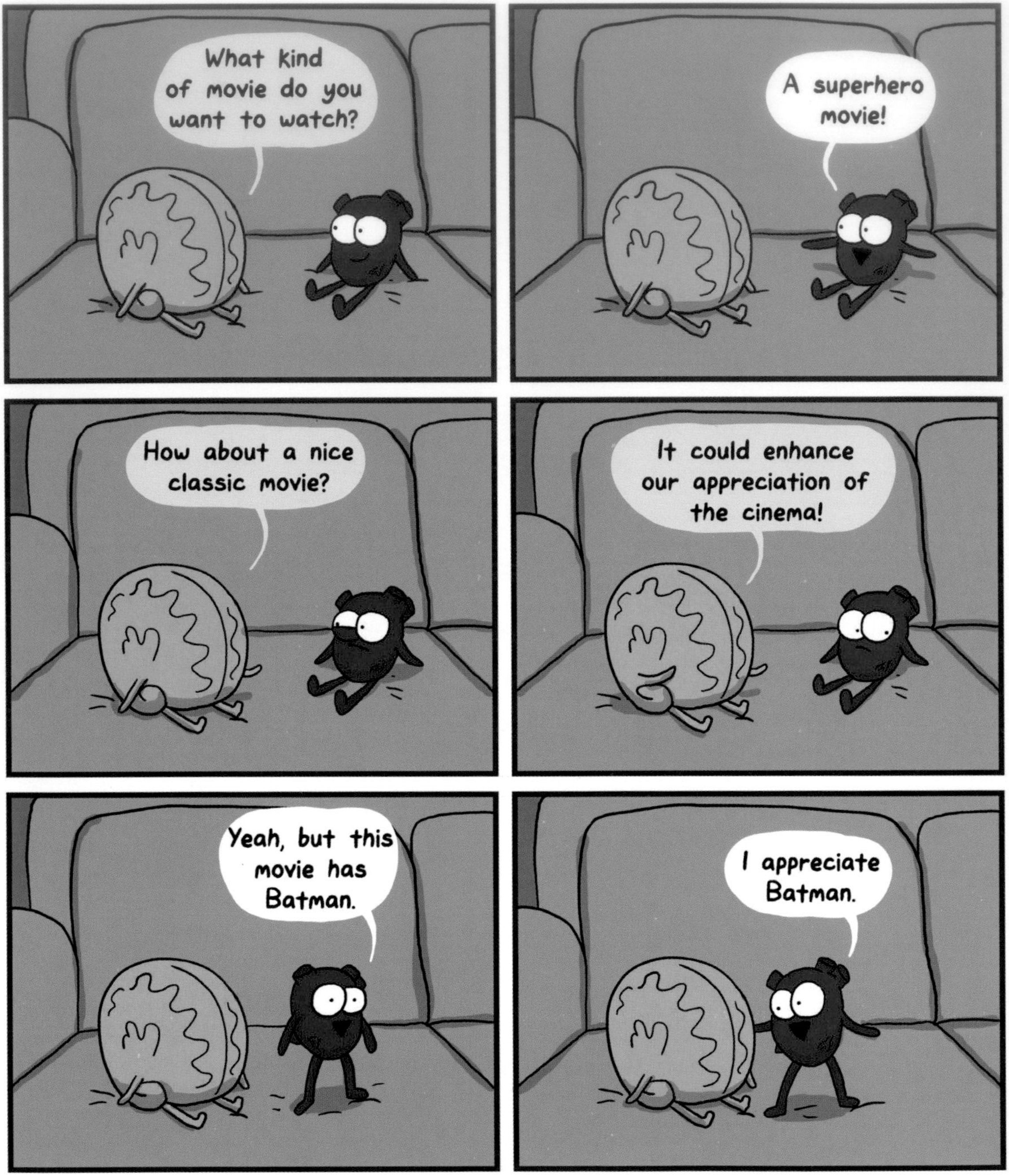
What kind of movie do you want to watch?
A superhero movie!
How about a nice classic movie?
It could enhance our appreciation of the cinema!
Yeah, but this movie has Batman.
I appreciate Batman.

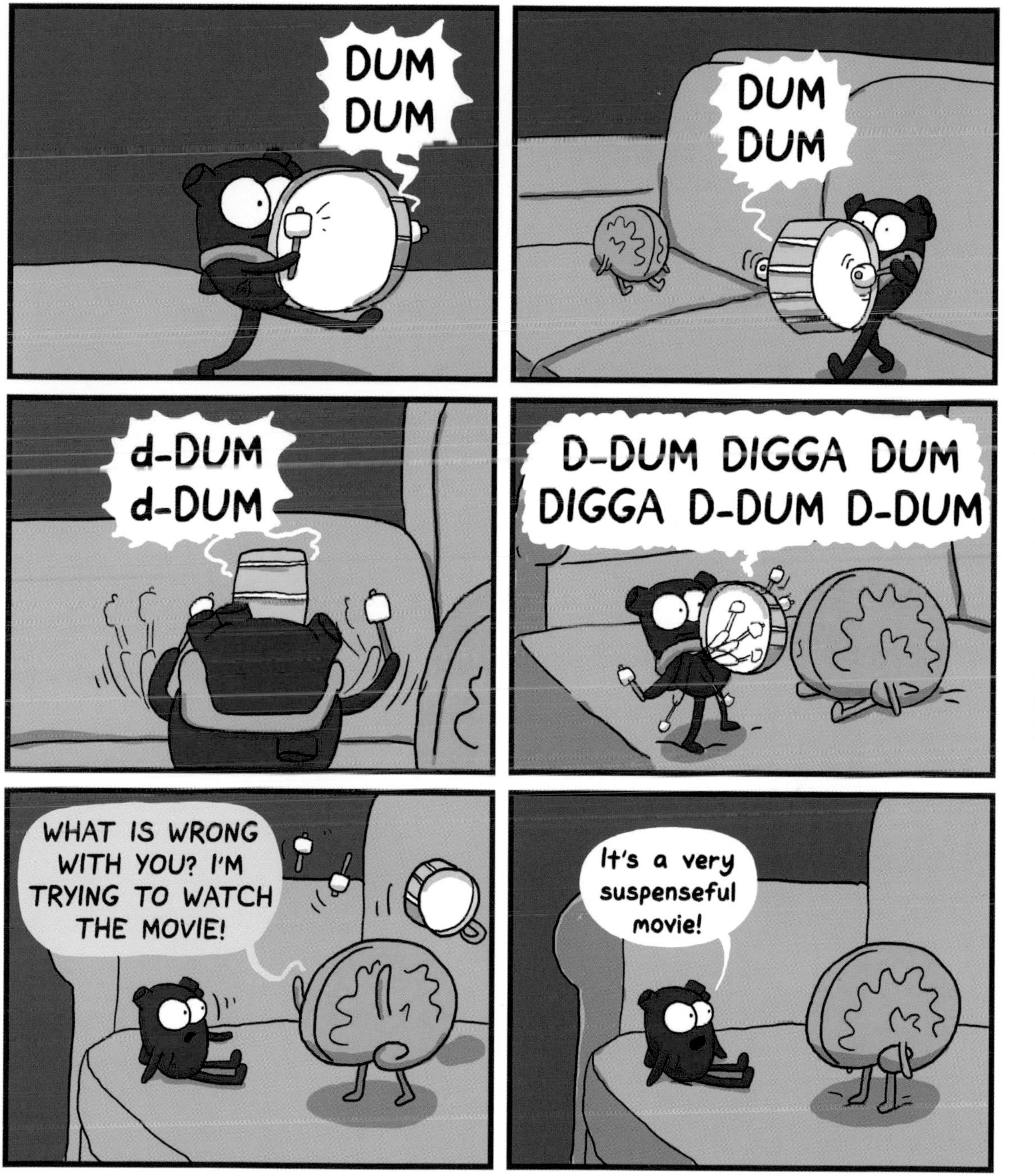
DUM DUM
DUM DUM
d-DUM d-DUM
D-DUM DIGGA DUM DIGGA D-DUM D-DUM
WHAT IS WRONG WITH YOU? I'M TRYING TO WATCH THE MOVIE!
It's a very suspenseful movie!

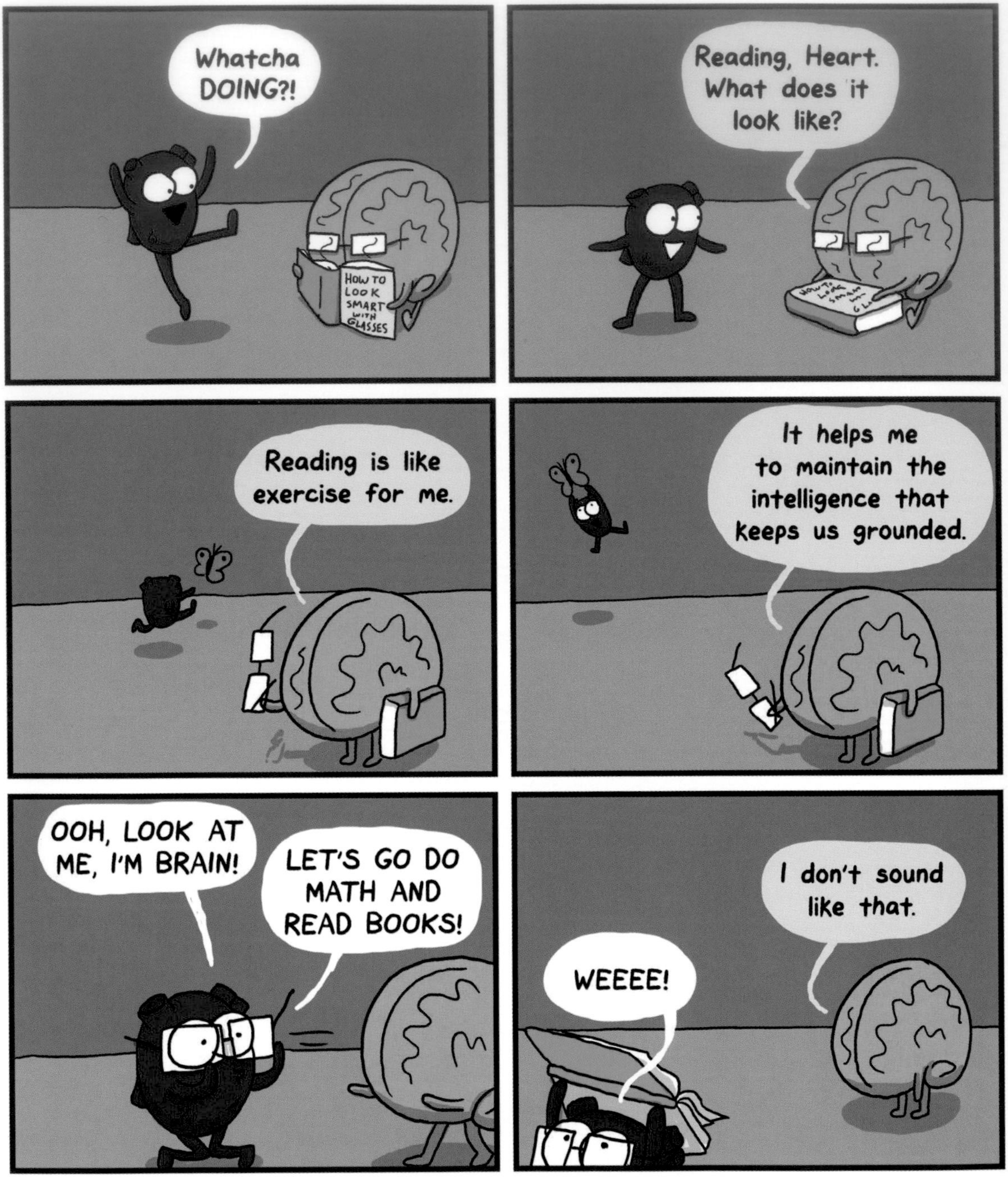
Whatcha DOING?!
HOW TO LOOK SMART WITH GLASSES
Reading, Heart. What does it look like?
Reading is like exercise for me.
It helps me to maintain the intelligence that keeps us grounded.
OOH, LOOK AT ME, I'M BRAIN!
LET'S GO DO MATH AND READ BOOKS!
WEEEE!
I don't sound like that.

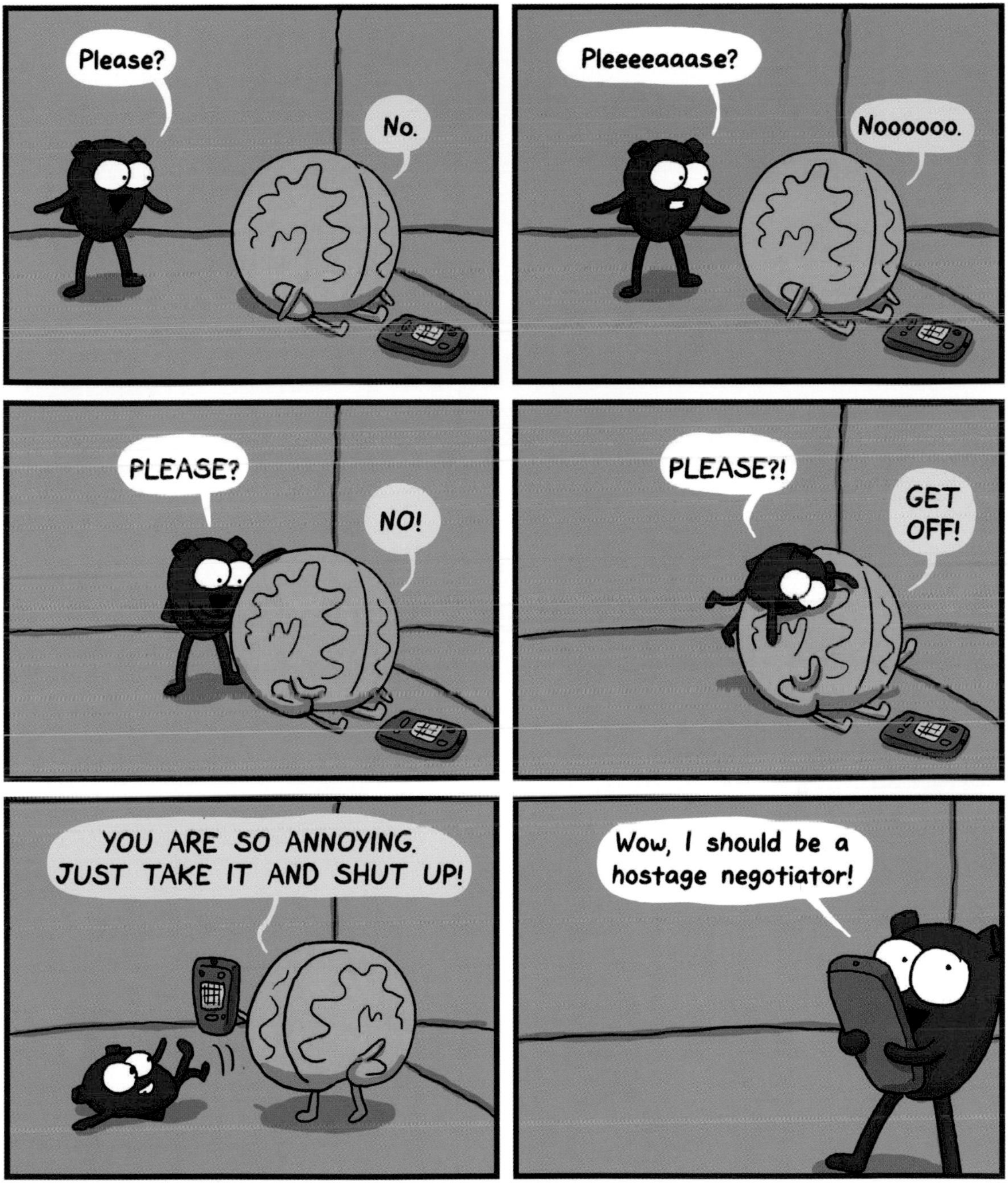
Please?
No.
Pleeeeaaase?
Noooooo.
PLEASE?
NO!
PLEASE?!
GET OFF!
YOU ARE SO ANNOYING. JUST TAKE IT AND SHUT UP!
Wow, I should be a hostage negotiator!

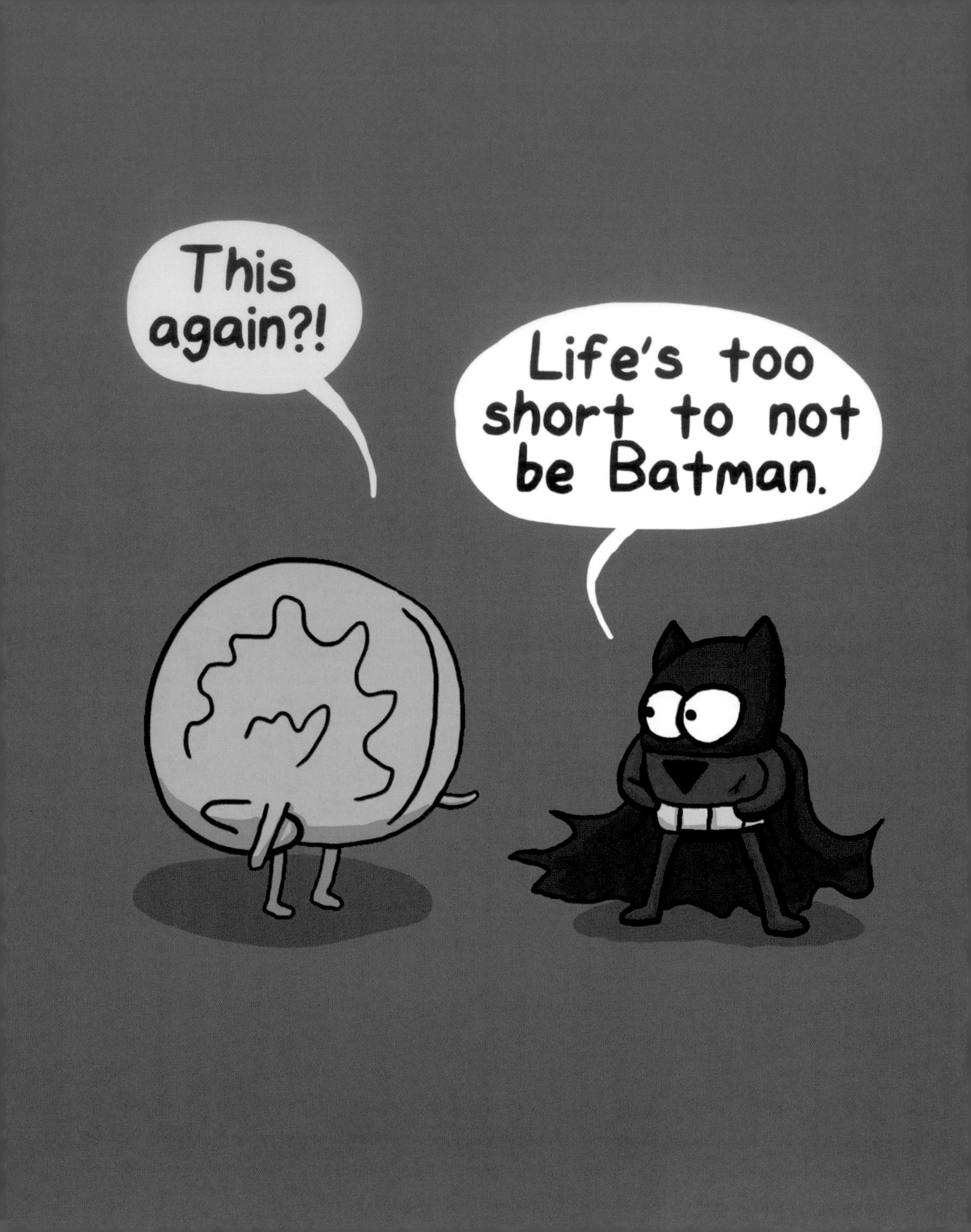
This again?!
Life's too short to not be Batman.

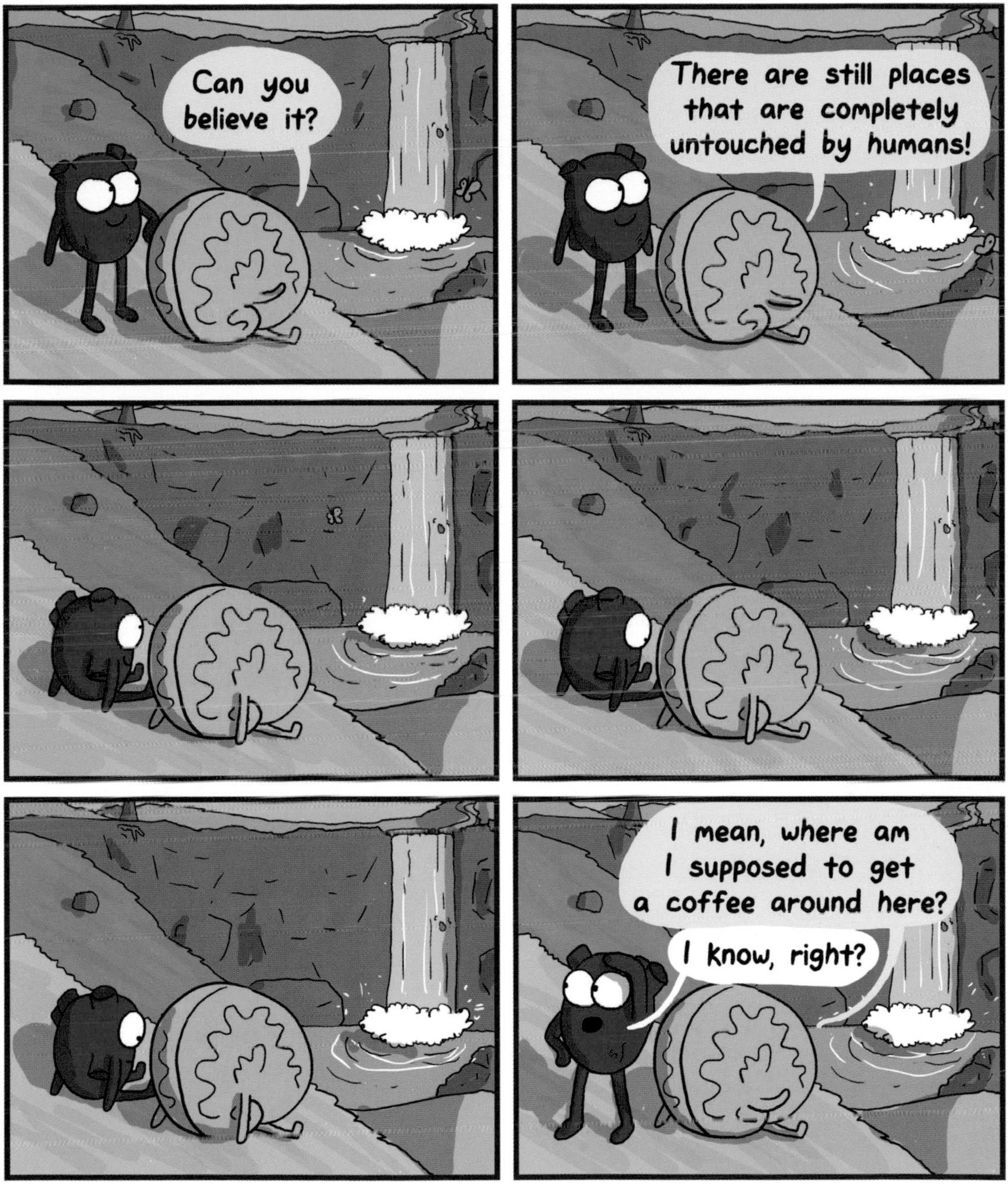
Can you believe it?
There are still places that are completely untouched by humans!
I mean, where am I supposed to get a coffee around here?
I know, right?

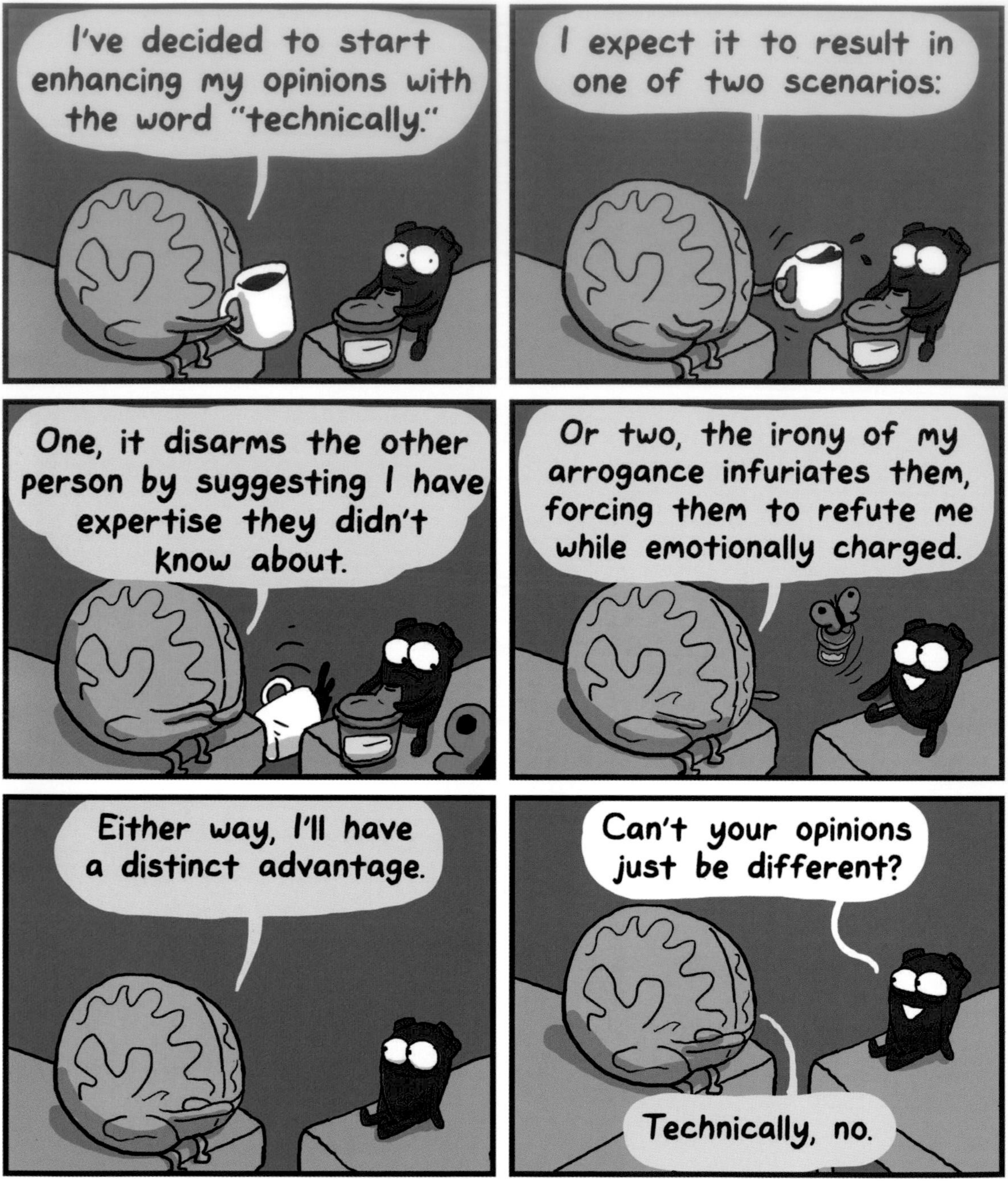
I've decided to start enhancing my opinions with the word "technically."
I expect it to result in one of two scenarios:
One, it disarms the other person by suggesting I have expertise they didn't know about.
Or two, the irony of my arrogance infuriates them, forcing them to refute me while emotionally charged.
Either way, I'll have a distinct advantage.
Can't your opinions just be different?
Technically, no.

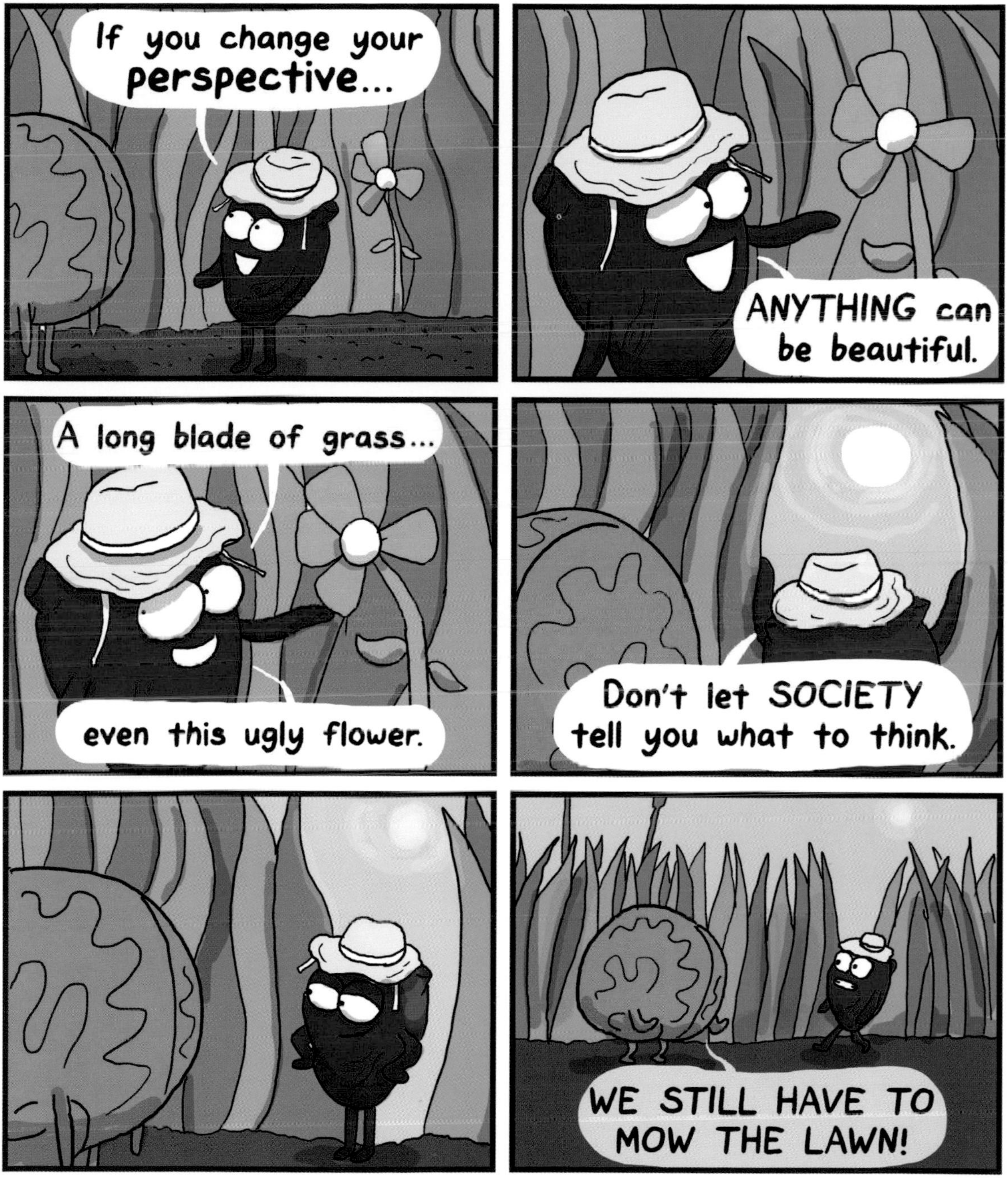
If you change your perspective...
ANYTHING can be beautiful.
A long blade of grass...
even this ugly flower.
Don't let SOCIETY tell you what to think.
WE STILL HAVE TO MOW THE LAWN!

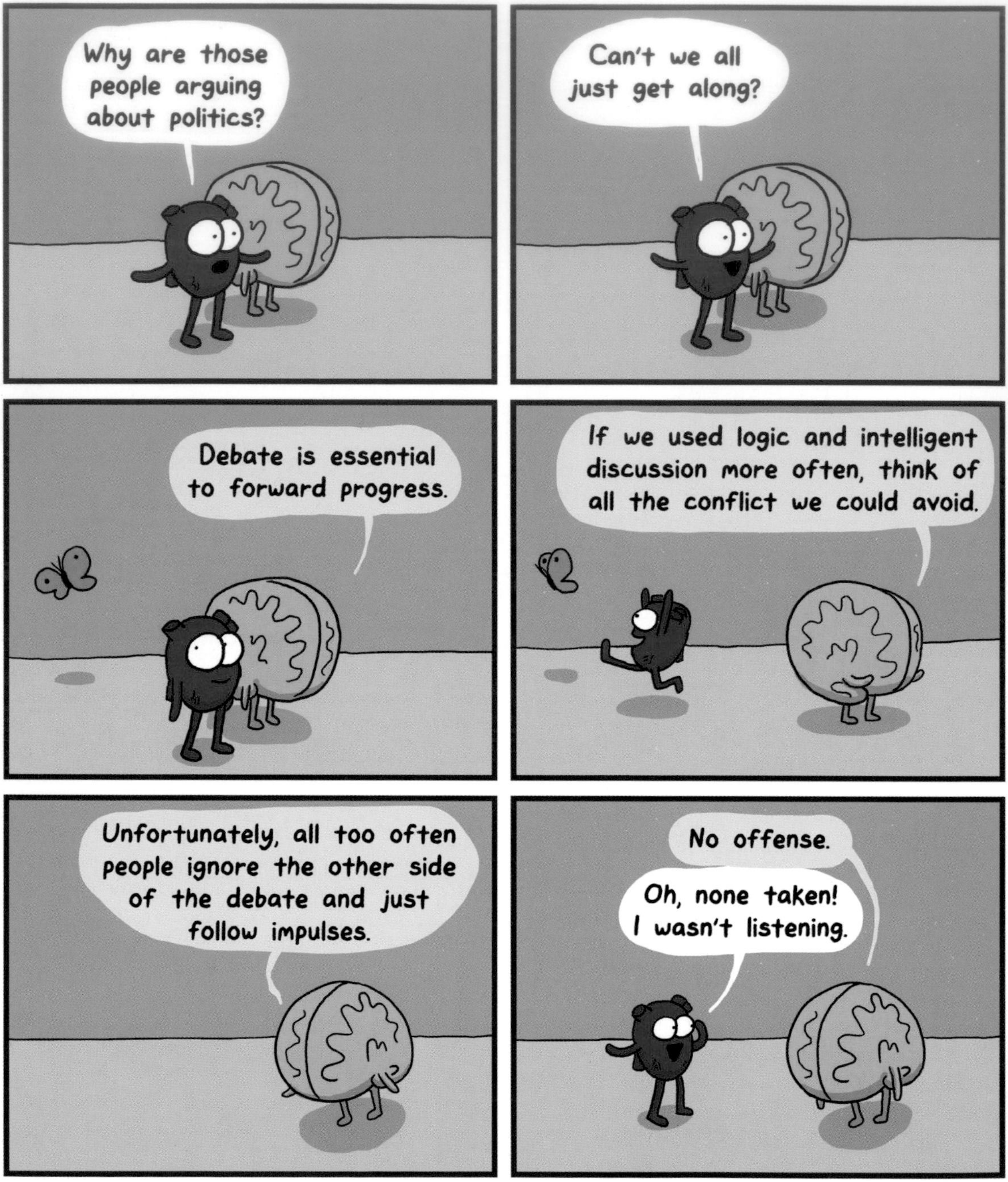
Why are those people arguing about politics?
Can't we all just get along?
Debate is essential to forward progress.
If we used logic and intelligent discussion more often, think of all the conflict we could avoid.
Unfortunately, all too often people ignore the other side of the debate and just follow impulses.
No offense.
Oh, none taken! I wasn't listening.

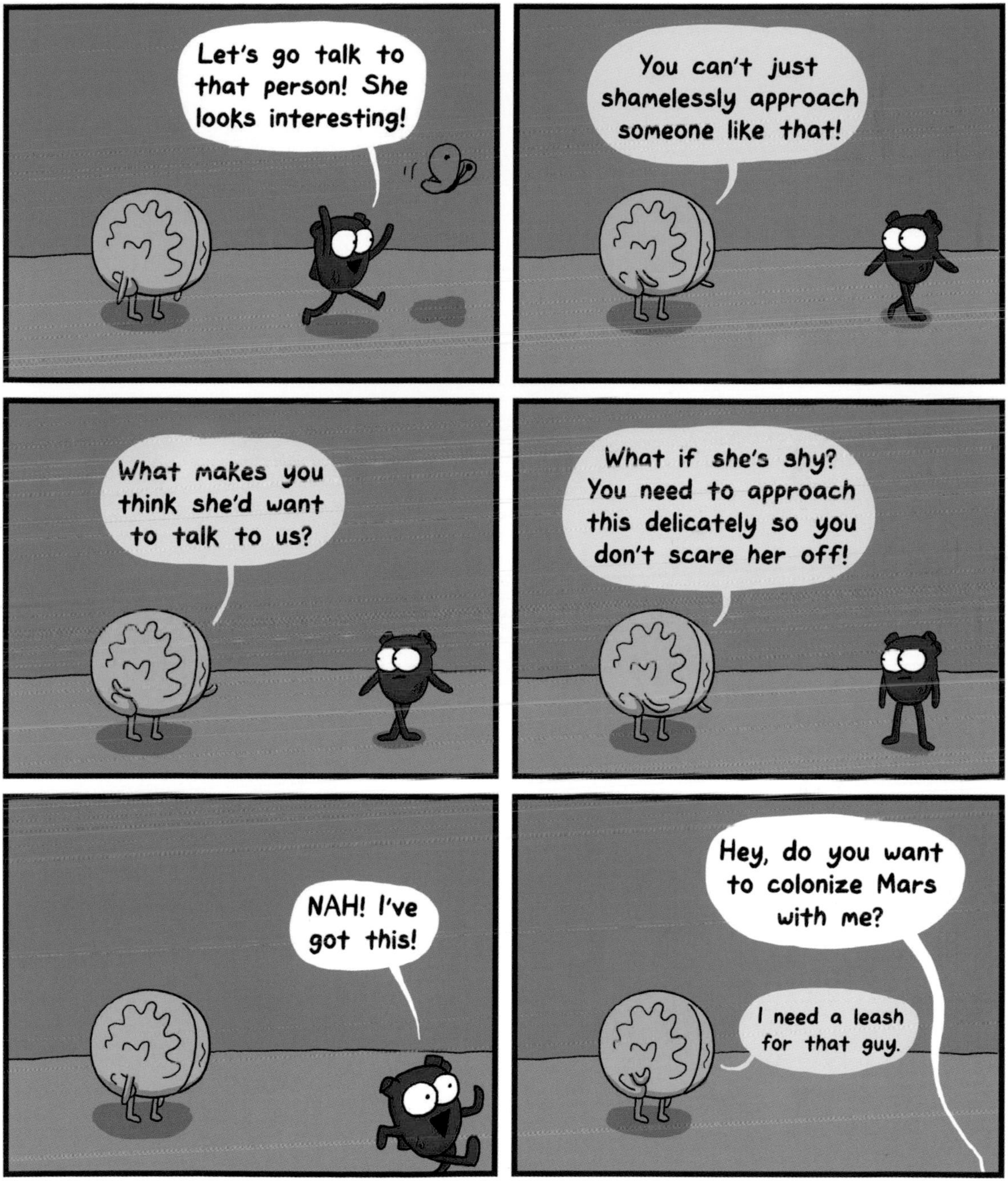
Let's go talk to that person! She looks interesting!
You can't just shamelessly approach someone like that!
What makes you think she'd want to talk to us?
What if she's shy? You need to approach this delicately so you don't scare her off!
NAH! I've got this!
Hey, do you want to colonize Mars with me?
I need a leash for that guy.

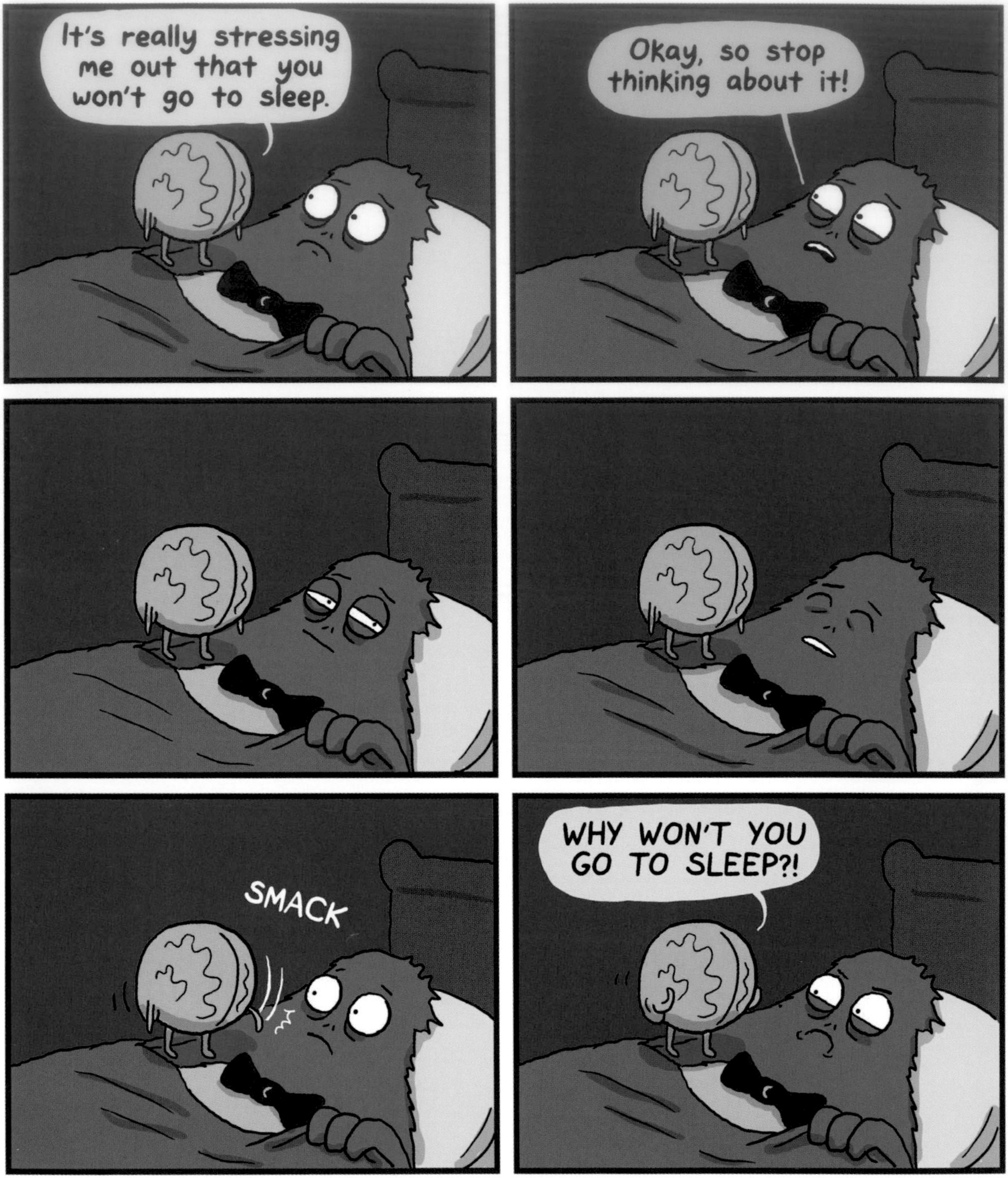
It's really stressing me out that you won't go to sleep.
Okay, so stop thinking about it!
SMACK
WHY WON'T YOU GO TO SLEEP?!

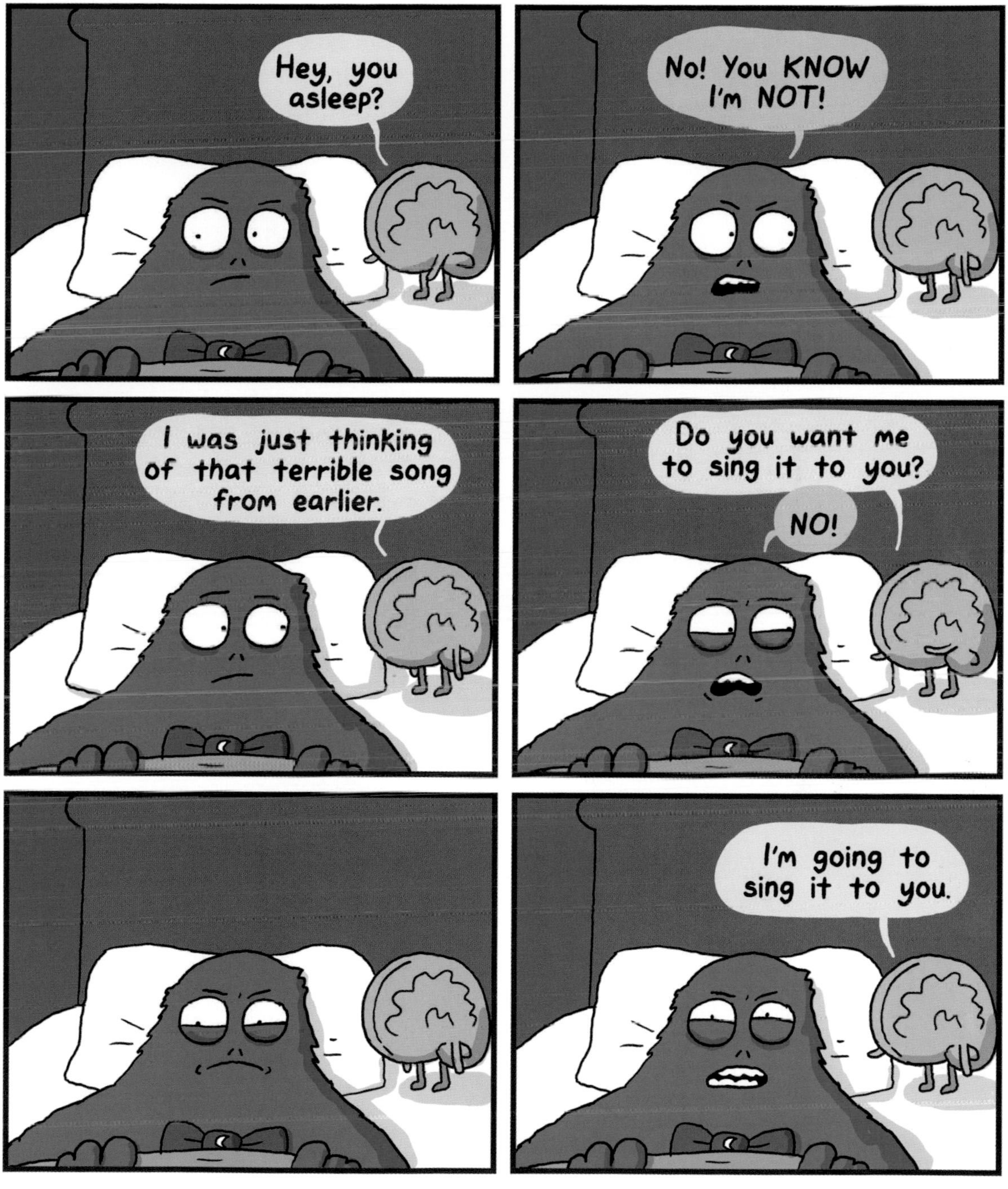
Hey, you asleep?
No! You KNOW I'm NOT!
I was just thinking of that terrible song from earlier.
Do you want me to sing it to you?
NO!
I'm going to sing it to you.

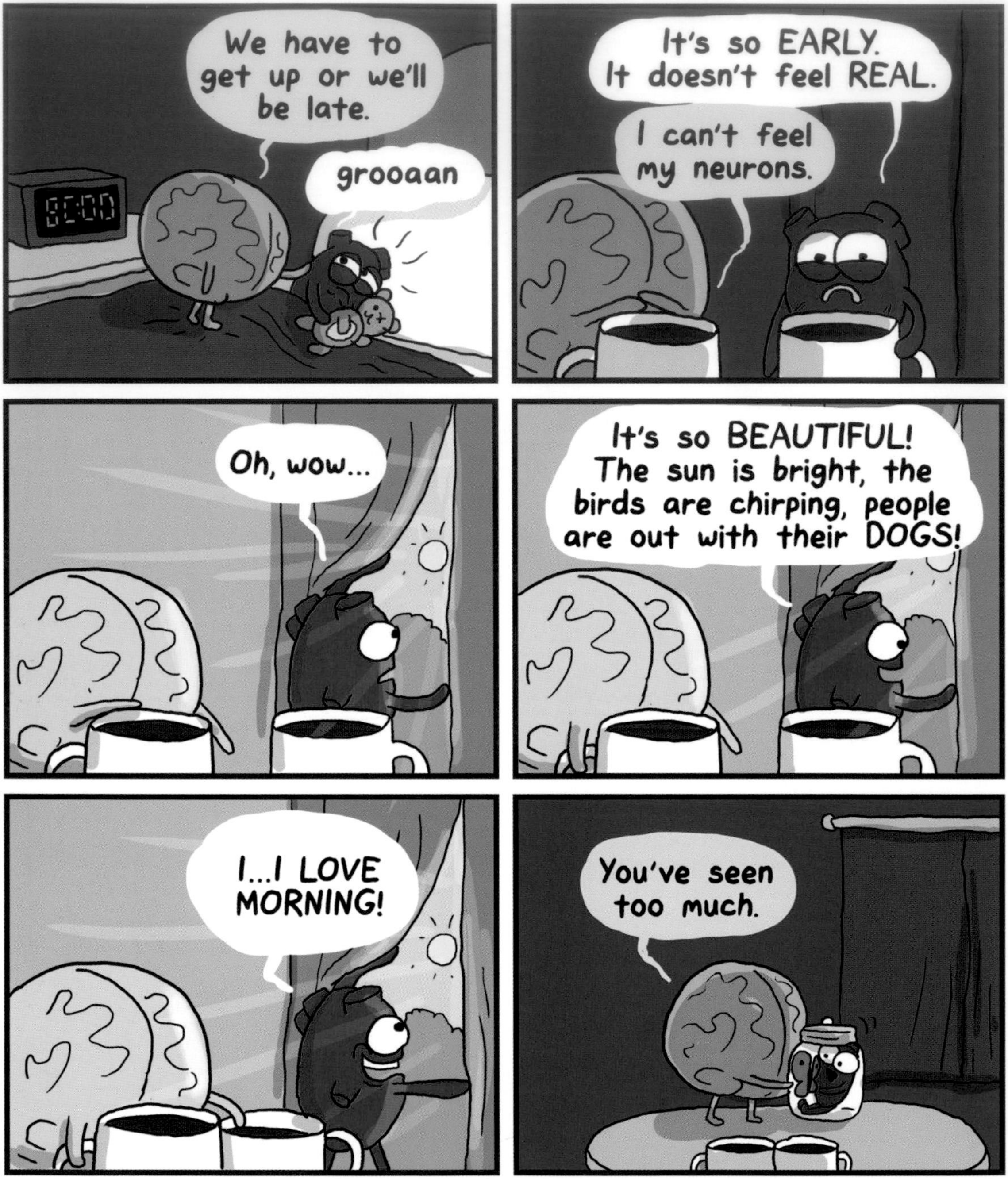
We have to get up or we'll be late.
grooaan
It's so EARLY. It doesn't feel REAL.
I can't feel my neurons.
Oh, wow...
It's so BEAUTIFUL! The sun is bright, the birds are chirping, people are out with their DOGS!
I...I LOVE MORNING!
You've seen too much.

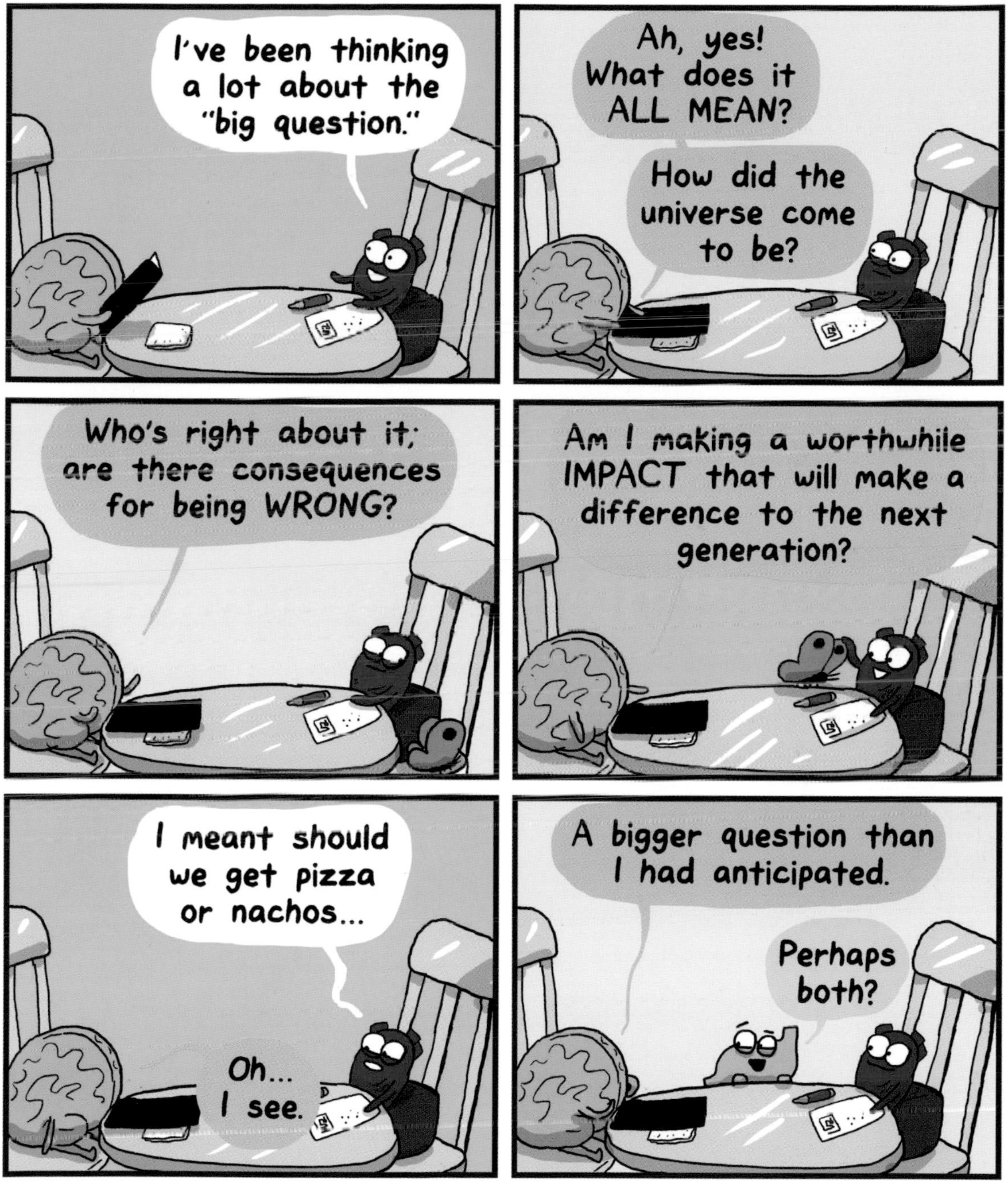
I've been thinking a lot about the "big question."
Ah, yes! What does it ALL MEAN?
How did the universe come to be?
Who's right about it; are there consequences for being WRONG?
Am I making a worthwhile IMPACT that will make a difference to the next generation?
I meant should we get pizza or nachos...
Oh... I see.
A bigger question than I had anticipated.
Perhaps both?

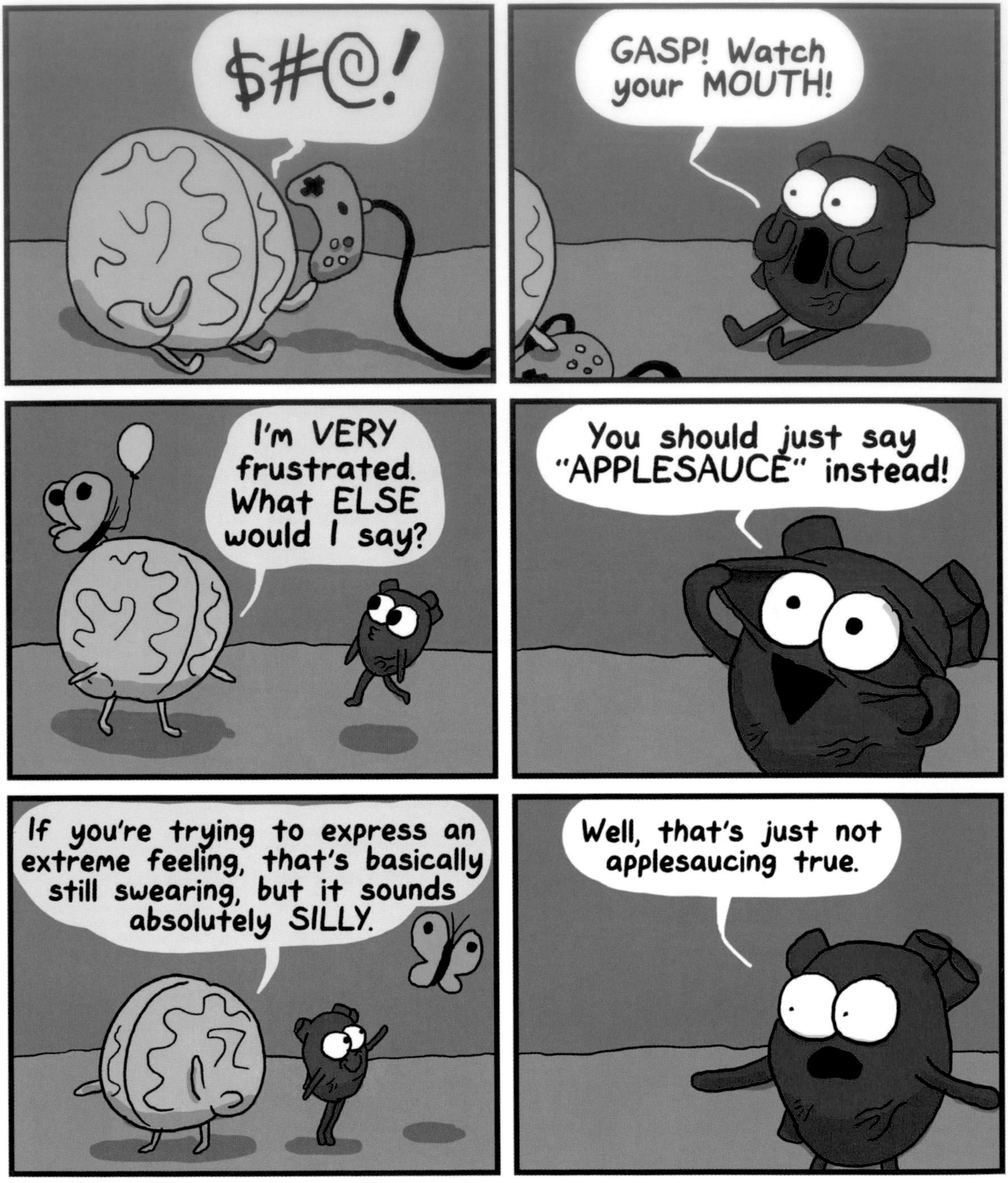
$#@!
GASP! Watch your MOUTH!
I'm VERY frustrated. What ELSE would I say?
You should just say "APPLESAUCE" instead!
If you're trying to express an extreme feeling, that's basically still swearing, but it sounds absolutely SILLY.
Well, that's just not applesaucing true.

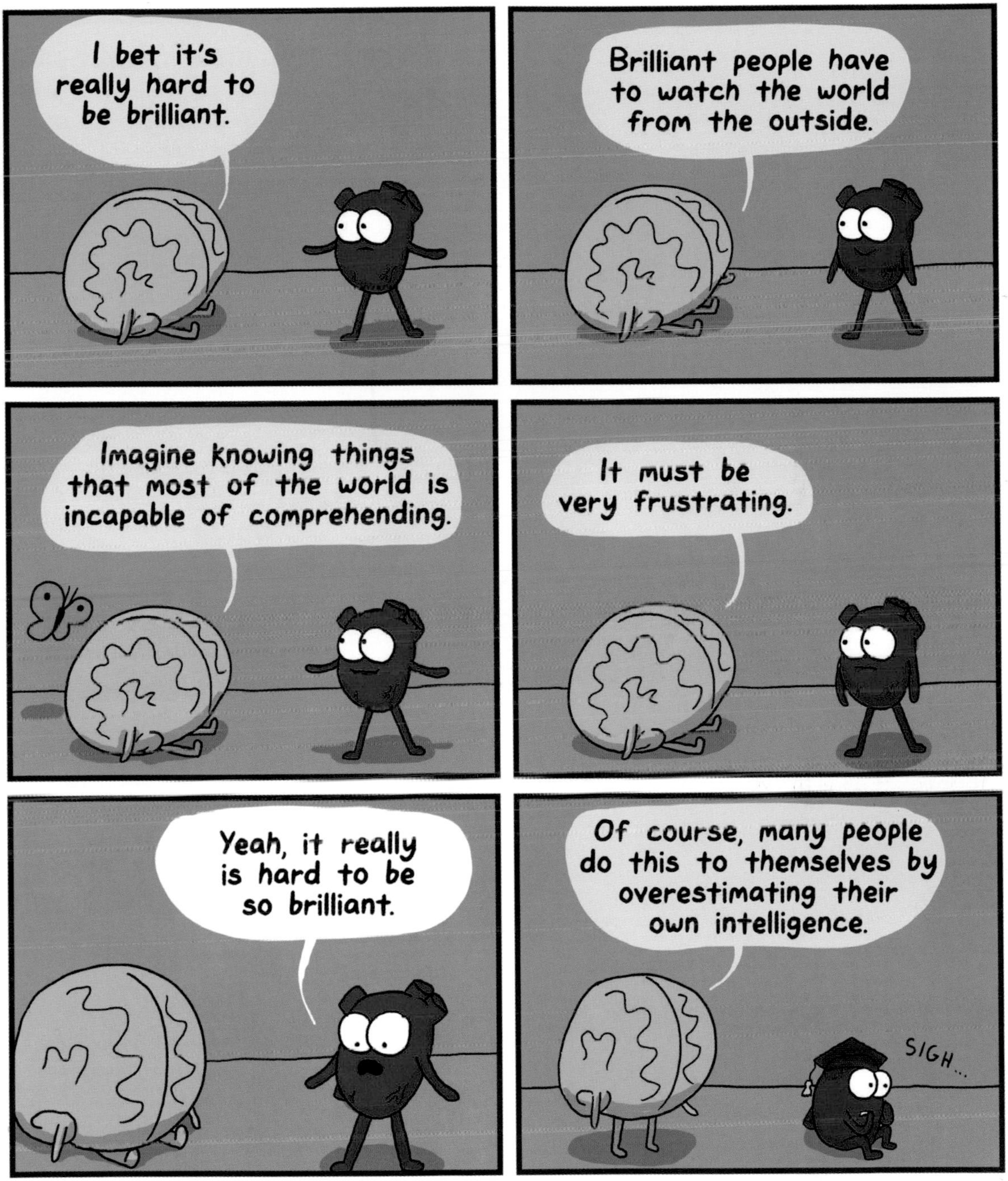
I bet it's really hard to be brilliant.
Brilliant people have to watch the world from the outside.
Imagine knowing things that most of the world is incapable of comprehending.
It must be very frustrating.
Yeah, it really is hard to be so brilliant.
Of course, many people do this to themselves by overestimating their own intelligence.
SIGH...

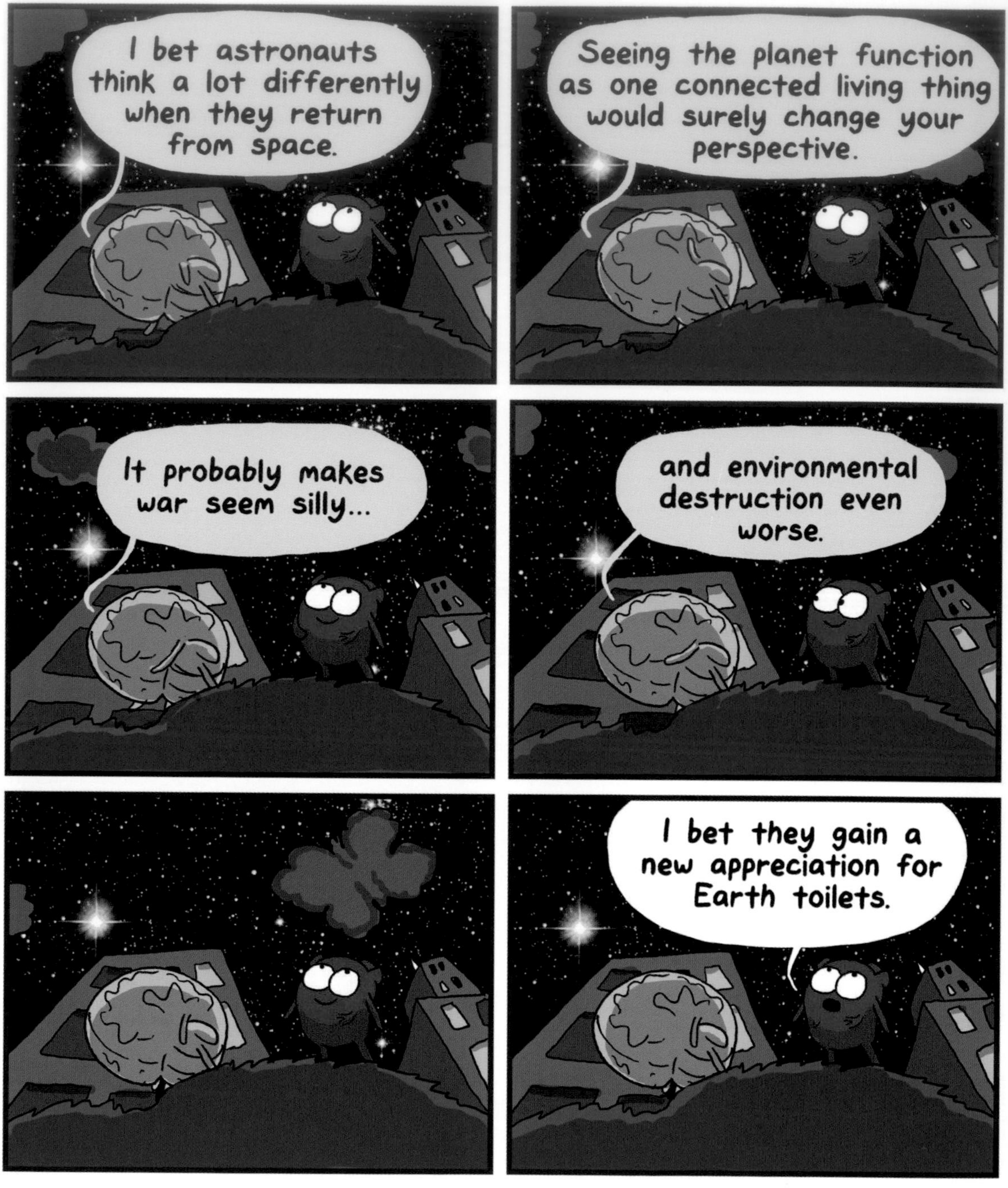
I bet astronauts think a lot differently when they return from space.
Seeing the planet function as one connected living thing would surely change your perspective.
It probably makes war seem silly...
and environmental destruction even worse.
I bet they gain a new appreciation for Earth toilets.

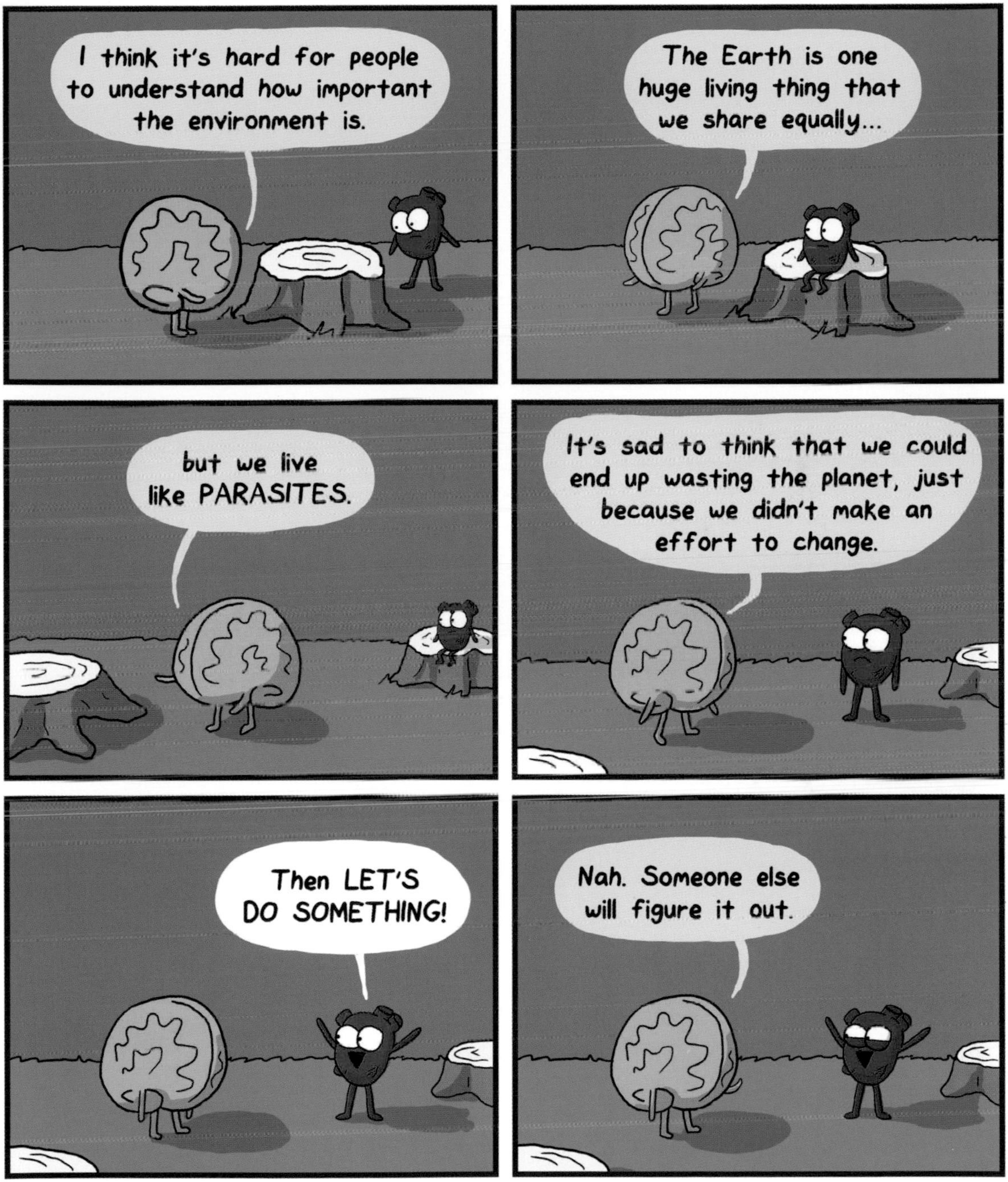
I think it's hard for people to understand how important the environment is.
The Earth is one huge living thing that we share equally...
but we live like PARASITES.
It's sad to think that we could end up wasting the planet, just because we didn't make an effort to change.
Then LET'S DO SOMETHING!
Nah. Someone else will figure it out.

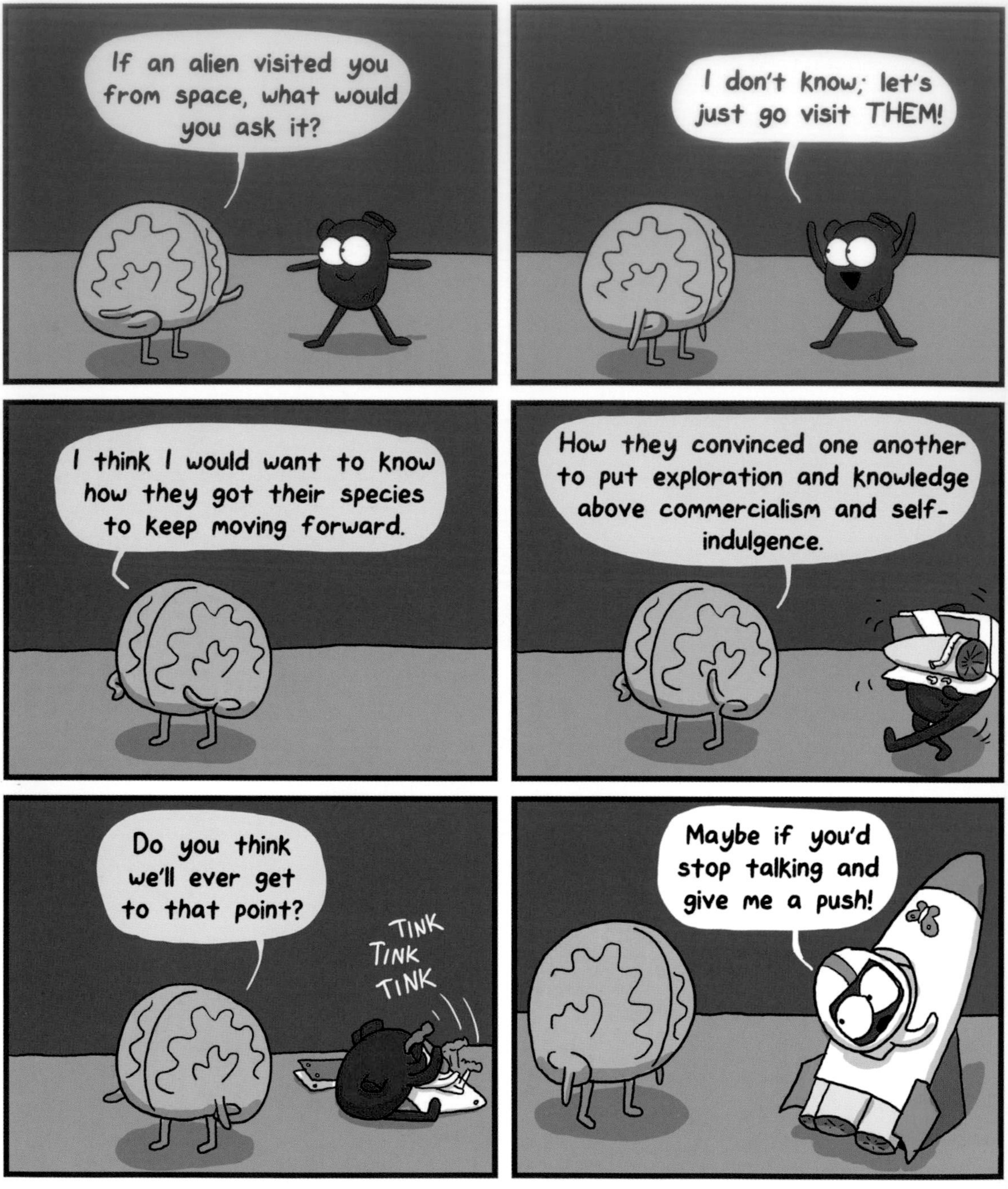
If an alien visited you from space, what would you ask it?
I don't know; let's just go visit THEM!
I think I would want to know how they got their species to keep moving forward.
How they convinced one another to put exploration and knowledge above commercialism and self-indulgence.
Do you think we'll ever get to that point?
TINK TINK TINK
Maybe if you'd stop talking and give me a push!

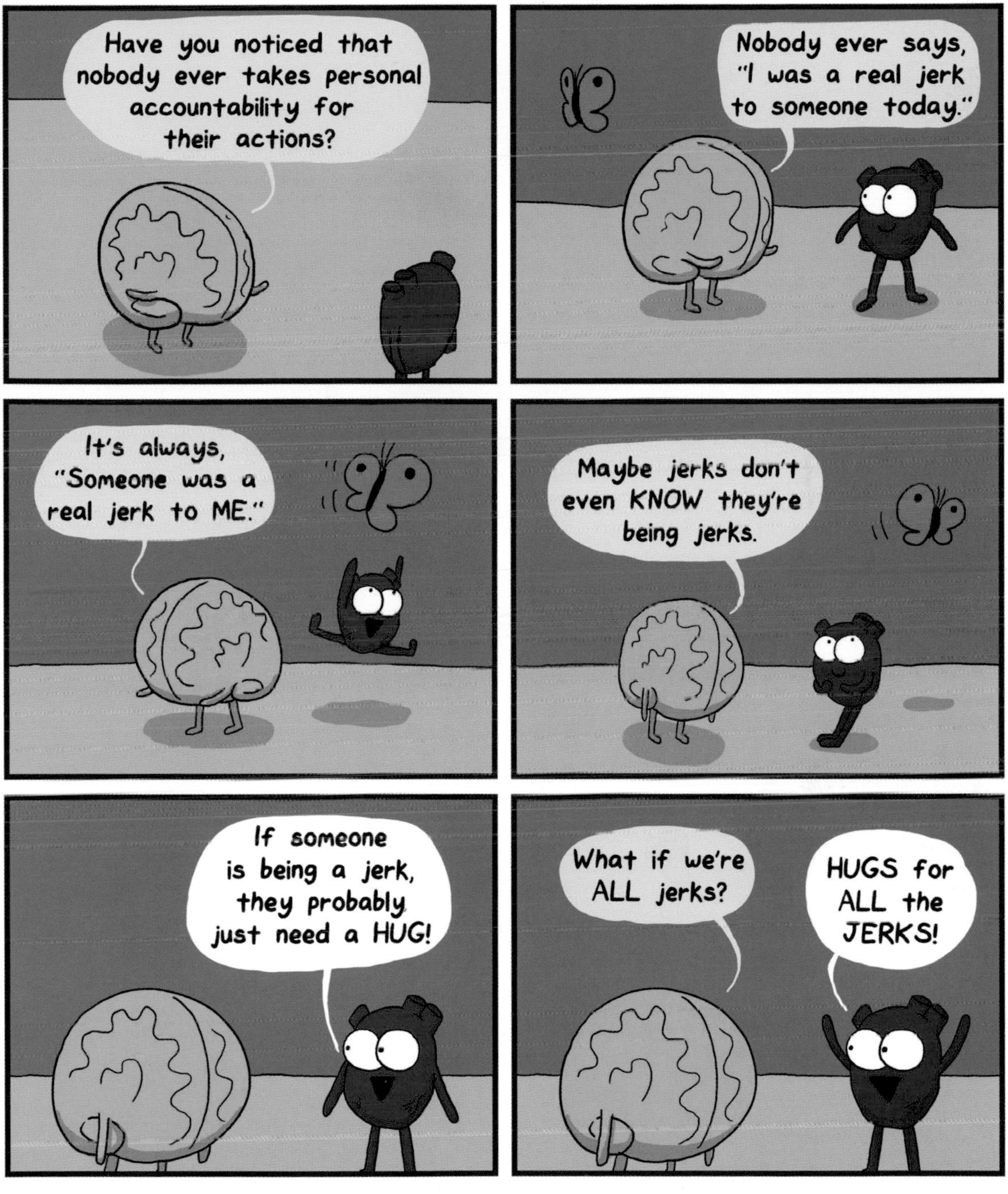
Have you noticed that nobody ever takes personal accountability for their actions?
Nobody ever says, "I was a real jerk to someone today."
It's always, "Someone was a real jerk to ME."
Maybe jerks don't even KNOW they're being jerks.
If someone is being a jerk, they probably just need a HUG!
What if we're ALL jerks?
HUGS for ALL the JERKS!

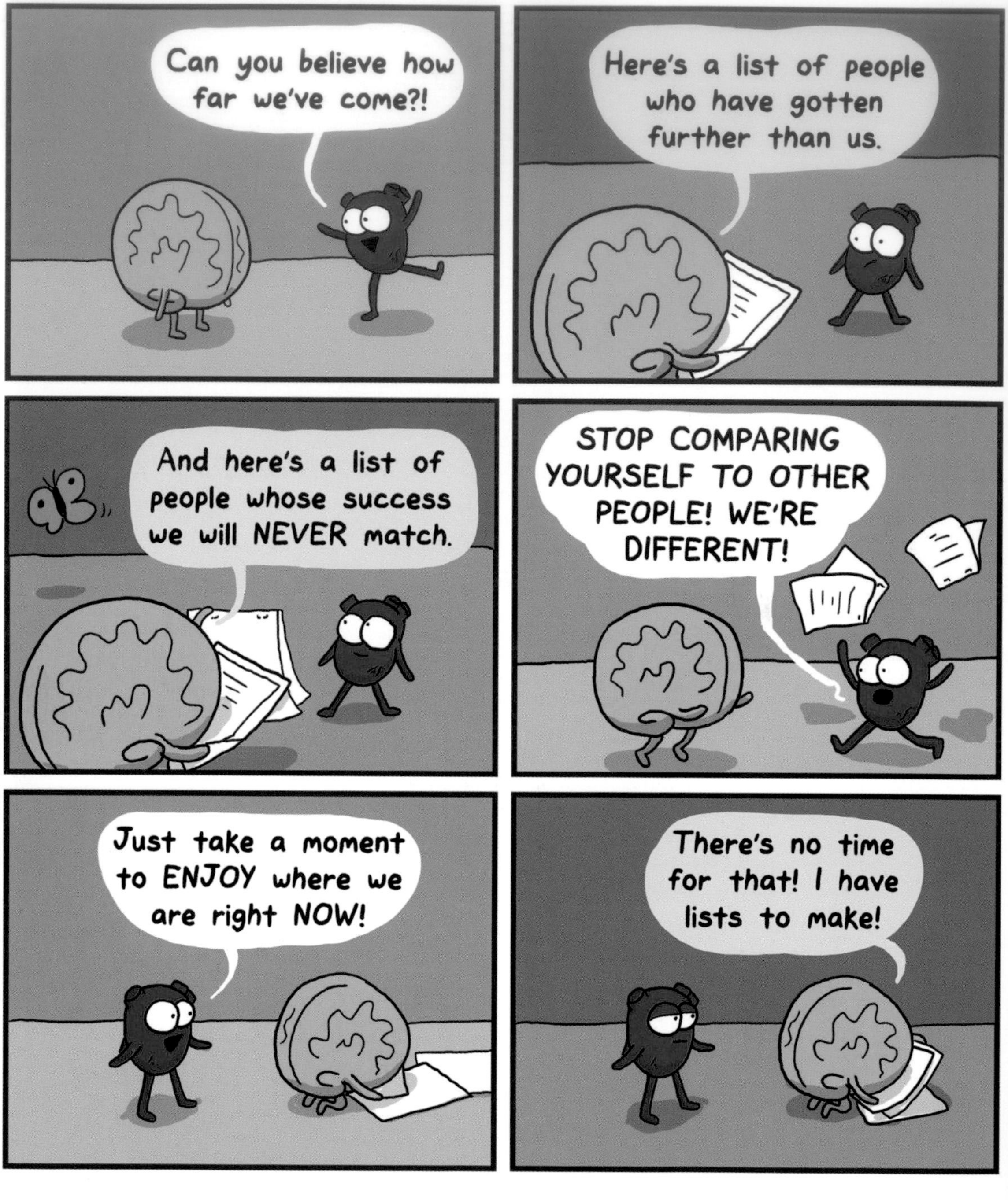

Can you believe how far we've come?!
Here's a list of people who have gotten further than us.
And here's a list of people whose success we will NEVER match.
STOP COMPARING YOURSELF TO OTHER PEOPLE! WE'RE DIFFERENT!
Just take a moment to ENJOY where we are right NOW!
There's no time for that! I have lists to make!

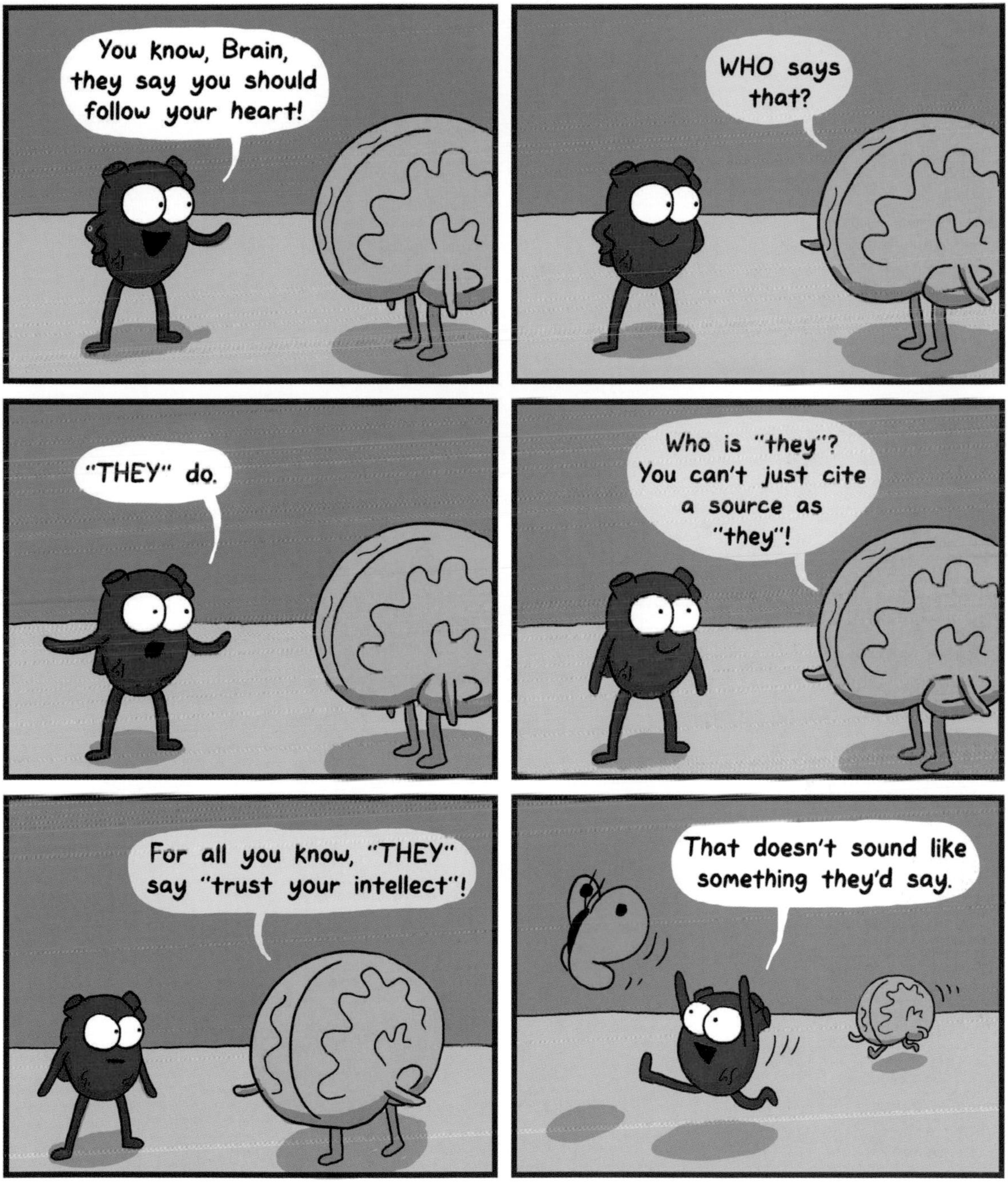
You know, Brain, they say you should follow your heart!
WHO says that?
"THEY" do.
Who is "they"? You can't just cite a source as "they"!
For all you know, "THEY" say "trust your intellect"!
That doesn't sound like something they'd say.

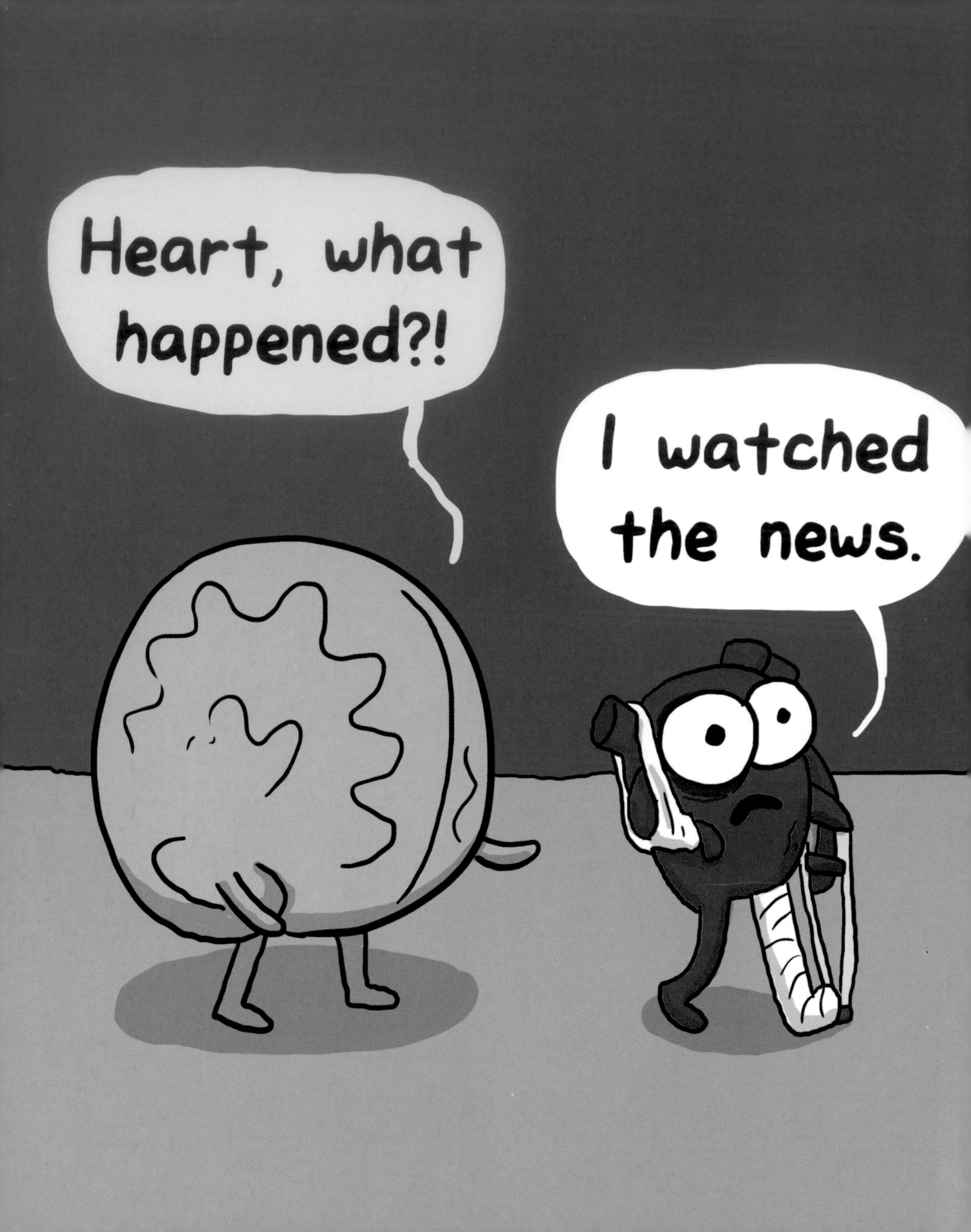
Heart, what happened?!
I watched the news.

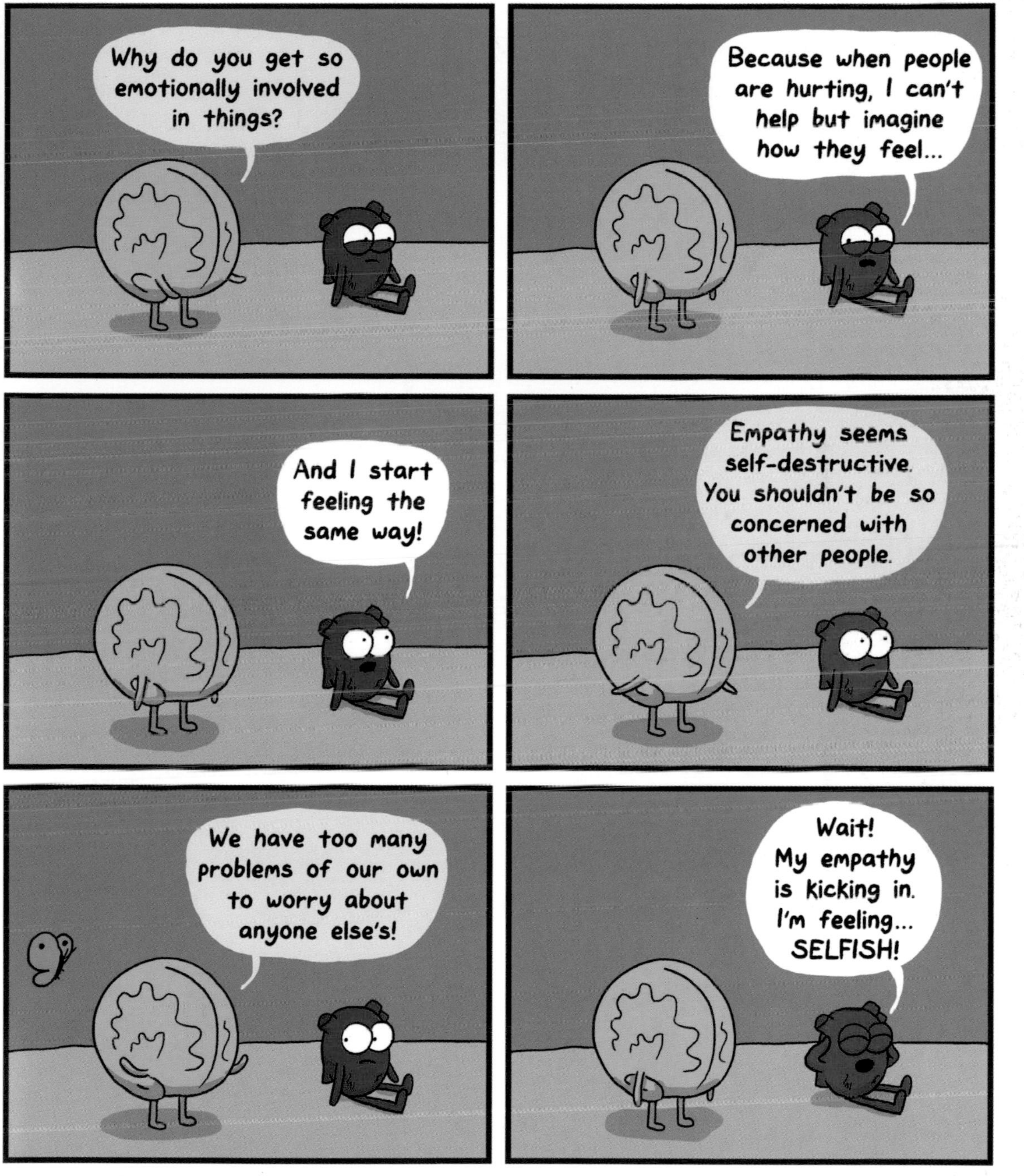
Why do you get so emotionally involved in things?
Because when people are hurting, I can't help but imagine how they feel...
And I start feeling the same way!
Empathy seems self-destructive. You shouldn't be so concerned with other people.
We have too many problems of our own to worry about anyone else's!
Wait! My empathy is kicking in. I'm feeling... SELFISH!

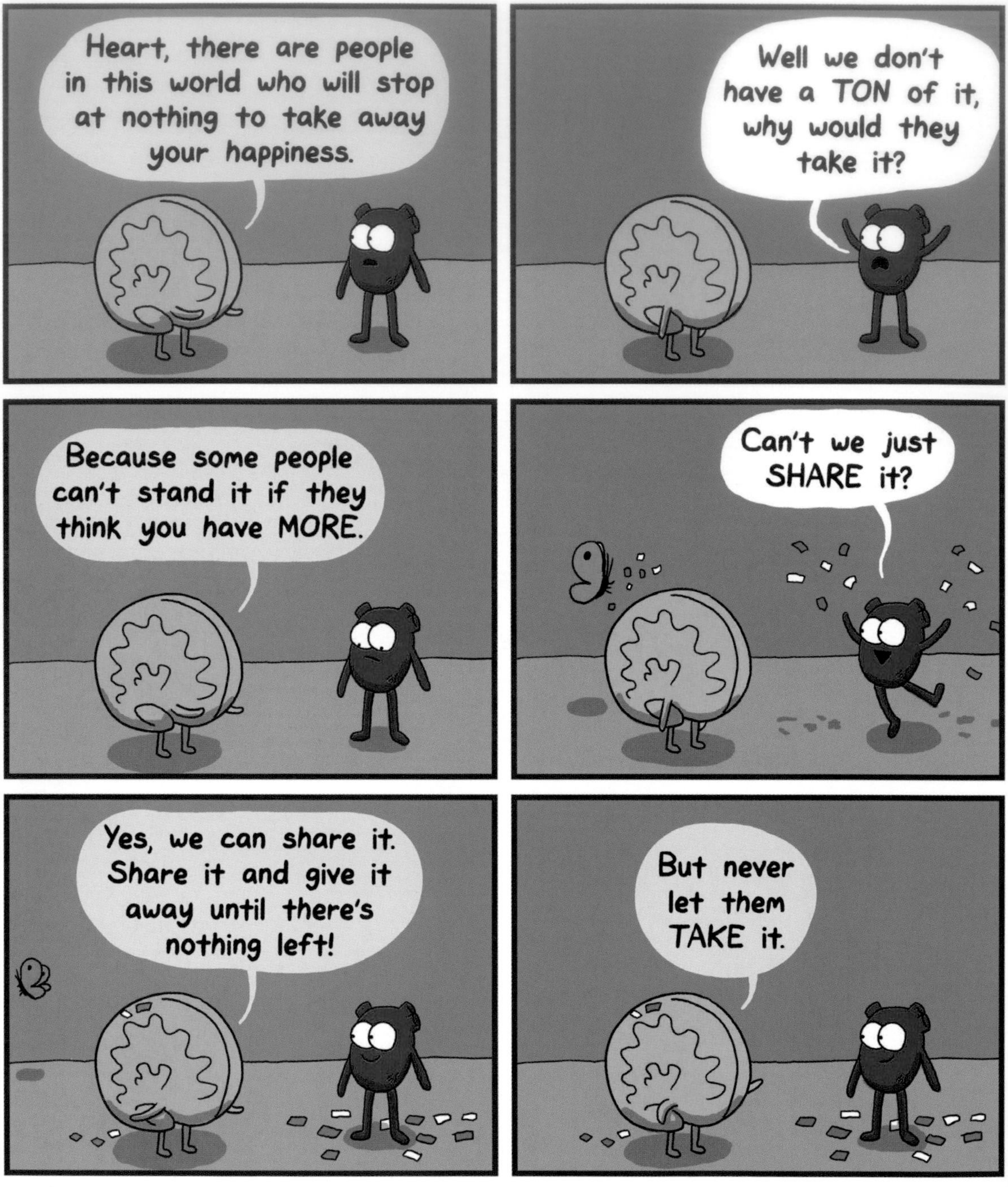
Heart, there are people in this world who will stop at nothing to take away your happiness.
Well we don't have a TON of it, why would they take it?
Because some people can't stand it if they think you have MORE.
Can't we just SHARE it?
Yes, we can share it. Share it and give it away until there's nothing left!
But never let them TAKE it.

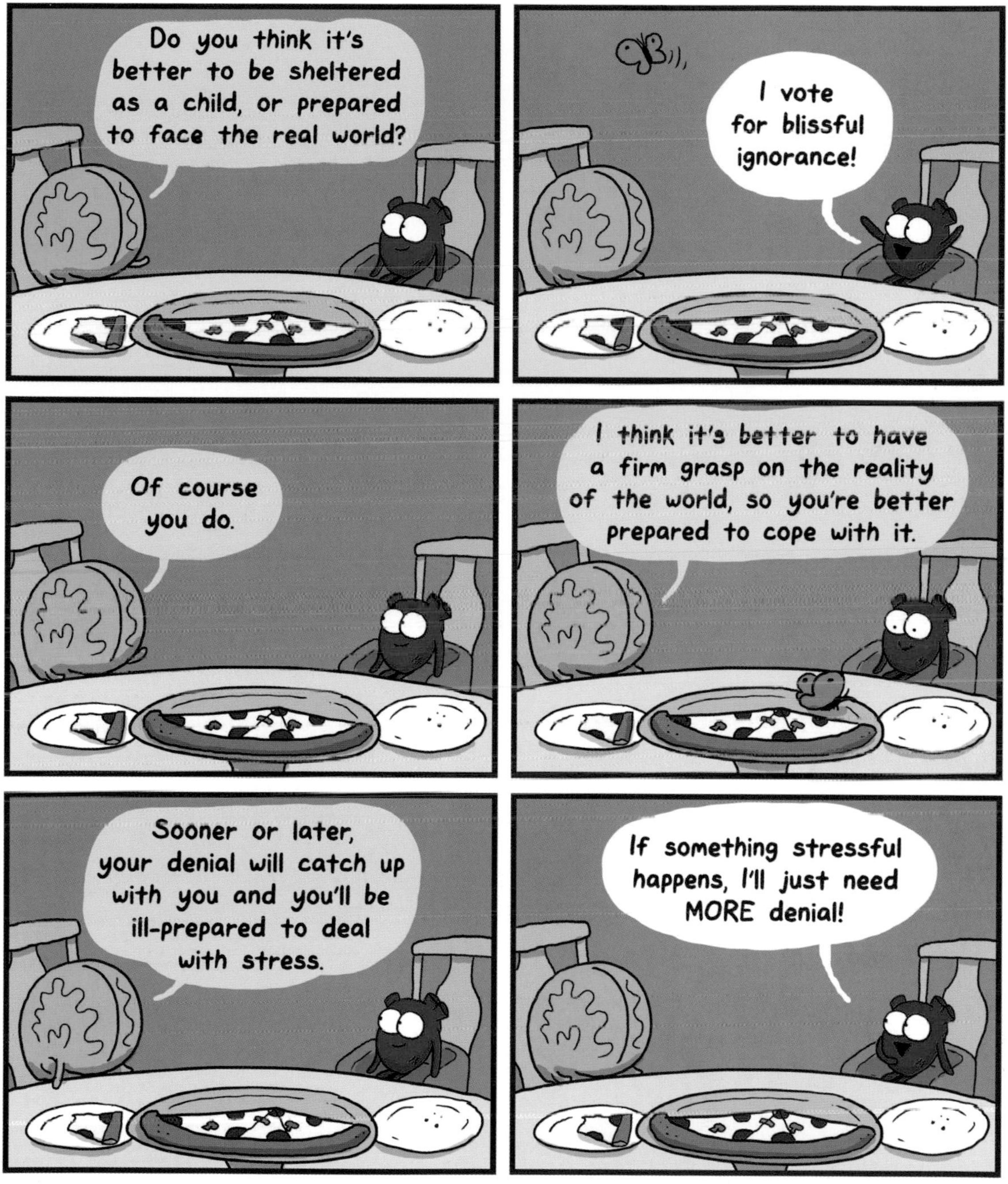
Do you think it's better to be sheltered as a child, or prepared to face the real world?
I vote for blissful ignorance!
Of course you do.
I think it's better to have a firm grasp on the reality of the world, so you're better prepared to cope with it.
Sooner or later, your denial will catch up with you and you'll be ill-prepared to deal with stress.
If something stressful happens, I'll just need MORE denial!

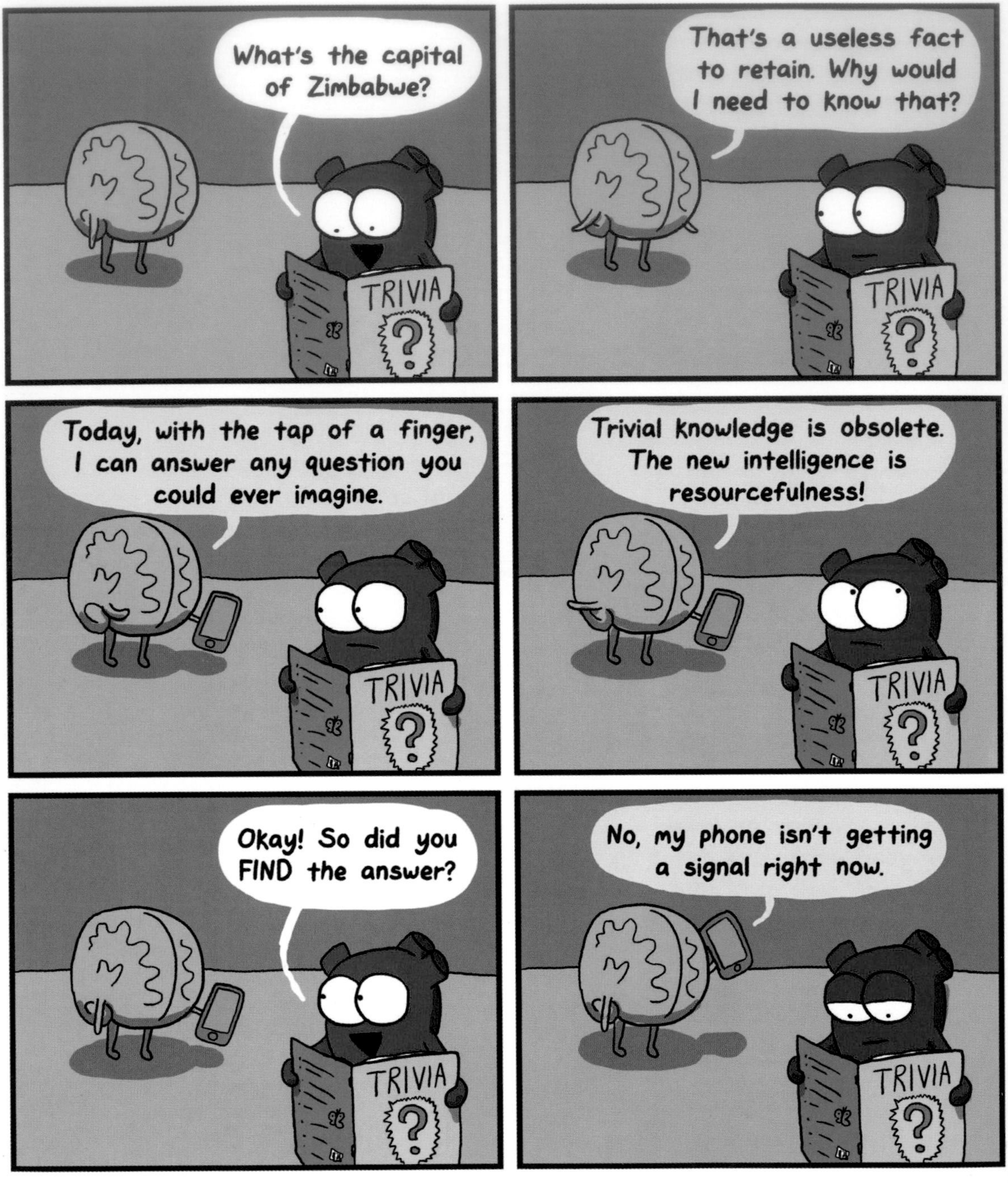
What's the capital of Zimbabwe?
That's a useless fact to retain. Why would I need to know that?
Today, with the tap of a finger, I can answer any question you could ever imagine.
Trivial knowledge is obsolete. The new intelligence is resourcefulness!
Okay! So did you FIND the answer?
No, my phone isn't getting a signal right now.
TRIVIA

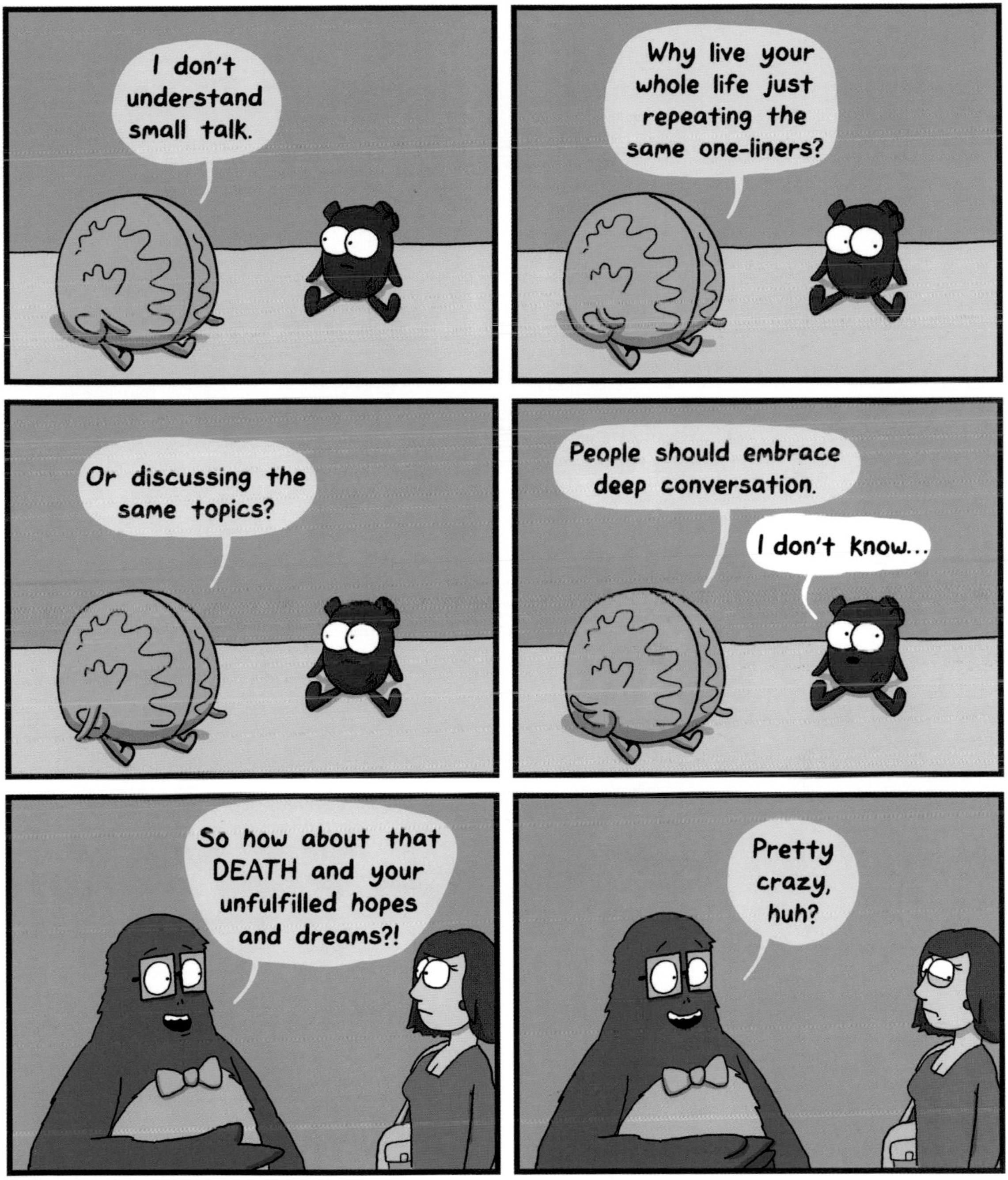
I don't understand small talk.
Why live your whole life just repeating the same one-liners?
Or discussing the same topics?
People should embrace deep conversation.
I don't know...
So how about that DEATH and your unfulfilled hopes and dreams?!
Pretty crazy, huh?

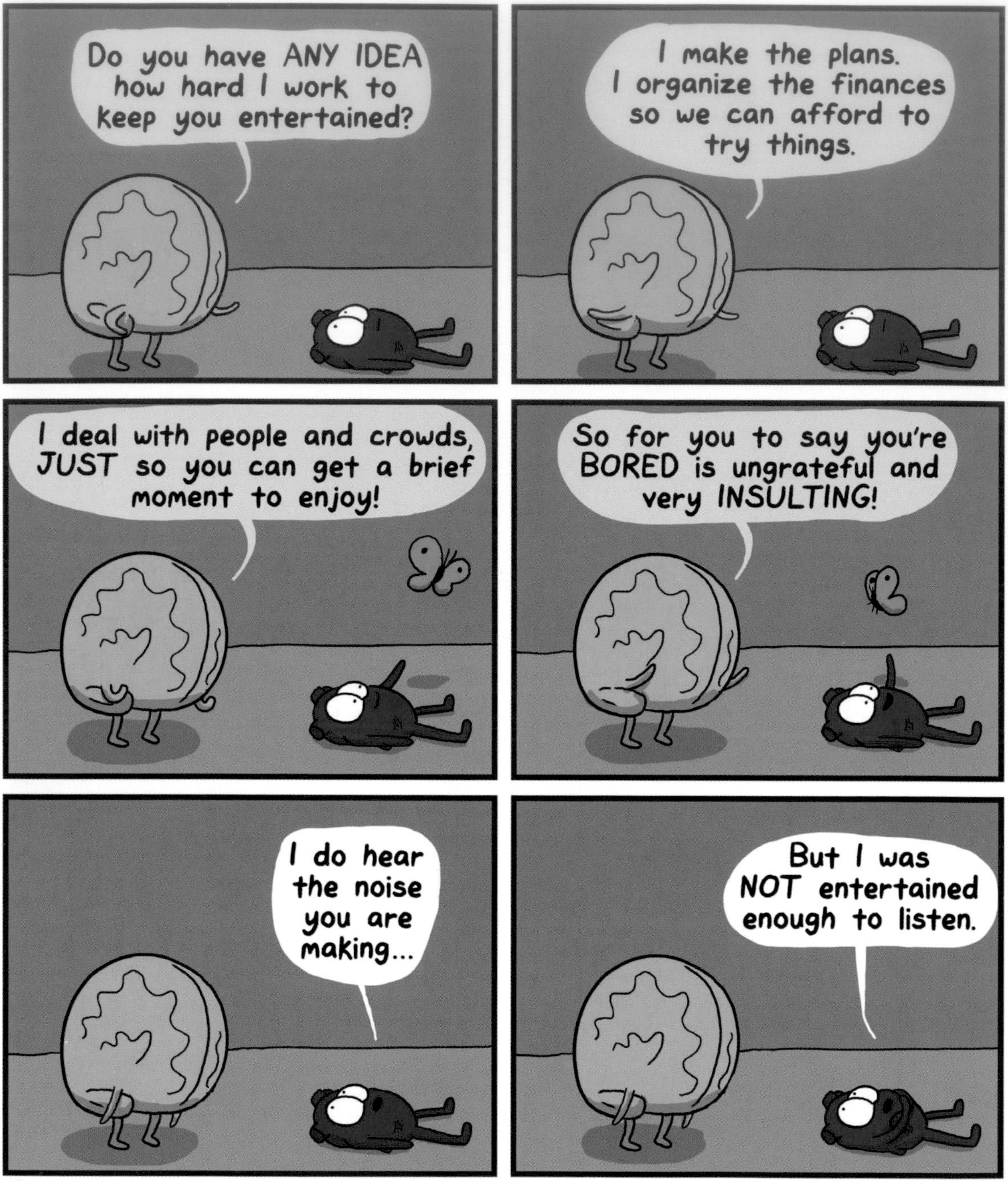
Do you have ANY IDEA how hard I work to keep you entertained?
I make the plans. I organize the finances so we can afford to try things.
I deal with people and crowds, JUST so you can get a brief moment to enjoy!
So for you to say you're BORED is ungrateful and very INSULTING!
I do hear the noise you are making...
But I was NOT entertained enough to listen.

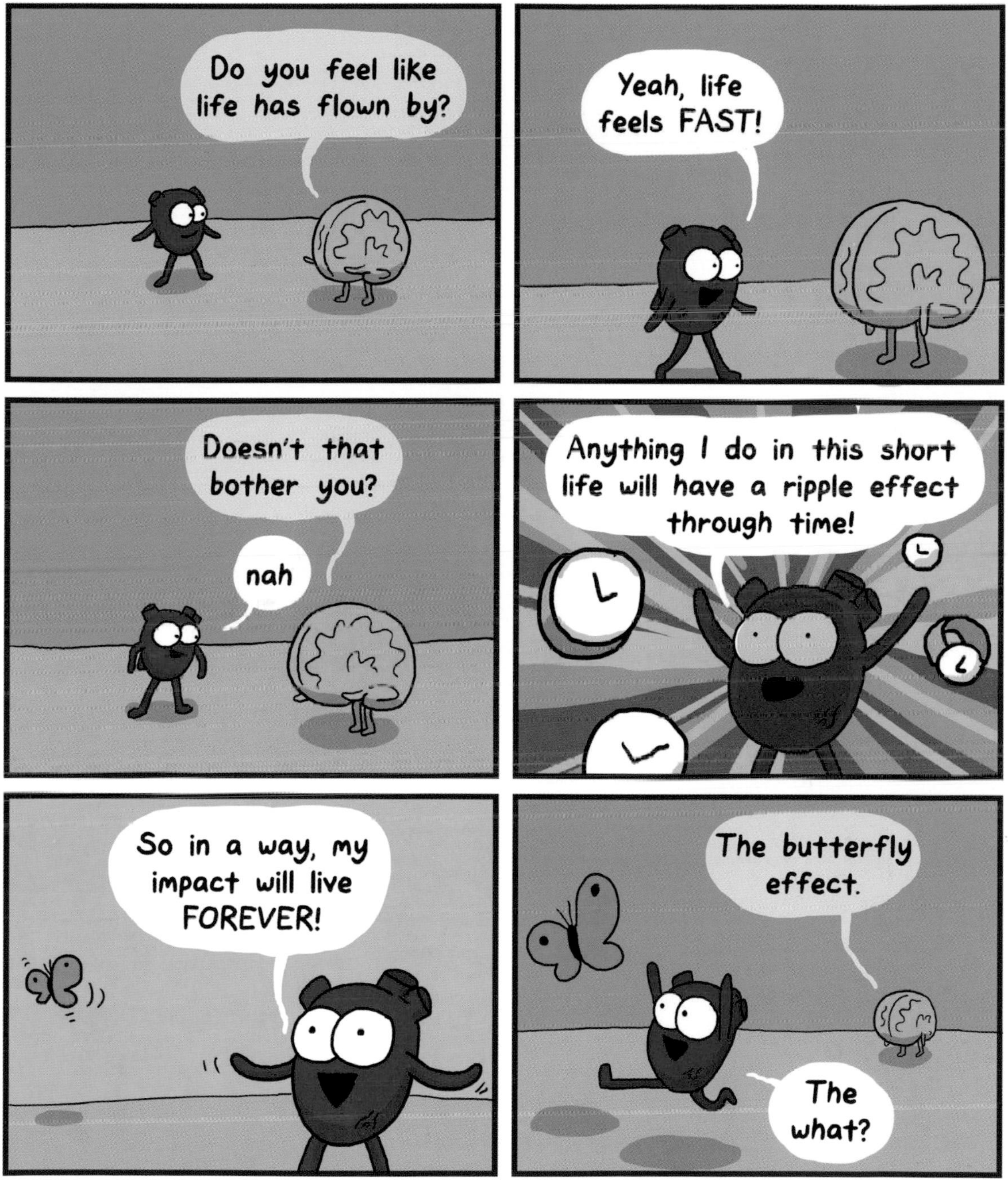
Do you feel like life has flown by?
Yeah, life feels FAST!
Doesn't that bother you?
nah
Anything I do in this short life will have a ripple effect through time!
So in a way, my impact will live FOREVER!
The butterfly effect.
The what?

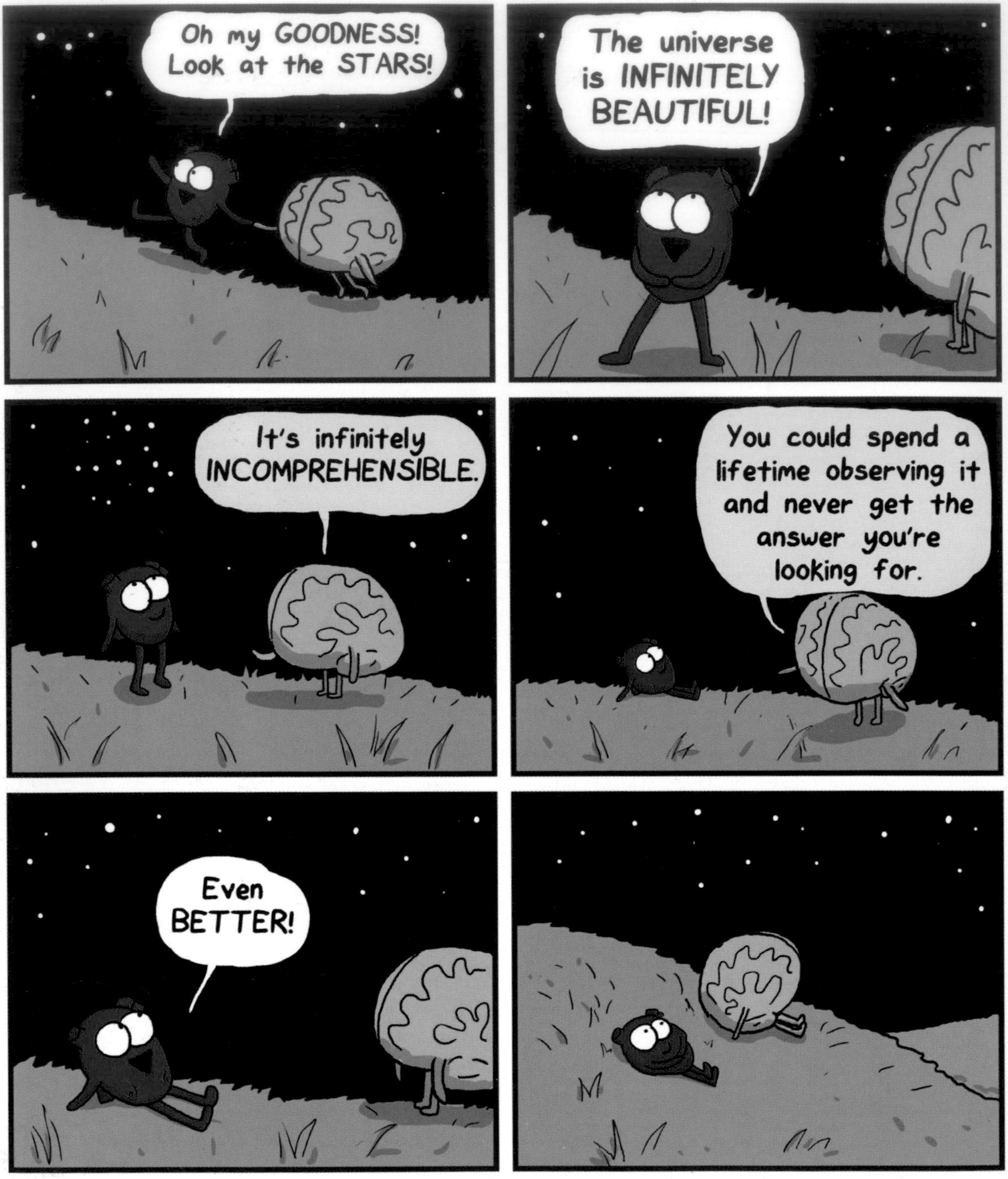
Oh my GOODNESS! Look at the STARS!
The universe is INFINITELY BEAUTIFUL!
It's infinitely INCOMPREHENSIBLE.
You could spend a lifetime observing it and never get the answer you're looking for.
Even BETTER!

The End

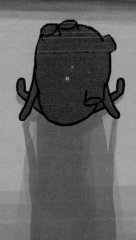

Heart and Brain

Andrews McMeel Publishing
a division of Andrews McMeel Universal
1130 Walnut Street, Kansas City, Missouri 64106

www.andrewsmcmeel.com

17 18 19 20 21 TEN 10 9 8 7 6

ISBN: 978-1-4494-7089-0

Library of Congress Control Number: 2015935792

ATTENTION: SCHOOLS AND BUSINESSES
Andrews McMeel books are available at quantity discounts with bulk purchase for educational, business, or sales promotional use. For information, please e-mail the Andrews McMeel Publishing Special Sales Department: specialsales@amuniversal.com.

theAwkwardYeti.com